April 2010

Perfect Pitch

Adweek and Brandweek Books are designed to present interesting, insightful books for the general business reader and for professionals in the worlds of media, marketing, and advertising.

These are innovative, creative books that address the challenges and opportunities of these industries, written by leaders in the business. Some of our writers head their own companies, others have worked their way up to the top of their field in large multinationals. They share a knowledge of their craft and a desire to enlighten others.

We hope readers will find these books as helpful and inspiring as *Adweek*, *Brandweek*, and *Mediaweek* magazines.

Published

Perfect Pitch

The art of selling ideas and winning new business

JON STEEL

AN
ADWEEK
BOOK

BICENTENNIAL
1807
WILEY
2007
BICENTENNIAL

John Wiley & Sons, Inc.

For general information on our other products and services please contact our
Customer Care Department within the U.S. at (800) 762-2974, outside the
United States at (317) 572-3993 or fax (317) 572-4002.

Wiley also publishes its books in a variety of electronic formats. Some content
that appears in print may not be available in electronic books. For more
information about Wiley products, visit our web site at www.wiley.com.

ISBN-13: 978-0-471-78976-5
ISBN-10: 0-471-78976-3

Printed in the United States of America

10   9   8   7   6   5

For Cameron and Hannah.

*May you grow up in a world
where people tell stories.*

CONTENTS

INTRODUCTION

THIS IS A TYPICAL CRAPPY PRESENTATION SLIDE, WITH A BOLD AND RATHER LENGTHY HEADLINE, OVER CRAMMED TEXT AND A STUPID CLIPART VISUAL

- THIS IS THE FIRST BULLET POINT, FURTHER DIVIDED INTO SUB-BULLETS
  - Hello
  - Welcome to "Perfect Pitch"
- THE SECOND BULLET POINT HAS A CLEVER LINK TO THE VISUAL
  - I hope the book gives you lots of ideas
- THE THIRD BULLET CONTAINS SOME GRATUITOUS DATA:
  - 84,805 words
  - 1,238 paragraphs
  - 6,774 lines
- IT'S USUAL TO END WITH A LINK TO THE NEXT SLIDE. SO WITH NO FURTHER ADO, LET'S MOVE ON TO THE INTRODUCTION

An Audience with Steve Jobs

I once met Steve Jobs.

It was in 1997, just after he had returned to Apple Computer as interim CEO, or iCEO as he liked to call it. He had been brought back to save the company, and one of the changes he thought was needed to accomplish this objective was to change Apple's advertising agency.

He invited two agencies to meet with him. One was Goodby, Silverstein & Partners, where I was a partner and director of planning. The other was TBWA\Chiat\Day, with whom Jobs had worked before at Apple, creating—among other award-winning work—the now-legendary *1984* commercial. The present situation was strange. We were convinced that Jobs was already committed to Chiat\Day; there was also the not-insignificant problem that Goodby, Silverstein was the agency for a competitor, Hewlett-Packard.

"Don't worry about that," Jobs had told Jeff Goodby on the telephone. "I know H-P's chairman. I can fix it."

We weren't convinced, but as none of us had ever met the famous Steve Jobs and wanted to, we took the meeting anyhow.

Two senior members of Apple's marketing department met us in the lobby. They had been hired by the previous regime and inherited by Jobs when he returned. I won't name them here, but I hope they are both now very happy and living in countries where they will not be able to read this book.

"Steve's running late," one of the marketing men said, ushering us into a darkened conference room. "We'll get you up to speed while we're waiting."

We took seats around one of those conference tables made up of four separate tables that never exactly fit together. At one end was a laptop and projector, which our host proceeded to boot up.

He went through the normal conference room audio-visual routine, where the computer worked and the projector did not ("No signal re-ceived"), then the projector picked up the signal and he couldn't find his file. We sat in silence as he accessed his desktop, and watched as he scrolled through what seemed like hundreds of files. Some of them had interesting names like "Cancun '96." Others, tagged with strange com-binations of numbers and abbreviated jargon, looked like a lot less fun. Finally he alighted on a file and brought up a title on the screen: *Agency Briefing*.

"I have a few slides," he said, without a trace of irony.

We were all a little surprised that we were being "briefed." From Steve Jobs' original telephone call, we had been prepared for a rela-tively informal chat. But maybe that would come when Jobs himself fi-nally appeared. Our host had no idea how late he would be; he did tell us, "Steve is very busy."

As it turned out, he was very, very busy. An hour and a half elapsed, and still there was no sign of him. For all that time, we endured what I can only describe as slow, lingering death by PowerPoint. The coffee did arrive, which gave us some small reason to continue living, but once it was gone no more was forthcoming. Our presenter seemed oblivious to our pain; in the half-light he brought up slide after slide, graph after graph, table after table, each densely packed with numbers and with commentary that he read verbatim. It was a lecture on the computer business and on Apple's product lineup. Occasionally his colleague would say something like, "If I could build on that," or "Let me drill down a little deeper," or "What we really bring to the table is. . . ."

The only thing I wanted him to bring to the table was more god-dammed coffee. Unfortunately, all he wanted to do was talk about core competencies, key learnings, net-nets, and win-wins, although it seemed to me that if there was any evidence of win-winning in the charts we were see-seeing, it was being done by companies other than Apple. My partners and I all knew before the computer had been switched on that Apple wasn't doing very well, because it had been well-documented in the press, and Jobs' return had been hailed as the hero returning to rescue his ailing company. But the presentation seemed to be designed, if not exactly to hide the problems, at least to make it difficult to identify them. The two men spoke optimistically of new strategies and paradigms that would enable Apple to "gain traction" once more.

At about the point when most of us were weighing the relative benefits of murder or suicide, the door opened. In came a man wearing jeans and a black polo neck sweater.

"I'm Steve," he said, although we knew that already. He shook hands with each of us, not acknowledging the fact that we had been waiting for him for almost two hours.

"We've been briefing them, Steve," said the senior of the two marketing guys as Jobs finished greeting us.

"I'm sure what they told you was crap," Jobs said, to us rather than to his two colleagues. Since it was the first time I had met him, I couldn't be sure, but he didn't seem to be joking.

"We brought some of our work to show you," Rich Silverstein said, trying to cut the air that seemed to have become a whole lot heavier.

"I've seen it," Jobs said. "I liked some of it."

Rich looked as if he wanted to say something but couldn't find the words.

"Okay," Jobs said, switching off the projector as he strode toward a dry-erase board on the conference room wall. He picked up a marker pen and tapped it in the air as he turned to face us.

"This company," he said, "is in deep shit. But I believe that if we do some simple things very well, we can save it, and we can grow it. I've asked you here today because I need your help. But let me tell you first what I'm going to do. My side of the bargain."

With the pen he drew 13 or 14 boxes on the board, telling us that each box represented a project into which Apple had invested millions and sometimes hundreds of millions of dollars. With the exception of the Newton, which was designed to turn a person's handwriting into typed text, most of the names were unfamiliar to us. They were names such as Cyberdog, OpenDoc, G4, iMac.

One by one, Jobs struck a line through the boxes. "In the past few days," he said, "I've killed this one, and this one, and this one. . . ." When he had finished, only two boxes remained.

Turning to face us again, he said, "We've got to go back to doing what we do best." As he paused, I found myself thanking God that he had said in plain English what his now-silent marketing colleagues had attempted to communicate with many charts and mentions of core competencies.

I was no longer thinking about coffee. *He* was like coffee. The energy in the room was palpable.

"The two projects that remain," he continued, "are for products we're calling the G4 and the iMac. They represent what we always wanted this company to be about; they're technologically superb and visually stunning. And I'm going to bet the future of this company on them."

All we had seen of the G4 and the iMac were two boxes, roughly drawn in black marker pen on a dry-erase board. But somehow we knew what he was talking about. We *felt* what he was talking about. We were excited too.

"So that's what I'm doing. What I've done," he said. "Now what do I want from you?"

Joining us at the table, he told us that, in its communications, Apple needed to say "thank you." He wanted to thank all the people who had stuck by the company and its products during a time when any sane individual would have predicted that Apple would shortly go out of business.

"We're an iconoclastic company," he said. "And these people are just like us. They don't care about being different. They *like* being different. I think we should recognize that and celebrate it. Thank them for hanging in with us."

That was it. Far from asking us to sell our company to him, Steve Jobs had pitched Apple to *us*. He had explained his strategy for the company in a little less than five minutes, and he told us how he saw the role of communications in not much more than 60 seconds.

The only visual aids he used were produced live using a marker pen and a dry-erase board. Yet they seemed as vivid as any expensively produced slides or blown-up photographs or videos we had ever seen.

In more than 20 years in the advertising business, I have never experienced a more focused, passionate, and inspiring presentation—at least, not in a conference room.

"I tell you what," one of my partners said as we walked to our cars a few minutes later, "He's brilliant, but he's an *asshole*. Did you see the way he treated those two guys?"

"He didn't want to watch our video," Silverstein said plaintively.

We all agreed that while Jobs may not have been the warmest, most caring client we had ever encountered, we couldn't remember the last time we met someone as smart, or as impressive. He had bigger things on his mind than our video, and after all, he had obviously thought enough of us to extend the initial invitation. And he was right about his colleagues' presentation. It was worthless, and it had appeared so even before Jobs had entered the room to show us all how a briefing should be done.

"H-P will never let us work for him," said Colin Probert, our president. He was always the pragmatist. But it was interesting how he said "work for *him*," not "work for Apple."

Jeff Goodby shrugged his shoulders. "I know," he said. "But the first thing we should do is buy Apple stock."

Later that day when I checked the stock price it was somewhere around $12 or $13 a share. Within months it was more than five times that. The rest, as they say, is history. Hewlett-Packard executives did indeed have problems with the concept of our working for Apple. Chiat\Day took on the account, which is probably what Jobs wanted anyhow. They relaunched the Apple brand to a doubting public under the line, "Think Different" (I wonder where that came from), and with a 60-second spot that celebrated "The crazy ones. The round pegs in the square holes." People like Einstein and Picasso, who, the commercial suggested, were united with Apple users in their willingness to stand out from the crowd, to do what others regarded as impossible. It was the celebration, the public thanks, that Jobs had spoken to us about.

Apple today is a very different company from the one we encountered in 1997. It's no exaggeration to say that the lion's share of its success is due to Steve Jobs, a man who believed passionately in the future of the company he founded, was able to attract the very best people to help him achieve his vision, and was able to remove any barriers—human or otherwise—that stood in his way. His presentation to us was compelling in every way.

Of course his personality is polarizing. But whatever you think of Steve Jobs the person, it would be impossible to think of him as anything but brilliant. As Bill Bernbach once said, "In this very real world, good doesn't drive out evil. Evil doesn't drive out good. But the energetic displaces the passive."

On which note I should add that the two marketing guys who "briefed" us had left Apple within a week of our meeting, perhaps taking their PowerPoint slides with them.

While those guys presented facts in the dullest way imaginable, Steve Jobs exuded passion and communicated an extraordinary sense of possibility. It was a dramatic juxtaposition: In one conference room, on the same afternoon, talking about the same company, I saw one presentation that has to be one of the worst I have ever witnessed. And I also saw one of the very best.

Saving the World from Bad Presentations

Every day, all over the world, millions of people make presentations to each other. Some are made by politicians, sports coaches, military personnel, and teachers trying to impart information and sell ideas. Others are given by street vendors, whose presentation might be informal but whose product is at least tangible: fruit, vegetables, imitation Rolex watches, sometimes even their own bodies. And even more are made by businesspeople. (Microsoft estimates that more than thirty million presentations are delivered worldwide each day using PowerPoint alone.) Businesspeople—speaking the language of business, addressing groups of other businesspeople, presenting a point of view in the hope of affecting their audience in a positive way. Even if some in the audience might not guess it, there is almost always a purpose: Perhaps the presenter wants to increase the audience's knowledge of a particular subject; maybe persuade them to agree to an uncomfortable course of action, usually to buy something.

In the world that I have inhabited for the past two decades, that of advertising, we make presentations—pitches—to persuade new clients to hire our agencies. We pitch campaign ideas to existing clients in the hope that they will produce them and extend our tenure. And in between we make countless other presentations to our clients and colleagues, helping them to understand market and category dynamics, competitive environments, and consumer motivations. Successful presentations can result in millions of dollars in revenue. Failure invariably means what our politically correct human resources people now term "downsizing," but which I still think of as loss of jobs, livelihoods, and sometimes self-respect. There's a lot at stake.

It's my job to make such presentations, and over the past 20 years I have probably made hundreds. I've provided the strategic heart of every new business pitch my agencies have made, and in recent years have taken on—rather unwillingly, I might add—the role of pitch leader. I've pitched and won business from global giants like Unilever, Pfizer, Nike, Sony, Pepsi, Anheuser-Busch, Samsung, Starbucks, and Hewlett-Packard; household names such as Porsche, Bell Helmets, Foster's Lager, Polaroid, DHL, Major League Baseball, and the National Basketball Association; more local and regional businesses like Chevys Fresh MexRestaurants, the Northern California Honda Dealers, the California Milk Processors (*got milk?*), SBC Communications, and Sutter Home Winery. Of the pitches I have made, my agencies have been awarded more than 90% of the available billings, more than $1 billion in total. This is in an industry where a successful agency's batting average would probably be lower than that of a leading baseball hitter. (One win out of three is considered very good.)

In case you are wondering what happened to my British humility, I must stress that these wins are far from being my responsibility alone. Like Ringo Starr, I'm lucky to have been in the right place at the right time. I have worked in some excellent agencies (Boase Massimi Pollitt in London, Goodby, Silverstein & Partners in San Francisco, Berlin Cameron/Red Cell in New York, and more recently with J. Walter Thompson in London). In each of those agencies I have worked with highly talented individuals, from whom I have learned a great deal and without any one of whom the agencies would have been less effective. So my purpose in mentioning the above is not to create the impression that I am a winning presenter, but rather that I know from firsthand experience how winning presentations are made.

Beyond making hundreds of presentations myself, I have also been on the receiving end of many more. I have been a member of a client team judging a series of pitches from public relations agencies; on another occasion I helped a client select a research partner. I have seen presentations from heads of Fortune 500 companies and others from trainees in their marketing departments. I've seen creative presentations, strategy presentations, research presentations, trend presentations, and financial presentations—even presentations on how to make a presentation.

And do you know what? I could count on one hand the number that I recall as being really inspiring. Most were at best instantly forgettable. At worst they were the kind of experiences that could only have been improved had I removed my own eyes with a blunt instrument and eaten them uncooked.

I don't think that I have been particularly unlucky. Other people tell me that their experience has been uncomfortably similar.

I had two main motives in writing this book, one of which my editor, Richard Narramore, described as "selfish and mercenary," the other as "humanitarian." I happen to think that the second is actually more selfish than the first, for reasons that I will explain, but for now let's stick with his descriptions.

First, here's the selfish, mercenary reason why this book exists: *Perfect Pitch* is designed to help people make better presentations—presentations that are persuasive and lead directly to business growth. That, I imagine, is the reason why most people will be interested in reading it. Call it selfish if you like, but growth—both corporate and personal—is the reason we're all in business. And this may be obvious, but although what I have to say is relevant to almost any kind of presentation, I am focusing particularly on new business presentations because those are the most important presentations we make; those are the ones where even the slightest improvement can make the greatest difference.

The second, humanitarian reason is that I would like you to suffer less on those occasions when you are not making the presentation yourself, but instead sitting in the audience. Saving the world from bad presentations might sound a little overambitious, but that's really why I'm sitting at my computer right now. I'll be honest with you— and this is where the humanitarian reason becomes well and truly selfish—I'm just plain sick of sitting through other people's shitty presentations. I apologize for the terminology, but I can't think of any more accurate or appropriate way to describe them. Remember that the people who are presenting to *me* every day, including the two ex-Apple employees, are all in the communications business. I can't begin to imagine the atrocities committed by those who don't even define themselves as professional communicators. There are people presenting at the moment I am writing this, and there will be people presenting at the moment you read it, who are to the art of presentation what Jack the Ripper was to medical research. I hope you will agree that they should be stopped.

Simple Human Communication

As you might have gathered from the above, my perspective on presentations as an advertising executive doesn't mean that the book should be of interest only to people from my industry. My intention is that it should be relevant to anyone who ever stands up in front of clients or colleagues and tries to convince them of something. Because in the end, whatever our business, whether we are trying to sell an advertising campaign, a new type of mutual fund, a new technology for clipping horses, or a human nose-and-ear trimmer, when we make a presentation we are selling ideas: new ideas on business growth; new ideas on financial security; new ideas on how to handle horses; new ideas on nasal hair control.

Whatever the nature of the business, the overall goal remains the same. Whether the desired response relates to advertising, investment, horses, or personal grooming, one key to success is common to all. A successful presentation engages the audience emotionally as well as rationally. The successful presenter is liked and trusted. In his or her hands, the audience *wants* to believe. And if everything goes according to plan, they may well want to buy before the presenter has even asked for the sale.

My starting point for this book is the belief that the methods we traditionally employ for our business presentations stand in the way of effective communication and persuasion. They don't render it impossible, but they do make things difficult. And maybe, just maybe, the problem results from the assumption that because we are making a *business* presentation, different rules apply. I don't accept the argument that business presentations should be very different from the other kinds of presentations we see in our daily lives—the ones we see on television, on the streets, in bars, and even in our own homes. And I see no reason at all—other than inertia, lack of imagination or sheer stupidity—why this situation should persist.

In the course of some 300 pages I will be asking you to look at a business presentation, not as a presentation but rather as a simple exercise in human communication. For role models I will ask you to look not just at other businesspeople, but instead at those who communicate most effectively in the context of real life.

I'll try to explain this by asking you a question.

What is the most moving, compelling, and ultimately persuasive argument you ever heard? Think about it. Think about all the times that someone has spoken to you, to try to persuade you to think something, or do something, that without their words you might never have considered. Think about all the times your mind has actually been changed, and think of all the arguments that failed to move you.

I'll bet that very few people who answer my question will respond with an example of an argument they heard in a conference room. It's sad, really, because if it's true that more than thirty million PowerPoint presentations are being made every day, that's an awful lot of time and money being wasted.

If I answer my own question, I can think of only one—the aforementioned encounter with Steve Jobs—that comes from the world of business, and his could hardly be described as a formal presentation. But there are many more from outside the business world that I will talk about in these pages, ranging from the speeches of Sir Winston Churchill and Dr. Martin Luther King, Jr., to the quiet persuasion of environmentalist Dr. Jane Goodall, the pitch of a London call girl, the late Johnnie Cochran's defense of O.J. Simpson, and Sebastian Coe's tale of the boyhood inspiration that led him to win two Olympic Gold medals and helped London secure the 2012 Olympic Games. All of these stories are a great deal more interesting and compelling than anything I ever heard at a conference table.

At its heart, therefore, *Perfect Pitch* is about the art of influencing people by storytelling, and it will be illustrated by examples drawn not only from the world of business but from this wider, infinitely more interesting world of human experience.

This book is not about the more technical aspects of presentation. If you're reading this in the hope of learning more about diction, posture, using the right hand gestures, and having great templates for your slides, then I must apologize. I don't deny that such things are important, but it's the last you will hear of them in these pages. I will assume that people who are trusted to present on behalf of their company are able to walk without dragging their knuckles on the ground, have the ability to talk loudly enough to be heard and clearly enough to be understood, and know enough not to place their hands down the front of their pants (or indeed anyone else's) while doing so. And as for "great templates," well, there's an oxymoron if ever I heard one.

Finally, *Perfect Pitch* is not a step-by-step guide to becoming a better presenter. It might be possible to use it that way, but my intention as I write is not to be prescriptive; I would prefer to share some observations on what seems to work for people whom I regard as highly effective communicators and, in so doing, open your mind to new ways of approaching your work. I'd like you to experiment, to find a combination of ideas and approaches that work best for you, given your specific business situation, your own skills and unique personality. And if you respond well to what I have to say, maybe the next time you are subjected to a bad presentation, you could approach the perpetrator and offer him or her a copy of this book. Remember—together we'll be performing an important public service. Not to mention putting my kids through college, for which I thank you.

Just to give you an idea of where the book will take you, Chapter 1, "Presentation Crimes," starts with an exploration of why many presentations fail. The reasons include basic lack of understanding of purpose on the part of the presenter, failure to understand the audience, and the absence of a simple, logical argument. I'll also examine common misconceptions about style, which manifest themselves in presenters talking at, rather than with, their audience, and in their belief that quantity is directly proportional to effectiveness.

Chapter 2, "Imperfect Pitch," shows how some of these basic errors and misconceptions combined to undermine the prosecution's argument in the famous (or infamous) case of *The People of the State of California v. Orenthal James Simpson*. It's a powerful analogy for new business presentations, with the prosecutors and defense teams as competing companies, the members of the jury as the audience, and the ultimate prize a favorable verdict.

Some of the world's best presenters will be put under the spotlight in Chapter 3. Enticingly named "Bill Clinton, Johnnie Cochran, and a London Hooker," it attempts to draw on the shared attributes and techniques of those who really know how to engage and move an audience, based on principles of simplicity, personalization, surprise, and, maybe most important of all, belief on the part of the presenter. Here the other side of the O.J. Simpson trial will be discussed: the successful strategy and execution of the defense team.

My own background in the advertising business is as a strategic planner, and that job entails bringing the target audience into the process of developing advertising ideas. In Chapter 4, "Making Connections," I'll bring some of the principles of planning to bear on the business of preparing a presentation. The presenter, like the advertiser, has to have a sound grasp of audience psychology. He or she also has to have the philosophical ability to turn vast amounts of information into a single compelling idea, in which the promise and the audience need seem almost interdependent. Finally, the presenter requires the skill of a playwright in writing the story (not to mention the confidence of a performer in the final presentation, but more on that subject later).

One of the most significant enemies of good presentation is our perception of lack of time for preparation. I use the word "perception" deliberately, because I fear that the problem is almost entirely of our own doing. Solving it is similarly within our grasp. In Chapter 5, "Trevor's Sledgehammer," I ask you to consider the barriers to our effectiveness thrown up by such modern necessities as e-mail, mobile phones, and personal communication devices, and suggest ways in which we might create both the time and space to become better thinkers, presenters, and listeners.

In Chapter 6, "We Will Fight Them in the Boardroom," I will focus on a relatively recent barrier to effective presentation: that of the presenter allowing technology to overwhelm his or her message. The emphasis here will be on the shortcomings of everyone's favorite presentation software. In a business culture obsessed with deadlines and deliverables, PowerPoint seems to be the default method of dealing with any problem—a kind of technological tail that wags the dog of good ideas. I'll suggest that PowerPoint is not only the easy option, but also the lazy option, showing how its cognitive style undermines intelligent argument. More constructively, I will also attempt to show how PowerPoint can be made to work better, given the application of a little thought and creativity.

Chapter 7, "Benign Dictatorship," is specifically about the art of leading a team presentation, although much of it remains relevant to the solo presenter. From deciding whether pitching is actually the right thing, to picking a team and giving responsibility, this chapter analyzes every stage of a pitch process. Obvious questions include those of how decisions should be made and the importance of rehearsal, but rather less obvious discussions shine a light on issues like knowing how and when to relax, and the positive effects of superstition.

When the winning of new business is concerned, many people know the date of their presentation and aim for that day as if it's Armageddon time. No plans are made beyond the end of the presentation except perhaps to identify the bar to visit when it's all over. Chapter 8 is about treating the presentation not as the end but instead as the beginning. "The Pitch and Beyond" is about the day of the presentation: owning the room, managing the presentation, handling questions, knowing what to leave behind and how to follow up.

In each of the first eight chapters I will offer a number of specific examples from presentations that I have worked on or observed to illustrate my points. In Chapter 9, however, I will focus on one presentation alone—a presentation I wish I had been a part of. London's bid for the 2012 Olympics was a pitch worth about $8 billion. I understand that there are some construction projects in the Middle East—like the archipelago project in Dubai—worth slightly more, but I think I'm safe in asserting that at least in the public and media domain, a new business pitch doesn't come any bigger than the bid to hold the Olympic Games.

London's presentation for the 2012 Games deserves the title "The Perfect Pitch." In its preparation and execution it was virtually flawless, while all of London's competitors made mistakes. It is a classic study in desire, belief, insight, and dedication, and as a Briton whose own children will be inspired by the athletes they see in 2012, I'm proud to tell the story here.

I hope that if you make it to the end of the book you will have found the journey stimulating, and that it will help both you (and your audience!) in future presentations—unless, of course, you happen to be pitching against me for an advertising account. Rest assured that I have kept one or two things to myself, not least the identity of a particular California Cabernet Sauvignon, which so far has a 100 percent winning record when consumed the night before a presentation.

Cheers.

Jon Steel
April, 2006

CHAPTER ONE

- **Presentation Crimes**
  - Why most presentations fail

Outrunning the Bear

Back in the mid-1990s, when I was with Goodby, Silverstein & Partners in San Francisco, our co-founder Jeff Goodby rose one day in our conference room and started a new business presentation with a story. You've probably heard it before.

Two men are hiking in a forest when they disturb a bear. It's that time of year when bears are easily upset, and true to form the bear comes after them. The men run for their lives. They have a good start on the animal, but four legs are better than two and the bear gets closer and closer. Suddenly one of the men stops, takes off his backpack, and sits down on a log.

"What the hell are you doing?" his friend asks, not wanting to stop. He can see the bear's fur boiling as it runs. Its teeth are bared. It's really close.

"I'm changing my shoes," he replies calmly, removing his heavy hiking boots and slipping on a pair of fancy Nike running shoes.

"You're crazy!" his friend shrieks, running to a spot behind a large tree. "You'll never outrun a bear, even in those."

"I don't have to outrun the bear," the man says, standing up and jogging alongside his friend. "I only have to outrun you."

While the tension in the room evaporated, Jeff was also making a serious point: our prospective client's competitive situation was not what it seemed. It was easy to be distracted by one particular competitor, but in fact victory over another, rather less obvious company, held the key to the client's success. At least that's what I think Jeff meant. We did win the client's business based largely on our recasting of the competitive context, so it must have helped.

There was, however, a higher meaning to this story: a subtext that we had discussed among ourselves as we prepared our presentation, and which should guide any company's new business activity.

It's the nature of almost every type of business that a presentation made to a prospective client is not made in isolation; other companies are always competing for the same business. It's also normal for these suitors to be set some kind of task. In the advertising business an agency will be asked to demonstrate an understanding of the client's category and competitive situation, to suggest an appropriate strategic direction, and create a campaign that brings this strategy to life. Outside of this world, garden designers might be asked to demonstrate their design philosophy through examples of previous work and also to create a new vision for the client's land. A realtor presenting to a business or homeowner to win the listing for their property will be expected to come up with a pricing strategy and marketing plan. Whatever the nature of the task, the time for completion will always be limited. It's a cliché to say that the pressure is intense, but clichés wouldn't be clichés if they weren't true. Advertising executives, garden designers, and realtors alike will be seduced by the extra income and prestige that success will bring; they will also fear failure, regarding the effect of defeat as the inverse of success. Defeat will ruin reputations, jobs will be lost, there will be no money for a Christmas party, and the kids' dental work will have to wait. Life will never be the same again.

This pressure causes many people to make the first and perhaps most critical error as they work towards their presentation. This is, in effect, to imagine the task they have been set as the bear chasing them through the forest. They believe that the best way to outrun this angry, hungry bear is by getting to the right answer, the perfect answer.

The Search for the Perfect Answer

I couldn't possibly criticize someone for wanting to solve a problem, to arrive at not just any old answer but the right answer. Perfectionism is a trait that is generally to be admired. In the context of new business presentations, however, it can be downright dangerous because when you are presenting in a competitive situation to any client, you don't have to be right. You just have to be more right than any of your competitors. Even just appearing to be more right, or maybe having the *potential* to be more right, is okay.

This is not just a jaded, cynical advertising guy talking. Aristotle died 2,283 years before I was born, and although to my knowledge he never worked in an advertising agency, he knew enough about persuasion to observe that a convincing impossibility is often preferable to an unconvincing possibility. In other words, although it hurts to say it, it's about winning, not accuracy.

I began my advertising career at a British agency named Boase Massimi Pollitt. (At the time of writing, more than twenty years later, it has become the London office of Doyle Dane Bernbach.) The agency was founded in the late 1960s on the belief that intelligent advertising decisions could not be made without the involvement of consumers. In creating account planners, whose job was to develop an intimate understanding of target consumers and bring it to bear at every stage of idea development, it changed the face of the industry. From BMP's unique combination of smart strategic thinking and brilliant creativity came many of Britain's most memorable advertising campaigns, for brands like Cadbury's Smash, Sony, John Smith's, Courage Best Bitter, Hofmeister Lager, and the Guardian newspaper. Many people in the industry referred to it—with affection, I think—as "the university of advertising."

The agency was very successful. By the early 1980s when I joined, it was one of Britain's top ten agencies by size, and widely regarded as one of the very best as measured by the quality of its work. By the middle of that decade, however, the growth had slowed. BMP was still being invited into a lot of major new business pitches, but it was failing to win. Time and time again the agency pitched. And time and time again the client came back with a resounding "no" for an answer.

The problem? Having developed a reputation for intelligence, the agency began, as Americans might say, to drink too much of its own Kool-Aid. The first task of every pitch seemed to be to prove just how much smarter the agency was than the client. The client's brief was wrong, and the agency would prove it. And from this new, improved agency brief, a strategy would be unveiled that would solve any problem to the 187th decimal place.

On one high-profile pitch to a national supermarket company, one of the agency's top strategic thinkers went away for what seemed like 40 days and 40 nights, eventually returning to our creative director with a tablet of stone on which he had written The Answer. Intellectually brilliant, his brief solved the eternal problems of retailing—even the ones the client hadn't thought of. If there had been a Nobel Prize for strategic direction to the supermarket industry this surely would have been a winner.

The creative director read it with interest. Then he said, "I can't write a fucking ad from that."

A few days later, the client was similarly unimpressed. The agency's presentation left him in no doubt that its executives regarded him as stupid, and he thanked them for their efforts by awarding his business to someone else.

In this case, and I suspect in many of BMP's other losing pitches at that time, the agency was probably correct in its point of view. The mistake it made was in contrasting its correctness with the client's errors, and while there is no doubt a time and a place for everything, a new business presentation is generally not the best time or place to tell a client that he or she is wrong. Another problem is that in almost any new business situation, however fast you are capable of learning, you will come to the presentation knowing less about the business at hand than every single member of the audience. Even if by some stroke of luck or genius you nail it so perfectly that a choir of angels spontaneously appears in the conference room to sing your name to the heavens, it is quite likely that no one will believe you.

Presentation Perfectionism

The second mistake presenters often make, after striving to find the perfect answer, is to try to make the perfect presentation.

It may seem strange that I would identify this as a mistake, when the title of this book is *Perfect Pitch*, but to me the success of a presentation is measured by its effect, not by its technical excellence. In her delightful book, *On Speaking Well*, Peggy Noonan (who wrote speeches for former Presidents Bush and Reagan) tells a story about Coco Chanel that illustrates this important distinction. Chanel believed that the hallmark of a great dress was that it didn't call too much attention to itself. Thus if a woman walked into a room wearing one of her dresses and everyone said, "What a fabulous dress!" she had failed. Success came when the woman walked into the room and people said, "You look fabulous!"

In the same way, a presenter fails if people say "What a great presentation!"

Back in 1983 when I was still a student at Nottingham University, I chaired a debate in which one of the speakers was Neil Kinnock, at that time the leader of the British Labour Party. He was an articulate, passionate orator, and for the 15 minutes that he spoke I, like most of the others in the room, was mesmerized. Some time later that same day, when someone asked me how Kinnock had performed, I replied that I had never heard a more impressive speaker.

"What did he talk about?" they asked.

And I didn't have a clue.

Many people have said of former U.S. President Bill Clinton that he is a brilliant speaker yet a poor presenter, because he often fails to make a clear point. His audiences are often moved by his speeches as I was by Neil Kinnock's, yet afterwards they are left grasping for meaning. As Peggy Noonan observes, "Clinton's biggest problem is that he rarely says anything that is intellectually interesting, that is genuinely deep and thoughtful. He has the intensity of a deep and thoughtful person without the depth of a deep and thoughtful person." Of course Peggy Noonan is a Republican, but I know what she means.

I will talk more about Bill Clinton in later chapters, because despite his occasional lapses into trying to say everything and please everyone rather than making a simple point, he is—at his best—one of the world's most engaging and persuasive presenters. For now, though, it should be enough to say that praise for being a great presenter, or making a great presentation, is not enough.

Much more desirable is the reaction that says, "You really made me think!" or "You have succeeded in changing my mind!" Or, simply, "You're hired!"

I hope that my pointing out Kinnock's or Clinton's inadequacies may come as a relief to any readers of this book who think they will never make a great presentation because they are not as good at public speaking as others they have heard. The ability to speak well in public is a means to an end, not an end in itself. It helps to be good at it—and I intend in the course of this book to offer advice that may help anyone to improve—but you should know that looking and sounding as good as Bill Clinton is not good enough if your presentation has no substance and if it doesn't succeed in communicating a clear and simple point.

This applies not only to individual presenters but also to presentations in general. I work in a business that is famous for "pitch theater," which often extends to building expensive sets, hiring Peruvian pipe ensembles, and generally spending a great deal of money on impressing a client. But any money spent on theater that is not directly related to the idea being communicated is generally money wasted. Turning a conference room into an airport departure lounge if you are presenting to British Airways might therefore be a good idea. One could argue that turning it into a tropical beach bar for the same pitch might also have some relevance. But creating a tropical beach bar for a presentation to executives from a company that makes shoe polish might be a little gratuitous. The same applies to expensive leave-behind books, which I will discuss in more detail in Chapter 8. I have seen fantastic books that bring the agency's idea to life in a very interesting and involving way and that the client will just have to read, savor, and keep; I have also seen books whose aim is simply to impress and which are expensive merely for the sake of it.

Great presentation!
Great room!
Great book!
But what's the point?

What's the Point?

A presentation does not begin at the moment when a presenter stands and says something original like "Good morning, ladies and gentlemen. Thank you very much for inviting us to present to you today." At least, the good ones don't. For the purposes of this book, I will explore "the presentation" not as just a single event but as a period extending from the moment the invitation to present is delivered, to the moment a decision is made. This period could extend over several months or even years. In the past two years I have worked on two separate new business projects where, each time, my team was given more than four months to prepare. After we had delivered our final pitch, one of these clients made a decision within two weeks. The other took another four months. In both cases, the work didn't stop when we handed out the leave-behind documents; we had to continue communicating the core idea to those who had been present and to others who had been absent, and we had to deal with the politics that are an inevitable part of any client decision-making process.

The purpose of any presentation is to take the key decision maker or makers from the place they currently occupy to the place where you want them to be. From Point A, where at worst they don't know you, understand you, or believe in your point of view, to some distant Point B, where they know, understand, *and* believe in you and are prepared to act upon that belief. From Point A, where you don't have their business, to Point B where you do. Point B is your objective. Point B is where you win.

This may sound obvious, but to take someone from Point A to Point B, as any airline pilot knows, it's helpful to know where the two points lie. You have to understand the decision makers' reasons for asking you to present, and what they will need to see and hear from you in order to make their decision in your favor. And having decided how far you need to take them, you will also have to figure out how to get them there. You can't just tell them where to go; you have to guide them carefully, sensitively, logically. And it's not enough to inform. The job of the person who wants to win is to persuade.

With that in mind, what follows is perhaps the most important lesson I have learned over the years of making new business presentations. It is also one of life's most important lessons, and you will see that it is a consistent theme of this book. It is this: successful communication and persuasion is not, as most people think, about being good at talking, having the gift of the gab. No, the best communicators, the best persuaders, are the best at what they do because invariably they are good *listeners*. As someone once told me, there's a reason why we all have one mouth and two ears. And even people who work in the notoriously voluble advertising business should try to use them in that proportion.

It sounds simple, but it's shocking how many companies and individuals lose sight of it. Let me illustrate the problem by example.

Let's imagine for a moment that I still live in Marin County, California. (As I look out on a cold, snowy day in England I can assure you that I imagine this often.) A colleague from out of town writes and asks for directions to the city of Oakland, and an estimate of how long the journey might take. This is the brief. Now I could answer this brief in a number of very different ways. For instance, I might write back saying, "Take the Richmond-San Rafael Bridge. The view's so much nicer than the Bay Bridge, there's less traffic, and it's cheaper."

I guess that very few people who have ever traveled to Oakland over the Richmond-San Rafael Bridge would disagree with this advice. The problem is that this route to Oakland is from Marin County, and in this case the person who asked the question will be coming from San Francisco. He also happens to be scared of heights, so he wouldn't want to cross any bridge, least of all keep his eyes open while doing so, and his Amish upbringing means that he prefers not to travel by car. All of these points render my directions completely useless. They are useless because they reflect my own personal preference on how to get to Oakland, not what my colleague needs. If I had stopped to think for long enough, I might have asked him one or two questions before sharing my wisdom.

A second way I might answer would be to say, "Don't go to Oakland! The traffic is terrible and it has some very bad neighborhoods."

Again, this is a personal point of view. Even if it's partially true, it's certainly not helpful. My colleague *has* to go to Oakland, and whether I like the place or not is irrelevant.

Assuming that I did know where he intended to start, and did not disapprove of his final destination, a third possibility might be to give him some detailed street directions in Oakland, followed by instructions on how to pay for a ferry ticket, then advice on getting a taxi in the East Bay, and finally directions to the ferry terminal in San Francisco. Even writing that is confusing. Imagine what it would be like to listen to and remember.

A fourth option would be for me to talk in some detail about the history of and methods used to construct the Bay Bridge; the geology and unique microclimate of Treasure Island, which lies in the middle of that bridge; the probability of an earthquake measuring more than 4.5 on the Richter scale striking in the time that it would take a person (on average and in ideal weather conditions) to cross from San Francisco to Oakland; and the diversity of bird life that may be visible while crossing the Bay. In this case, what I have to say may actually take longer than the journey itself.

Finally, and much more sensibly, I might respond with some questions of my own. Where will you be coming from? What time do you need to be there? Would you prefer to travel by road, rail, or by ferry? By asking such questions I can tailor my response to the particular needs of my colleague. And if he is interested in knowing more about the bird life of San Francisco Bay I can buy him a book for his birthday.

This example is not as far-fetched as it might seem, because every day, in conference rooms all over the world, people are making presentations—many of them extremely important, career-, company-, and life-defining presentations—which treat their audience as I treated this imaginary colleague in the first four examples.

They fail to find out what the audience really wants, or needs, to hear.

They lecture, as opposed to communicating.

Their presentations lack a clear flow.

They believe success to be directly proportional to detail.

Think of these as *presentation crimes.* They are crimes against the audience and crimes against those whose livelihoods rest upon a successful outcome. Just one of these crimes can condemn the perpetrator to failure; in combination, failure is virtually guaranteed. I will examine them separately before focusing in Chapter 2 on one famous example of how getting them wrong can end in disaster: the presentation of the case for the prosecution in the 1994–1995 trial for murder of O.J. Simpson.

Failing to Understand the Needs of the Audience

A few years ago, on a commercial flight out of San Francisco, I rather uncharacteristically listened to the advice of the cabin staff before take-off, and took the time to read the safety card in the seat-back pocket in front of me. In the part outlining the procedures that should be followed in case of an emergency, one sentence read:

> If you are seated in an exit row and you are unable to read this card, please call a member of the cabin crew.

It doesn't take long to figure out how many blind or illiterate passengers would be likely to respond as requested to instructions that they couldn't read. It's a classic example of someone failing to consider the needs of their audience; if the airline is thinking about its safety procedures so carefully, I hate to think how it might instruct its maintenance crews to service the engines.

Many presenters offer similar disregard to the needs of their audience, and have apparently been doing so for thousands of years. In *Rhetoric,* Aristotle wrote of *pathos,* the ability of the successful persuader to connect emotionally to an audience. His perspective was that if an audience didn't like you, they were unlikely to listen, even less to act upon what you had to say. Such emotional connections are impossible if you do not know your audience. You have to understand exactly why they have asked you to present: why they might be dissatisfied with their current business partner, what keeps them awake at night, what they expect to hear from you, what they think they want to hear from you, and what they need to hear. (The final three are very often quite different, and it's critical to understand the reasons why.) You have to do your homework before you meet, and when you do meet you have to ask questions. And it does help to listen to the answers.

If you think about it, a successful presentation has a great deal in common with a successful first date. The aim of both is to impress the other party enough to progress to a further meeting, and, all other things being equal, appearing to be more interested in hearing about the other person than talking about yourself is a pretty reliable strategy. Of course you also have to use knowledge to your advantage. On your first date, if you know that she volunteers at an animal shelter on the weekend, it's probably advisable not to spend all evening telling her about the way you used to shoot birds, rabbits, and the occasional stray cat on your dad's farm. If he told you that he's allergic to shellfish, you might want to hold off on the oyster stew. Similarly, the client who is legendary for his middle-American values and whose brand's core audience is aged over fifty might not enjoy a reel full of video game commercials packed with fart and belch references. And a devoutly Catholic client might not appreciate the stripping nun you have organized to perform at the end of dinner.

If these examples seem ridiculous, it's probably because they are. But they also happen to be true. I know the people involved and hope that they will appreciate my not naming them. The first dates I mentioned were, not surprisingly, last dates, of which one ended in a hospital emergency room. And the stripping nun incident, at a London dinner held in honor of Renault clients from Italy at the time of a major international review, is still talked about by those from the agency who were there. None of whom, incidentally, worked much on the Renault business thereafter.

The chances of a presentation successfully taking the audience to your desired Point B are greatly reduced if you cannot discipline yourself to see and hear everything you do and say from the point of view of each and every member of your audience. This applies at every stage of the process, from the very first meeting to the final presentation and beyond. Your every word, your every action, will pass through the filter of their experience, expectations, prejudices, hopes and fears. It's thus not what you say that is important. It's how they will receive it. And how they will process it.

Lecturing Rather Than Communicating

Many people regard the purpose of presentations as imparting information. They assume that when they speak, the audience will listen. The audience will believe. The audience will act.

If only it were that simple.

In 1991 I was part of a team from the then-named Goodby, Berlin & Silverstein, making a new business presentation to the National Basketball Association in the United States. Andy Berlin opened the meeting; his task was to introduce his colleagues and give Commissioner David Stern and his team a short preview of what was to come. I should point out that at his best, which is probably 95 percent of the time, Andy is one of the most engaging, effective presenters I have ever seen. Unfortunately, this was one of the other times and, uncharacteristically tense, he proceeded not just to preview the presentation but to deliver it himself in some detail. About forty minutes into this "brief" introduction, he turned to me and announced to the audience that I would now be presenting the agency's strategic recommendations.

Given that he had already presented most of them for me, I too had developed quite a serious case of stage fright. This wasn't helped when, about two sentences into a presentation that I knew had to be revised as I delivered it, David Stern said loudly and theatrically, "You've brought a *Brit* to talk to me about basketball?"

I responded with a reasonably well-received joke about knowing the difference between Karl Malone, Moses Malone, and Bugsy Malone (for the non-aficionado, Bugsy Malone was a movie character, not an NBA star), but for the rest of the time that I was on my feet I was too busy mentally rewriting and improvising to be able to recall exactly what I said. I was, however, aware of Andy Berlin becoming more and more agitated. He knew—as we all did—that we were failing spectacularly, but he couldn't figure out how to get it back on track.

What I didn't see was the note he passed to copywriter Dave O'Hare, who was supposed to follow me by presenting our proposed campaign. It read:

> O'Hare: Be enthusiastic. Tell them what a great campaign it is. Sell the fucker hard. And I mean hard.

O'Hare scribbled a reply that he couldn't do that. It wasn't his style to sell anything hard.

Andy's finger prodded his original words on the note. Tell. Them. What. A. Great. Campaign. It. Is. Anyone who has met him will know that Andy Berlin is a large man, with quite persuasive fingers.

A few minutes later, when I had finished repeating Andy's introduction, O'Hare rose.

"Thanks, Jon," he said, through a strange, fixed smile. "We have a great campaign for you today. We're really excited by it. And what's great. . . ."

"Stop!" Commissioner Stern rose to his feet, stopping him in his tracks. "I tell you what. I'm going to tell you the funniest joke in the world. It's really funny. Maybe the funniest joke you have ever heard. Shall I tell it to you?"

"Point taken," Andy said quickly. "Come on, O'Hare. Just show the work, will you?"

Strangely enough, we went on to win the NBA pitch, because David Stern and his team really did like the idea we presented, and for some reason they were prepared to forgive our earlier transgressions. And several years later, with his new agency in New York, Andy won the business for a second time, based in large part on the excellent relationship he forged with David Stern after that rockiest of starts.

But that first time we really didn't deserve to win. Our presentation was chaotic, and when Andy told Dave O'Hare to "sell the fucker hard," he was asking him to do what O'Hare instinctively knew that he should never do—namely, to tell the audience what to think, rather than allowing them to draw their own conclusions.

Many presentations are based on the simple but erroneous view of communication as something that happens successfully when a sender delivers a message to a recipient and elicits a response that mirrors the message. In the NBA example described above, Andy Berlin is the sender, David Stern is the recipient, and the message is "It's a wonderful campaign." The desired response? The message echoes back as David Stern says, "It's a wonderful campaign!"

It didn't happen that way because in fact, as Jeremy Bullmore points out in an excellent chapter in his book, *More Bull More*, "The Consumer Has a Mind as Well as a Stomach," a message is a double-edged sword, because it can mean two quite different things and we can't always distinguish between them. A message is something that a sender might put into a piece of communication, but it is also something that the recipient might take out. And unfortunately for the presenters who do not understand these things, the two are not always the same.

For example, my son happens to go to school with a child whose doting, somewhat myopic parents have convinced him that he is God's gift to sport in general, and God's gift to the sport of rugby in particular. Thus if this boy walks into the classroom and says, "I'm the best rugby player in the school," he thinks that the message has duly been delivered and everyone will be convinced of his brilliance. The problem—for him—is that while his message is indeed received, his audience then processes it in a way that he doesn't expect. Rather than nodding their heads and saying, "Yes, he sure is the best rugby player in the school," they raise their eyebrows, remember all the times he missed tackles or dropped the ball, and think something like, "you arrogant little prick." These ten-year-old schoolboys are far from being the passive recipients of information that their annoying little friend assumes. Like any audience that is still listening, they are active participants in his communication.

Jeremy Bullmore, in his book mentioned earlier, describes the act of communication not as a message delivered and received, but rather as the provision of a stimulus, which invites the participation of the audience and elicits a response. Such a stimulus may come in the form of words. It may also be provided by a smile, by perspiration, by dress, by tone of voice or, in the above example of the schoolboy, by knocking the crap out of an opponent with a tackle that causes everyone to say, "What a fantastic rugby player!" The way humans exchange information and form opinions in their life outside of business is very complex and extremely subtle. It would be naïve to think that they behave any differently once they enter a conference room.

My own rather simplistic version of the stimulus and response mechanism is to ask people to see their presentations in the form of punctuation. Many presentations come in the form of the period, or full stop, implying the end of a thought. These are the presentations that assume passive reception on the part of the audience. Other, better presentations, take on the form of the question mark. They signal the start of a new thought: an invitation, a challenge to the audience to get involved, to bring something of themselves to your communication. They are going to do it anyhow, so why not make it work for you? As Bullmore says, you should aim to make your audience willing accomplices in your presentation.

Perhaps the best advice ever offered to presenters on this subject is that of the Japanese philosopher Saki. He said, "When baiting the mousetrap with cheese, always be sure to leave room for the mouse."

Lacking a Clear Flow

The members of the audience will spend more time thinking about why the presenter is talking about a particular subject than about what they are being told.

It will start at Point A and will end at Point B, and the presenter will figure out a logical way to get them there, one idea at a time.

PowerPoint presents a particular problem for presenters who allow its limitations to dictate structure and content.

Bad presenters provide their audience with no map, and no signposts.

How many times have you found yourself in a presentation asking, "How the heck did we get *here?*"

A good presentation, like a good movie, will have a clear start, middle, and end.

Andy Berlin's introduction to the NBA was intended to provide direction, but because he expanded it to include almost every point each one of the team was going to make, it created chaos.

When a presenter starts jumping around between ideas, and layering one on top of another, it becomes very confusing for the audience.

Just like this section.

Too Much Detail

The final cardinal sin of the presenter is to provide too much detail. This stems from the belief that in order to succeed it is necessary to communicate absolutely everything you know, and everything that every single member of your audience might possibly want to know.

This belief manifests itself in chart after chart of numbers, detailed technical explanations, and a word count that would bore the hind legs off a donkey; most of it is totally unnecessary in the achievement of the objectives, and more often than not it is counter-productive.

I am confident in assuming that at some time in your career, you too have been the victim of this particular presentation crime. But in the interests of brevity and because I now want to talk about O.J. Simpson, I will say no more on the subject except to note the famous words of Ludwig Mies van der Rohe:

Less is more.

I hope that in the following pages I offer enough (but not too many) examples of effective communication and persuasion to convince you that where presentation is concerned, Mies van der Rohe was absolutely right.

CHAPTER TWO

- **Imperfect Pitch**
  - The People of the State of California v. Orenthal James Simpson

The Case for the Prosecution

More than ten years have passed since I, like millions of others in the United States, watched the bizarre CNN coverage of O.J. Simpson driving slowly down a Southern California freeway in a white Ford Bronco, accompanied by a phalanx of law enforcement and television vehicles, being cheered by members of the general public from every shoulder, exit ramp, and overpass. This was just the beginning. In the months that followed, the nation was gripped by the trial; it became perhaps the most public, the most talked-about, in legal history. The principal characters became household names—not just the accused, whose legendary status was already assured thanks to his strength and speed when carrying a football, but the judge, the prosecutors, the defense attorneys, the victims, and key witnesses. Overseas, people who knew O.J. Simpson only as an actor in the *Naked Gun* movies became caught up in the excitement. It was rare for me to talk to a friend in Europe without being asked, "What's going on in the trial?"

While others were interested because they thought Kato Kaelin was cute, or because they liked to gossip about Marcia Clark's dress sense, I was drawn for another reason. To me it was a new business pitch in all but name. The prosecution and defense were competing agencies; large teams of people worked invisibly but feverishly behind the scenes while their senior executives basked in the limelight. The members of the jury and their alternates were the audience; at the end there would be twelve key decision makers. The verdict was Point B, the ultimate prize. At just over a year in duration, the trial did take a little longer than most new business pitches—although not all—and it was certainly higher profile than most. Yet it was won and lost for exactly the same reasons that advertising agencies, landscape architects, and hair care product salesmen win and lose when they present to potential clients.

In this chapter I want to focus exclusively on the strategy and execution of the prosecution team, led by Marcia Clark. Obviously the prosecutors' actions alone can't explain the "not guilty" verdict that was delivered on October 3, 1995, but they are illustrative of many of the common errors made by presenters, the so-called "presentation crimes" outlined in Chapter 1. In the Simpson trial, these errors were exacerbated by a smart strategy and consistent, almost perfect execution on the part of the late Johnnie Cochran and his defense team. These positive lessons in presentation provided by Cochran and his team will be explored in Chapter 3. For now, though, let's look at some of the fundamental mistakes made by Clark and her colleagues in prosecuting O.J. Simpson—mistakes that as presenters we should all strive to avoid.

Mistake Number One: Not Listening to the Audience

O.J. Simpson was arrested on Friday, June 17, 1994, and charged with the murder of his ex-wife, Nicole Brown Simpson, and her friend, Ronald Goldman. More than three months then passed before Judge Lance Ito opened proceedings on September 26.

The first stage of the trial was the selection of a jury from a pool of more than nine hundred potential jurors. In the three months since Simpson's arrest, both the prosecution and defense had used consultants to advise them on the optimum composition of the jury, and these deliberations had centered on the sensitive issue of ethnicity. Early public opinion polls had suggested that opinions on the Simpson case divided sharply along race lines, with white respondents generally regarding him as guilty and black respondents convinced of his innocence.

The presumption of Simpson's innocence on the part of the African-American community did not seem to worry Marcia Clark. As Jeffrey Toobin points out in his excellent article, "The Marcia Clark Verdict," published in *The New Yorker* in September 1996, Clark believed that over the years she had developed a particularly strong affinity for black female jurors. "In case after case, she saw their smiles, their nods, their sympathy." Her strategy in many of the cases she had prosecuted was to evoke the humanity and suffering of victims, and create an emotional bond between these victims, the jurors, and herself. Going into the Simpson case, she believed that she could succeed once more with this approach. She wanted a disproportionate number of black women on the jury, based on the theory that black women were disproportionately victims of domestic violence themselves. With this experience—either direct or indirect—she believed that they would relate to the suffering of Nicole Brown Simpson and embrace the victim as one of their own. Given O.J. Simpson's well-documented history of domestic violence, and the volume of evidence connecting him to the murder scene, she was confident of both touching black female jurors on a personal level and getting a conviction.

While Clark's desire to involve jurors on a personal level was exactly right in theory, the circumstances of this case were different from most of those she had tried in the past. The occasions where she had succeeded in connecting to black female jurors were often those where the accused was the kind of predator who could conceivably have threatened the jurors themselves. O. J. Simpson, the football hero and movie star, was not like any of those other alleged murderers. Perhaps even more significant, the social and cultural context in which the trial took place had changed.

One of the most important truths of any presentation—whether it takes place in a legal, business or political setting—is that it does not exist in a vacuum. Presenters who pay attention to the effects of external social, economic, and cultural forces—and understand how to use them to their advantage—tend to succeed, while those who ignore or try to fight against them invariably fail. This was a vital lesson that Marcia Clark chose to ignore.

Just two years before O.J. Simpson was arrested, the United States had experienced its most violent and destructive rioting since the 1863 Draft Riots in New York City. These riots took place in Los Angeles, and when the fires were finally extinguished more than 50 people were dead, hundreds injured, 7,000 arrested, and more than $1 billion in property damage had been sustained. The violence was in response to the acquittal of four Los Angeles Police Department officers, who had been caught on video beating an apparently defenseless African-American man named Rodney King. To most impartial observers, it seemed like an open-and-shut case. The officers were easily identifiable, and as the video was shown again and again on television, polls showed that more than 90 percent of the population of Los Angeles believed that they had used "excessive force." But a largely white jury in Simi Valley acquitted them, and a furious African-American community took to the streets in protest. Even though two of the officers were eventually convicted on federal civil rights charges, the incident and first trial had left many African-Americans in Los Angeles with lingering feelings of institutional racism in the Los Angeles Police Department and judicial system. These were feelings that Clark would have to fight if she went ahead with her strategy of selecting a largely African-American jury.

In July, 1994, a month after Simpson was arrested, Clark was present during some research organized by a jury consultant to assess possible jury reactions to key facts in the Simpson case. The results, described by Jeffrey Toobin in *The New Yorker*, were possibly more "stark and overwhelming" than those of the public opinion polls. Among the mock jurors, whites were for conviction, blacks for acquittal. Even when, as an experiment, four black jurors were given additional "evidence" that established with absolute certainty that it was Simpson's blood on a glove found at the murder scene, three of the four refused to change their "not guilty" vote. Contrary to what Clark had expected, black women in this and later research actually defended Simpson's history of domestic violence, saying that a bit of "slapping around" is a natural part of most relationships, and that a history of hitting his wife certainly didn't make him a murderer. These jurors seemed to have more empathy with O.J.—for whom many still expressed their admiration—than they did toward his ex-wife. Indeed, their feelings toward Nicole Brown Simpson seemed to border on antipathy; in their eyes, such a beautiful, rich white woman was almost more threatening than the accused.

When these same jurors were asked for their opinions of Marcia Clark herself (as I might ask clients for their opinions of individual members of my pitch team, lest I prejudice my chances by fielding someone whom the client takes objection to), many of them described her as harsh, strident. Maybe this was because for many of these black women, O.J. Simpson was the epitome of African-American virility and success. And Marcia Clark, like all those other jealous white people, was trying to emasculate him.

For many, one word seemed to fit her perfectly.

Bitch.

Marcia Clark knew all of this when she entered Judge Lance Ito's courtroom on the morning of September 26, 1994. Yet she went ahead with jury selection as she had planned from the very start. When the final 12 members of the jury retired just over a year later to consider their verdict, one of the 12 was an African-American man. There was a Latino man and two Caucasian women. The remaining eight were all African-American women—this in a county where African Americans amount to 11 percent of the total population and just over 30 percent of the jury pool

The seeds of Marcia Clark's failure were sown before a single item of evidence was shown in Judge Ito's courtroom. To be fair, her mistakes were not unique: Many presenters, in situations much less tense than this, opt for the comfort and confidence provided by the tried-and-tested approach, without stopping to consider its suitability to new and different circumstances. Many presenters also find it hard to look beyond the expected parameters of their subject. Clark saw the O.J. Simpson trial as a simple exercise in proving a man's guilt, while the defense team—as we will see in Chapter 3—took the wider view. They opened their eyes and ears, saw and listened, and adapted. Meanwhile, Clark and her team buried their heads in the sand of righteous idealism.

Clark decided to recruit a jury which, in the wider context of Angeleno and American race relations, was less likely to convict O.J. Simpson than a jury of similar composition might have done just two years previously. She then adopted a strategy—that of portraying Simpson as an instrument of domestic violence—which these jurors were predisposed to reject. She did so in a manner that alienated many of them, just as she had alienated their "test" equivalents in the pre-trial research. And when it became clear that her strategy was not working, she was not flexible enough to change.

In business, I have never had the opportunity to select an audience. I can't even imagine the circumstances under which that might happen. But it is simply impossible to make a successful presentation without first understanding the audience—their preconceptions, their prejudices, the reasons why you are presenting to them at all, the reasons why they might not want to listen. It's the first rule of the advertising business that the only important opinion is that of the person hearing or seeing a commercial message, yet even in my business that rule is often ignored when a presentation is being prepared. Whatever the context of the presentation, you ignore the feelings of the audience at your peril. Furthermore, a successful strategy for presentation is based not necessarily on what you believe, or even on what is right, but rather on what is most likely to take the audience, both individually and collectively, to your desired destination.

In the Simpson trial, it was Marcia Clark's failure to identify the correct final landing point for her audience that represented the second fatal flaw in her case.

Mistake Number Two: Not Recognizing the Real Destination

When Marcia Clark spoke to reporters shortly after Simpson's arrest in June 1994, she spoke emphatically of his guilt. "It was premeditated murder," she said at a press conference at the Los Angeles Criminal Courts Building. "That is what we will prove."

She believed this passionately, and everything about her subsequent strategy was geared towards having the jurors believe it too. She and her prosecution colleagues spent 23 weeks presenting evidence to prove that O.J. Simpson killed Nicole Brown Simpson and Ronald Goldman in a most violent and premeditated manner. It seems like a reasonable enough strategy—after all, isn't that the job of the prosecution, to prove that the accused is guilty? In this case, though, Clark should have heard enough from the reactions of the focus groups and mock juries before the trial opened to know that it was not enough for the jurors to believe that Simpson had wielded the knife that killed his ex-wife and Ronald Goldman.

This is a fundamental issue in any presentation. It is not enough for the client to believe that your point of view is right, that your advertising campaign is better than the other agency's, or that your garden design is better than that of your award-winning competitor. That belief has to be turned into action. With the advertising example, the client has to believe so strongly in the superiority of your work that he or she is willing to fire the existing agency—a notoriously difficult thing to do—and then hire you ahead of the others in the review process. (Or, conversely, rehire you when the entire review was set up as a means of getting rid of you.) The desired outcome is therefore not doing the best work, or even making the best presentation, but rather getting hired. Similarly, a young garden designer might present fantastic ideas, only to be beaten by someone who has won countless awards at the Chelsea Flower Show and who—even in the light of a substandard presentation—just seems like a more reliable choice. I know I'm repeating myself, but it's an important enough point to bear not just repetition, but repeated repetition.

It's not just about being right.

It's not only about being the best.

It's about winning.

As I mentioned in Chapter 1, being right and being the best are admirable objectives, and nine times out of ten they will indeed carry you to victory. In later chapters I will talk more about how to arrive at the correct solution, and how to make a better, more persuasive presentation. For now, though, I want to leave you with the essential message that being right and being the best will never guarantee victory. I can tell you that from bitter personal experience. You haven't won until your client has signed the first check.

To win the O.J. Simpson case, Marcia Clark and her team had to do more than give Simpson a motive and tie him to the scene, the weapon, the bloodstains, the infamous bloody glove. Of course they had to convince the jurors beyond reasonable doubt that Simpson had killed his ex-wife and her friend, but more than that *they had to persuade them to return a guilty verdict.* The desired belief and the desired action are very different, and would have required equally different strategies on the part of the prosecution. Unfortunately for the prosecution, the only people who really seemed to understand this were the members of O.J. Simpson's defense team, who did not set out to prove that Simpson was innocent, but rather to make it too uncomfortable for the jurors to return a "Guilty" verdict. It proved to be a critical distinction.

It may seem like I'm splitting hairs over definitions of guilt or innocence, making semantic arguments to explain the outcome of a trial that due to external factors alone might well have been over before it even began. But there is no more important issue to consider when preparing any presentation. It is a basic truth of human nature that imparting information is not enough to make someone believe. It is equally true that belief—even if that belief is passionately held, and passionately argued—is no sure indicator of behavior.

I have encountered numerous examples of these contradictions in the business world. When I worked on the California Milk Processors' *got milk?* campaign in the 1990s, I saw dairy industry campaigns from all over the world that sought to halt the decline in milk sales by persuading people that milk was good for them. The effect of many of these campaigns was to increase the percentage of people believing that milk was good for their bones, skin, teeth, and hair, and even to increase the numbers of those claiming that they intended to consume more. These improved attitudes, however, were matched only by a continued decline in consumption. So knowing about milk's nutritional benefits was not enough. Believing that they should drink more was insufficient incentive to take a trip to the grocery store. By contrast, my agency's *got milk?* campaign set out with the express aim of changing behavior: persuading people to buy more milk, and persuading them to consume more. Exactly how we did it, our client said, did not matter in the slightest. The end would justify the means. Our proposed solution was to create desire for milk through the kinds of food that had never been previously featured in milk advertising on health grounds (peanut butter and jelly sandwiches, brownies, chocolate chip cookies, and the like), but which were all perfect companions to milk. We proposed stimulating increased purchase by reminding people how terrible it was to run out of milk—a situation made infinitely worse in the presence of one of those companion foods. The resulting campaign succeeded in increasing milk sales in California for the first time in decades, because its objectives and strategy were set in a context of truth. It was based on the way that people really use milk—not the way they have been taught to talk about it.*

Similarly, more recently, I was part of a team pitching to Unilever for its global laundry business. For brands like Persil in the U.K. and Omo across much of the rest of the world, Unilever had been running an interesting, controversially counter-intuitive campaign based on the idea that getting dirty is an important part of a child's development. While other laundry brands were talking degrees of whiteness, Unilever was championing the act of getting dirty under the banner of "Dirt is Good." Our research across the world showed that the core target of mothers readily agreed with this idea. "Yes, it's so important for children to get dirty," they told us. "We encourage it."

When we talked to their children, however, they seemed to have rather a different perspective. "When we come home dirty," they said, "mom gets real upset."

It seemed that the idea of "Dirt is Good" resonated on an intellectual level. It was an idea that every mother could agree on . . . when it pertained to other people's children. But when *her* child appeared at the door with dirty knees—well, that was a different story. The task was clear: if the campaign were to achieve its full potential, Unilever's communication had to take mothers beyond rational agreement and have them become *active participants*. Again, belief had to be converted into action.

Outside of the business world, my life and probably yours are filled with such contradictions. Forty-five million Americans still smoke

---

*For more on the *got milk?* campaign, see my book, *Truth, Lies, and Advertising,* Chapter 7.

cigarettes, and I'd bet the majority of them not only know that smoking is bad for them but would also rather give up than keep on smoking. They know, they believe, but they just keep on lighting up. And why does the number of gymnasium members exceed the number of users by more than two to one? We know why we should go, we believe that we should, yet our actions suggest otherwise.

My point is that people generally don't make decisions based solely on rational evidence, any more than the O.J. Simpson jury voted on the body of evidence presented by Marcia Clark and her colleagues in 1995. Even minor decisions are influenced by emotional factors and by the cultural context in which they are to be taken.

In part, Marcia Clark failed to convince the Simpson jury because she didn't understand the critical nature of this cultural context. In part she failed because she believed that it was enough to prove Simpson's guilt. But she also failed because she presented her case in a way that prejudiced the majority of the jurors against her.

Mistake Number Three: Lecturing the Audience

There is no doubt that Marcia Clark is a very accomplished trial lawyer. Her track record before the Simpson case was impressive, and her opening statement in the Simpson trial, where she described the trail of blood "where there should be no blood . . . a trail of blood from Bundy through (Simpson's) own Ford Bronco and into his house in Rockingham is devastating proof of his guilt," was generally admired by experienced legal observers and commentators. Unfortunately, Clark also had an arrogant streak that had led to her rejecting the advice of jury consultants and researchers before the trial, and that arrogance accompanied her into the courtroom.

In the pre-trial research, mock jurors had been asked for their opinions of Clark from what they had seen on television coverage of the case. Many of them had reacted negatively, describing her as strident and harsh in the way she had publicly proclaimed Simpson's guilt. This may have been influenced by a number of factors, including the rather stern manner—mostly dark business suits—in which she dressed, her tightly permed hair (which was to soften later—perhaps too late—in the trial), and a brusque speech pattern. On the basis that all of this might be somewhat intimidating to those jurors with less education than herself, several of her prosecution colleagues and paid advisors recommended a lighter approach. These recommendations were not heeded.

From the early days of the trial, much of the prosecution's evidence was presented in a style suggesting to the jurors that the prosecutors thought they were dumb. In part this was a function of Clark's personal manner, but it was also manifested in the inordinate amount of time taken, and number of witnesses called, to establish facts that could almost be regarded as given. Speaking after the trial, defense attorney Robert Shapiro offered as the most blatant example of this the eight days of evidence offered to establish that Nicole Brown Simpson and Ronald Goldman had died as a result of multiple stab wounds. No one on the jury would have doubted this, and as creative as Shapiro and his defense team were, even they would have been hard pushed to suggest an alternative explanation.

A line I have often heard in relation to bringing up children is "know when to fight your battles." Let the small stuff go, and save your energy for the really important issues. That advice is equally pertinent for presentations. If the members of your audience already know something, then you should simply acknowledge it and move on. Even if they don't know it, it is sometime best to acknowledge it—as something that intelligent, knowledgeable people like the ones sitting before you are *sure* to know—and move on. Trust me—they will nod their heads as if they have known it all their lives. Save your energy for the big, contentious issues, because proving the obvious, reproving it, and proving it again just to be sure, will make any audience member wonder how stupid you really believe them to be.

An important issue here is respect—more specifically, the audience's perception of the amount of respect you are paying them. I will talk more about this in later chapters, but in any presentation, every single member of the audience has to feel that nothing is more important to you than what you are saying, and no person in the world is more important than the one who is watching and listening to you right now. Everything you do and say has to appear to be for their benefit.

In the Simpson trial, Marcia Clark herself handled many of the early witnesses, but for a period of almost three months, while the prosecution was presenting its forensic evidence, she left the presentation to other prosecutors. During this period she was often late for court, which left many of the jurors with the impression that she did not respect them. They had been sequestered for the duration of the trial, with no contact with the outside world, and every morning they were roused early by Sheriff's Department officials to ensure their punctual arrival in court. Many observers noted the frosty stares Clark drew from the jurors as she belatedly took her seat. Again, it's a small thing—and unrelated to the substantive evidence of the trial—but it made a huge difference. I have seen a new business pitch fall apart because one of the agency partners stepped outside the room to take a call, or because another—who was not a part of that day's pitch team— did not even drop by to say "hi." I've seen clients enraged by the fact that during the presentation one of our senior team members seemed more interested in his BlackBerry than in anything anyone else in the room was saying. And tardiness in almost any context is interpreted as sloppy and disrespectful.

If Marcia Clark had been late only once or twice, she could have explained it in terms that many of the jurors would have understood, and which may even have endeared her to them. She was a single working mother, and even high-profile attorneys have kids who get sick or caregivers who let them down. But no such explanation was forthcoming; Clark was habitually late, and apparently without contrition.

As the trial developed, it was clear to most courtroom observers that the prosecution had lost the initiative in the case. The evidence had taken 24 weeks to present, the forensic and DNA evidence in particular had been lengthy and confusing, and in cross-examination defense lawyers had very successfully turned the jurors' attention away from the evidence and instead towards issues of race and of police incompetence. In the face of carefully measured provocation from the defense,

Clark had become increasingly frustrated, and this frustration was obvious in her exasperated responses.

As Johnnie Cochran said on the day that the prosecution rested, "We did pretty well—on their case."

When the time came for the defense to present its case, which it did in less than half the time taken by the prosecution, Clark seemed to channel her frustration into her cross-examination of the witnesses. People who had met with Simpson in the days leading up to the murder were treated as if they, not he, were on trial. One young couple, who happened to have walked home from their first date on a route that took them past the murder scene about 15 minutes after the prosecution contended the murder had taken place, testified that they had not seen a body. To protect her chronology, Clark tried to discredit them, virtually accusing them of drinking so much over dinner that their memories were impaired, or making the whole thing up for the sake of publicity.

Because the 15 minutes in question did not really make much difference—Simpson could still have committed the murder after the couple passed and got home in time for his "alibi limo" to the airport—such aggressive questioning was really unnecessary.

It's reminiscent of a new business pitch conducted about 1990, by Goodby, Berlin and Silverstein. At the end of the presentation, one of the clients—who had obviously been engaged by what we had said—asked a simple question: "Do you have a direct marketing capability?"

My immediate instinct was that this was asked out of interest rather than for any more ominous reason. It was really no big deal. Unfortunately, one of my colleagues whom I will call Bill, saw the question otherwise. He immediately launched into a defense of our ability to handle the client's business, our excellent track record in working in partnership with other companies, the unimportance of direct marketing relative to the required task, the need to concentrate on the big strategic issues rather than minor executional considerations, his surprise that the client would have asked that particular question when we had been at pains to point out the need for an anthemic television campaign (maybe the client hadn't understood?), and the need for an agency to concentrate on what it really does best.

No one could get a word in edgewise for about ten minutes. When he finally stopped to take breath, Andy Berlin spoke to the now stony-faced client.

"What Bill means," he said, "is *no*."

Berlin, unlike Marcia Clark, knew when he was beaten.

Mistake Number Four: Boring the Audience

On May 8, 1995, Court TV reported, "Court became biology class Monday as the prosecution's first DNA expert lectured to the jury on her specialty."

Does that set off any alarm bells?

In all the years I have been working in the advertising business, I cannot recall a single occasion where a TV producer has taken the floor in a new business pitch and explained the long and tedious process by which TV commercials are made. I have bought a number of cars since that battered, blue compact Volvo in 1985, and I still know nothing about the workings of the internal combustion engine. Is this behavior sloppy? Have my agencies been deficient in not explaining the technicalities of TV production, and have I risked the small fortune I have expended on cars by not taking the trouble to really understand how they work? I think not.

In week 16 of the Simpson trial, Dr. Robin Cotton, the laboratory director of Cellmark Diagnostics and a PhD in molecular biology and biochemistry, took to the stand to explain the process of RFLP, or Restriction Fragment Link Polymorphism, which she said was the most effective and accurate method of testing deoxyribonucleic acid (DNA). She also explained the so-called PCR test, which takes less time to perform and requires a smaller blood sample. For her presentation she used many large boards, with complex diagrams showing double helixes and multi- (and I mean *multi-*) syllabic words. For six days she testified, showing how the odds of a blood spot found near the victims' bodies belonging to anyone other than O.J. Simpson were in excess of one in 170 million. The chances of blood spots found on Simpson's socks coming from anyone other than his ex-wife were a staggering one in 9.7 billion.

She was still talking in week seventeen, finally making way for a second DNA expert from the California Department of Justice to cover much of the same ground. Gary Sims explained how the Restriction Fragment Link Polymorphism tests done at the California lab were different from the Restriction Fragment Link Polymorphism tests carried out by Dr. Cotton's Cellmark Diagnostics. On May 18, he combined the test results to give new odds on the blood on O.J. Simpson's sock belonging to anyone other than Nicole Brown Simpson—one out of 21 billion.

The numbers are impressive, but from the very start of the trial they had been undermined by defense assertions of racially motivated conspiracy, forensic incompetence, and contamination. What does one in 21 billion really mean if there's a greater chance that a racist cop planted the evidence?

The truth is that with all the explanation, all the science, the prosecution numbed the jury to the point where even the most powerful conclusions had little effect. I have just described the contributions of Dr. Robin Cotton and Gary Sims to the Simpson trial in just two paragraphs, and I imagine that you found those paragraphs as tiring to read as I found them to write. Now imagine what it was like having to sit on an uncomfortable seat and listen to that kind of stuff for an entire day. And the day after that. And every day for the best part of three weeks.

Speaking after the trial, Robert Shapiro said, "The prosecution bored the jury on the forensic evidence. Rather than qualifying a witness as an expert and asking for an opinion of the results, they tried to explain to a lay jury the science that was nearly impossible to understand . . . when you bore a jury, you lose a jury."

And when you bore an audience in a new business presentation, you lose the business.

Even in the summing up of the case, Marcia Clark and Christopher Darden methodically re-presented the basic elements of the prosecution's case, describing each item of evidence as interlocking pieces that connected to prove Simpson's guilt, and culminating in the presentation of a complex visual that summarized all the points of unrefuted evidence. "What we have here is logic, and evidence, and common sense," Clark told the jury.

In response, the defense told a story. A story of lies, ineptitude, and corruption. Of a bigoted LAPD officer who hated O.J. Simpson enough to frame him for murder. Johnnie Cochran quoted the bible and tried on O.J.'s black knit cap to show that it hardly worked as a disguise. He invoked Adolf Hitler while describing Mark Fuhrman as a "lying, perjuring, genocidal racist." Leaning towards the jury he said, "If you grew up in America you know that there are Fuhrmans out there." He talked about the failed experiment where the prosecution had asked Simpson to try on the bloody glove, and Simpson hadn't been able to pull it on. "If it doesn't fit," he said, "you must acquit." His colleague Barry Scheck asked the jurors how many cockroaches they would have to find in a plate of spaghetti before they refused to eat it.

"This," he said, "is reasonable doubt."

Finally, in contrast to Clark's entreaty to decide on logic, evidence, and common sense, Cochran urged the jurors to vote not just with their intellect but with their hearts and feelings as well.

And, after deliberating for less than four hours, that's exactly what they did.

CHAPTER THREE

- Bill Clinton, Johnnie Cochran, and a London Hooker

  - Learning from the world's best presenters

The Science of Successful Presentation

In the introduction to *Physics for Poets*, Robert March writes:

> A scientist . . . is supposed to be looking for the *truth* about nature. But not all truths are equal. Some we call *deep* truths, and these are the ones that are also *beautiful*. An idea must be more than right—it must also be pretty if it is to create much excitement in the world of science. For the search for truth is not simply a matter of discovering facts. You must also understand their significance, and then persuade others that your way of looking at them is valid. It is always easier to persuade people to believe in something new when they find it beautiful, especially if it runs counter to their established beliefs.

Truth. Beauty. Excitement. Significance. Persuasion.

I was fascinated to see words such as these being used to describe the process of "selling" new scientific ideas. First, because it had never occurred to me that significant scientific breakthroughs needed to be sold at all, and second, because my own experience of science was that it was more fact-filled, analytical, and process-driven than it was beautiful. The only scientific excitement I ever experienced was back in the heady days before health and safety legislation, when 12-year-old grammar school pupils could still light the tubes of the chemistry laboratory Bunsen burners to make flamethrowers, and burn holes in each other's school blazers using hydrochloric acid. Much to our delight, even our teacher, Mr. Ackroyd, once managed to set his hair alight during a demonstration on laboratory safety.

Once out in the real world, though, we are surrounded by the results of the kind of science to which Robert March refers: genuinely exciting ideas that have changed the way we all live and work, but which at the time of their conception were often extremely difficult to sell.

A wonderful insight into the process of gaining acceptance for groundbreaking ideas is given in *The Double Helix*, where Nobel Prize Winner James Watson describes the concern he shared with his partner, Francis Crick, that their proposed structure of DNA "might turn out to be superficially very dull, suggesting nothing about either its replication or its function in controlling cell biochemistry." Later, having uncovered the possibility of the double helix, his concern turned to "delight and amazement" at the emergence of an answer that was "simple, as well as pretty." Both men understood that the inherent beauty of what they had discovered would prove equally captivating to those who would sit in judgment on their work.

The most successful presenters seem to achieve their success by very straightforward means. First, they understand how to *involve* the members of their audience on a basic human level. They engage them as accomplices, inviting them to bring their own experiences to the communication to make it personal, and to arrive at the logical and emotional conclusion themselves. Second, they keep it *simple*. Abraham Lincoln's Gettysburg Address was less than three hundred words in length and took only two to three minutes to deliver. Beauty and simplicity, as Watson and Crick knew only too well, invariably walk hand in hand. Third, we all know that in beauty also lies *surprise*, and in surprise lies the energy that will change a mind, convince, inspire, recruit, or persuade. Great presenters have the ability to tell you something that you already know, in a way that gives it new and more powerful meaning. Their evocation of the familiar creates a comfortable environment for listening; the unique twist that they give it provides the catalyst for action. And finally, the most persuasive presentations are built on *belief*. The secret of eloquence, an American congressman named Bourke Cochran once told Churchill, lies in believing passionately in what you're talking about. The first and most important audience for your presentation is arguably the one that faces you in the mirror each morning, because after all, if you don't believe it yourself, why should anyone else? In *The Double He-*

lix, James Watson talks freely of the "youthful arrogance" displayed in the presentation of his work, but that was really only a reflection of his enthusiasm and his belief in the importance of what he was doing. Such enthusiasm is infectious.

Using the enormity of an American presidential election campaign, Johnnie Cochran's defense of O.J. Simpson, and the sales pitch of a London call girl, I will explore these four pillars of effective presentation—involving the audience, simplicity, surprise, and belief. Although I will deal with them separately, you will see that they are often, by necessity, intertwined. While I wouldn't go as far as to say that if you neglect to build your presentation on all four of these pillars you will fail, I do believe that in ignoring any one of them you will make it much, *much* more difficult to succeed.

Involving the Audience

In 1992, Arkansas Governor Bill Clinton was running for the U.S. presidency against incumbent President George H. W. Bush. (Bush Senior.) A pivotal point in the campaign came on the night of the second nationally televised debate, during which the President and his opponent faced questions live from a studio audience.

One woman asked the candidates a rather confusing question. "How has the national debt affected each of your lives?" she said. "And if it hasn't, how can you honestly find a cure for the economic problems of the common people if you have no experience in what's ailing them?"

President Bush was in the unenviable position of having to answer first. "I'm sure it has," he said, sitting on his stool in the middle of the stage. "I love my grandchildren. I'm not sure I get the question . . . well, listen, you oughta be in the White House for a day and hear what I hear . . ." He struggled for a while longer, talking around the question but never directly addressing it.

Finally it was Clinton's turn. He got down from his stool, walked toward the woman, and said, "Tell me—how has it affected you again?"

She talked, and for every problem that she raised, he responded with an aspect of his economic plan, phrased not in big, global terms, but in the language and experience of his questioner, and of the millions of ordinary Americans who faced the same issues in their lives.

Many political commentators believe that, in that moment, Bill Clinton won the American presidency.

It was because he made it personal. He involved the woman who asked the question, and the studio audience, and the wider audience outside, by asking a question himself and then setting his response in the context of *her* life and problems. He didn't talk at her, as President Bush had done, but rather talked *with* her. In having a real conversation with her, he engaged her as an accomplice. And in doing that, he raised millions of voters' hopes and expectations as part of a new American dream, a dream that could only be realized, they concluded, if they voted for Governor Clinton.

My former partner Rich Silverstein used to talk about effective advertising using the analogy of those dot-to-dot games we all used to play as children. I'm sure you remember joining numbered dot to numbered dot, trying to guess what you're drawing as the picture slowly emerges. Dot, to dot, to dot . . . then, with just one stroke of the pencil, it is suddenly clear. You have a picture of a badger. Silverstein always used to say that it was important for us to join enough of the dots in our advertising to avoid confusion (and as a result rejection), but to leave enough dots for the viewers or listeners to join for themselves. Into the gaps between the dots of advertising they should insert their own experience, hopes, fears, joys, and sorrows, and thus embrace the communication by becoming a part of it.

As Phillip Khan-Panni correctly observes in his book on professional public speaking, *Stand and Deliver*, "the audience is never listening to what you are saying. They are listening for what it means for them." This means that the presenter has to be more than relevant; he or she must also be inclusive. This philosophy is shared by the producer and director of many of the most critically acclaimed and biggest-grossing movies of all time. When once asked the secret to his success, Steven Spielberg said, "I make movies for the masses. But I talk to them one at a time." This approach is essential in every form of communication, and that includes presentation. As a presenter, you should not be trying to connect to "an audience," as every member of that audience will be different. Instead, you should be trying to connect to each and every individual who comprises that audience.

How do you do that?

It can be achieved in a number of ways, the first and most obvious of which, as mentioned in Chapter 1 and demonstrated by Governor Clinton, is for the presenter to finish a sentence with a question mark rather than a period. A question mark invites participation, whereas a period ends a thought. In case you're wondering, I don't mean that *every* sentence needs to be a question—that would be ridiculous. No, I mean that a few well-chosen questions can be a very powerful tool.

I remember one new business pitch in San Francisco in the mid-1990s, for which the client had briefed us to cover a number of different topics. We had points of view on all of them, but were finding it difficult to tie them together in a logical sequence. As the presentation day drew closer, someone had the bright idea of inviting the client to make the decision for us. On the day of the pitch, we covered one wall of our conference room with boards on which were written questions about the client's topics and, in addition, two or three more of our own. The client was simply asked to pick which question he was most interested in hearing us answer. For example, he had asked us to demonstrate an understanding of the competitive context. Our question implied that our opinion might well differ from his own:

Who are we *really* competing with?

This approach had three key benefits: first, the client was engaged and directly involved throughout the presentation; second, he naturally gravitated towards the most important issues and we spent more time on those than the ones he left until last, making our presentation as a whole seem more relevant and substantive; and finally, the whole question and answer format seemed to provide a natural invitation for informal discussion. In other words, the presentation became a conversation.

Sometimes, of course, you won't need words at all. A critical part of

Bill Clinton's communication in the presidential debate came from his body language; unlike President Bush, he did not stay detached from the audience on his stool, but walked over to the questioner and had a conversation *at her level*. The symbolism of that act was as powerful, arguably more so, than his subsequent words.

It's unfortunate that many conference rooms and auditoriums are set up in a way that inhibits such physical bonding. Lecterns are set on detached stages, presenters are naturally placed at the head of long conference tables, and members of the audience are separated from the presenter by vast expanses of open space or polished mahogany. None of these situations is conducive to audience involvement. It's rare, though, to see a presenter actively try to reduce this distance. I will talk more about this in Chapter 8, but room layout and distance are important tools in presentation; they can be changed to great effect.

This brings me back for a moment to the O.J. Simpson trial. As described in the previous chapter, Marcia Clark and her team of prosecutors took a total of 24 weeks to present the evidence that they believed would convince the jurors of Simpson's guilt. Convinced that the evidence would speak for itself, they presented it to the jurors in painstaking—and at times excruciating—detail. The style and complexity of their presentation may have alienated some jurors and it may have distanced others. What is undeniable is that the prosecution failed to *involve* any of the jurors in its case.

In marked contrast the defense team, led by Johnnie Cochran, adopted a strategy that sought to involve the jurors on several different levels. From their own pre-trial research, Cochrane and his colleagues knew that Marcia Clark was prone to talking in the manner of a schoolteacher explaining advanced mathematical theory to intellectually challenged children. So they set out to be more likeable. They also recognized that the jurors' attention span was limited, so they tried to find more concise, poetic ways of presenting their point of view. Right from the start, their aim was not to prove Simpson innocent, but rather to convince the largely African-American jury that a guilty verdict would not just be against Simpson, but against the entire African-American community. The jurors didn't have to believe in Simpson's innocence, only in the unfairness of his conviction.

In any presentation, having the members of the audience like you enough to want to listen to what you have to say is essential. In advertising agency pitches, it is common for presentations to be made by teams representing both agency management and representatives of its different disciplines, and decisions on who will present tend to be made on grounds of seniority or even on the basis of not upsetting anyone. When people have done a lot of the background work, they tend to assume that they will be making the presentation. It's a kind of reward for all their hard work. To be prevented from presenting would be tantamount to punishment. In many cases, however, it is wrong to bow to this assumption or this pressure. The presentation should always be made by the best presenter, as identified by the answer to this simple question:

Of all the potential choices, which person will be most likely to engage with the audience and communicate the ideas most effectively?

In the advertising agency world this question is complicated by the fact that most clients—quite correctly—want the presentation team to be the team that would continue to work on the business if the agency is appointed. My way of dealing with this is to give a role to everyone who will work on the client's business going forward, but give the major roles to those who are the most engaging, likeable presenters—the people who are more likely to win us the business in the first place.

In the slightly simpler world of the O.J. Simpson trial (simpler only in the sense that the decision was not the prelude to a continued working relationship), it is no exaggeration to say that one of the key reasons for Simpson's acquittal was that the jurors liked Johnnie Cochran more than they liked Marcia Clark. The same could be said of John F. Kennedy's victory over Richard Nixon in the 1960 Presidential election, and Bill Clinton's over George H.W. Bush more than thirty years later. High on the list of deciding factors was the fact that the voters simply liked Kennedy and Clinton more when they compared them to their opponents in the debates.

An obvious question here is how such people make themselves

more likeable, and how a presenter who doesn't have the confidence of Johnnie Cochran, or the good looks and easy manner of Kennedy or Clinton, might succeed. Well, I have seen many very confident and capable presenters fail. I've seen many good-looking, confident, and capable presenters fail. The truth is that what people value in attorneys, politicians, and even advertising agency presenters, is what they also value in other areas of their life. Naturally in the professional context some technical expertise or experience may be a prerequisite, but in general we vote, hire employees, and engage agencies, house painters, or car mechanics in the same way that we choose our friends. We do so on the basis of warmth, humor, ease of conversation, shared interests, and a feeling that they like us, or would like us if they got the opportunity. And we tend to make these judgments very, very quickly.

Thus, in the Simpson case, most of the jurors decided in the first few days of the trial that they did not like Marcia Clark. (Many had probably decided this at the time of jury selection and possibly, on the basis of television interviews they had seen, even earlier.) At the same time, they probably decided that they quite liked Johnnie Cochran and some of his colleagues. Having established this human bond, Cochran and his team exploited it to devastating effect, by asking the African-American members of the jury to bring to their deliberations all their experience (direct and indirect) of prejudice against their community. Even if Cochran could not prove that O.J. Simpson had been the victim of a conspiracy at the hands of L.A.P.D. officers, he could at least convince the jurors that such a conspiracy was possible. In the courtroom Cochran had a prosecution witness, L.A.P.D. officer Mark Fuhrman, who in the course of the trial was famously exposed as a racist. In the jurors' minds were recent memories of the Rodney King beatings and the acquittal of the offending officers by a white jury in Simi Valley. And Cochran also knew that each and every juror would have his or her own experiences of racial epithets, of being pulled over by cops at times when a Caucasian driver might have been allowed to pass, and of the similar stories of friends, family, and neighbors. None of their experiences and stories appeared on the log of evidence for the O.J. Simpson trial, but these, skillfully suggested by Cochran, were the reason for Simpson's acquittal.

While Marcia Clark and her team made a presentation, Johnnie Cochran told a story. And because the jurors became personally involved (as African-Americans who in today's United States still believe that there is one law for the black man and another for the white), they believed the story of the defense more than they believed the prosecution's hard facts.

Whenever I make a presentation, I invariably use personal stories. When I first did it, it was not a conscious decision, but I learned that by demonstrating the relevance of the situation to my own life and experience, I subconsciously invited my audience to do the same, and to listen to what I had to say as *people* rather than as business executives.

If, for example, I quoted an old saying of my grandmother, I did so knowing that everyone I was talking to had a grandmother too, and that their grandmother probably had a collection of sayings similar to my own. If I was talking to a group of Americans about the value of the time that children spend getting dirty, I could evoke my own memories of playing on the beach or by a lake as a child, when my mother and father were relaxed and getting covered in sand too, and the parents in the audience would not only remember the same activities, they would also feel the guilt of parents who wish they spent more time actively playing with their children instead of being passive spectators. Through just one personal anecdote, I could bring *their* memories and *their* emotions rushing to my aid. There's no more powerful alliance.

In opening himself up to an audience—however briefly—a presenter might provide a memorable metaphor for his (or her) understanding of their problem, the methods the presenter proposes to use in addressing it, or even a recommended solution. But much more important, if it's done right, it creates a common bond. In Chapter 9 you will see the power of a personal story told by Sebastian Coe in his presentation to the International Olympic Committee; it was instrumental in bringing the Games to London.

Keeping It Simple

In his book, *Eating the Big Fish*, my friend Adam Morgan tells a story about Picasso that I have stolen and used many times to illustrate a vital point, not only about creativity but also about the business of communication. I will continue to tell it for as long as people persist in inviting me to stand up and talk about effective communication.

Here it is.

One day Picasso welcomes a visitor to his studio. On the floor in the middle of the studio is a large block of unhewn rock. The visitor asks Picasso what he intends to do with it.

"From that rock, I will sculpt a lion," the great artist replies.

The visitor is taken aback. It's hard for him to imagine how anyone could create *anything* from such a rock. In obvious awe of Picasso, he asks the master nervously what—how—where one might start the process of creating a lion from such an unpromising block of rock.

"Oh, it's very simple," Picasso replies. "I just take a chisel and knock off all the bits that don't look like a lion."

I often use that story to illustrate my belief that creativity is not, as many people believe, a process of invention from nothing. Instead, it's a painstaking exercise in reduction, of removing all the bits that don't look like a good idea.

The same, I have always argued, is true of communications in general and presentations in particular. You may remember the phrase that political consultant James Carville placed front and center of Bill Clinton's 1992 election campaign. A sheet of paper was pinned to the wall of the campaign "war room," on which Carville had scrawled four words: *It's the economy, Stupid!* In other words, the U.S. economy was the most important and indeed only issue on which Clinton and his team should contest the election. Carville believed passionately that if he could successfully keep the focus on the economy, then his candidate would win. Conversely, if Clinton and his team allowed themselves to be deflected from this central issue, they would lose. The purpose of the paper pinned to the wall was to remind Clinton and his advisors that every time they were asked to speak, they should speak about the economy. Every time they were asked a question, even a question about marital infidelity (*especially* a question about marital infidelity), their answer should return to the economy. The message was simple: with Clinton in the White House, the U.S. and its people would prosper; under President Bush it would continue to languish.

Some people might argue that such an approach to communication is one-dimensional and, at least theoretically, indeed it is. But in many ways, the key to successful communication is how well you deal with choices—first recognizing that a choice has to be made, and then making the right one.

To people who work in the advertising business, the theory that single-minded communication works better than that which attempts to communicate a number of ideas simultaneously is far from revolutionary. For decades, Volkswagen's advertising has consistently communicated reliability. Whatever its specific message, whether it be about a desktop computer, a laptop or an iPod, Apple's advertising has always championed creativity. Avis built its reputation—and continues to focus its communication today—on the line, "We try harder." More recently, a strategy for building milk sales in California based on the idea that you should buy more because it's a real pain in the ass to run out of it, is articulated simply (with no need for further explanation) with the words, *got milk?*

These are all simple ideas, simply stated. But the desire of agencies to simplify messages in this way, to focus on one single, compelling idea, is probably the cause of more heated discussion between agencies and their clients than even the issue of remuneration. Many clients feel that one idea alone may not be enough to persuade everyone; others may argue that if they have paid such vast sums for TV time, they should really get their money's worth. Communicating one idea isn't such a great return on investment—why can't they communicate two? Three? Four? If they're on air anyhow, why not squeeze in a few extra points? After all, there's just so much to say about their product.

But there's always more to say about any product. Any candidate. Any alleged criminal. The question is, what exactly do you gain by saying more?

Jeff Manning, the marketing executive responsible for the *got milk?* campaign, could have fallen into the same trap that caught countless dairy advertisers before him, and asked—nay, *demanded*—that in addition to any fancy creative ideas our agency might have wanted to pursue, his advertising should also list milk's nutritional credentials and health benefits. But if he had, he would most likely have failed as his predecessors had failed before him. Similarly, Bill Clinton and his advisors could have pinned up a sheet of paper on the wall of their campaign headquarters, saying "It's about the economy, foreign policy, healthcare, crime, welfare reform, and immigration, Stupid!" Which would indeed have been stupid, as it was when Clinton subsequently talked about all of those things and many more in his 1995 State of the Union Address, prompting a political commentator in the *Washington Post* to write, "It was a speech about everything, and therefore about nothing."

That is the point. It's an irrefutable truth of communication, whether you are talking to an audience of millions on network television, or an audience of one at your own kitchen table, that the more separate points you attempt to make, the less your audience will take in.

I always liken this to the throwing and catching of a tennis ball. If I throw one ball to you, it's quite likely that you will catch it. Now if I throw you two simultaneously (unless you are a professional juggler) it will be quite difficult for you to catch both. Much more likely, in your confusion over which one to catch with which hand, which one to catch first and which one to catch second, you will succeed in catching neither. If I throw three, it's odds-on that all will hit the floor. If you don't believe me, try it with a friend. You'll find that pens and books about advertising work just as well for this exercise, although they may be more likely to cause injury or damage to property when dropped.

Simple does not, and I repeat does not, mean dumb. It's a tragedy that many of the people I meet in business, particularly those who are younger and trying extra hard to impress, go out of their way to use long words, complex words, and lots of them, to show me how intelligent they are. Industry jargon oozes from their lips like snot from the nose of a cold-stricken baby: they tell me of the paradigms they have shifted; together, they suggest, we might develop scenarios of our collective pathways; we should optimize and maximize; in fact we could do many things ending in "ize." And why bother saying it in 20 words when it can be said in seven hundred and thirty-eight?

In *On Speaking Well*, Peggy Noonan writes of this phenomenon:

> "As you grow older and life itself becomes more elaborate and complex, you find yourself using simpler words. And this is not only because your brain cells are dying. It is also, for some of us, because you have grown used to life, even comfortable with it, and understand that it comes down to essentials, that the big things count and the rest is commentary, and that way down deep in the heart of life's extraordinary complexity is . . . extraordinary simplicity."

It's strange, when you think about it, how many of life's most important, most emotionally charged moments are captured in the simplest of phrases:

"I love you."

"I do."

"It's a girl."

"I'm leaving."

"He's dead."

Think too about the greatest speeches in our history, the speeches that really changed the world. Those who wrote and delivered them never used words for words' sake; the central ideas were always stated in the simplest, plainest of language.

For example, when listing his Commandments, the prophet Moses resisted a temptation to which many of us have been known to succumb, and stopped at ten. And of those ten, relative to modern standards, many are disappointingly short on both detail and syllables. ("Thou shalt not kill." "Thou shalt not commit adultery.") In today's world I doubt that they would be stated as succinctly. The attorneys would ensure that everything was defined, clarified, and assisted by the correct legal language, and the resulting tablets of stone would cover a football field.

Simple ideas have more impact than complicated ideas. They are more memorable in the short term, they are easier to pass on by word of mouth, and in the longer term they endure.

"I have a dream."

"We shall fight on the beaches."

"*Ich bin ein Berliner.*"

In his summing up in the O.J. Simpson trial, Johnnie Cochran left the jurors with one short, unforgettable phrase ringing in their ears. If the rest of the case for the defense had been an advertisement, this was Cochran's tagline.

Earlier in the trial, prosecution attorneys had attempted a piece of theater that had backfired spectacularly. Much of the prosecutors' attention had been focused on the so-called "bloody glove," found at O.J. Simpson's Rockingham estate by detective Mark Fuhrman on the night of the murders. They had attempted to prove—through weeks of laborious DNA evidence—that the blood on this glove belonged to both O.J. Simpson and his alleged victims. Realizing too late that much, if not all, of this scientific evidence was passing over the heads of the jurors, the prosecution team decided to take a gamble and fit Simpson to the glove in a more literal, physical way. They asked him to put it on his hand.

In one of the trial's most dramatic moments, Simpson struggled to pull the glove on to his enormous hand. The glove was too small. Prosecutors argued that having been soaked in blood and left to dry in a laboratory for several months, it would not be surprising if the glove had shrunk. Simpson's failure to fit his hand inside didn't mean that it did not fit him . . . but they should really have thought of that before conducting the experiment. Having already dismissed the prosecution's forensic evidence in general as flawed because of police corruption and forensic incompetence, Johnnie Cochran brought the jurors back to the issue of the bloody glove in his summing up. This was one of the prosecution's most important pieces of evidence. It connected Simpson to his ex-wife (it was alleged that she had bought the gloves for him as a gift years before), to the murder scene, to a violent struggle, and to the blood of his victims. But what did that all mean, Cochran asked, if the glove is too small for Simpson to even pull it onto his hand?

"If it doesn't fit," he said. "You must acquit."
He fought science with poetry. And he won.

The Incalculable Value of Surprise

One of the most famous symbols of Britain, recognizable all over the world, is the red telephone box. At one time these proud symbols of empire and technological progress dotted every city street and village green. For millions of Britons, before home telephones became commonplace, they were the only link to the outside world. Later on, when we all had phones in our living rooms, they provided the only guarantee of privacy. I remember making my first trembling call to a girlfriend from the box in my village, dropping my coins on the floor when her father answered the phone. (He never did like me.) From another phone box I learned that I had achieved the necessary grades to gain entrance to the university of my choice. Even though many were used for unspeakable things that bore no relation to telephone calls, and even though most of them reeked of stale cigarette smoke and, worse, urine, they still hold a special place in our hearts.

Today, however, the days of the venerable red telephone box seem numbered. In the name of progress and hygiene, many have been replaced by the kind of open, characterless booths that can be found pretty much anywhere in the world. And in this era of the ubiquitous mobile phone, even these "new and improved" fresh-air booths seem almost anachronistic. Maybe their presence is sustained by the millions of foreign tourists whose mobile phones are not set up for international calling, or whose phones are incompatible with British networks. I'd like to think so, because what I see every day as I walk to my office in London suggests only one other major use: The London telephone box has become an advertising medium for the city's prostitutes. (See Figure 3.1.)

It is hard to find a telephone box in London that is not completely covered in printed cards offering all manner of interesting experiences. Typically they consist of a picture, a telephone number, and a description—sometimes coded, sometimes more explicit—of what exactly is

FIGURE 3.1 Photo of the inside of a London phone box, showing the advertisement known as "Tart cards."

on offer. These "tart cards" are a relatively modern phenomenon, although they do have their roots in earlier times. In Victorian London, prostitutes solicited by distributing business cards describing their services to music halls and theaters. In the twentieth century, the windows of newsagents were the medium of choice, with discrete handwritten notes advertising "French lessons," "private tuition," and "personal services." Printed cards began to appear in the city's telephone booths only in the mid-1980s, when a loophole in the law meant that they were technically not illegal. As Caroline Archer points out in her fascinating book, *Tart Cards*, "It was an effective and cheap way for the girls to advertise their services; and it was both logical and helpful for the customer, to move the cards directly to the technological interface necessary to arrange business." Since 2001 it has been a criminal offense for anyone to put up tart cards in telephone boxes, punishable by heavy fines and several months in jail, but the law has had little effect. As fast as telephone company cleaners or community groups remove them, they reappear.

So why, I hear you asking, should I be talking about this?

First, I should point out that my interest in these printed cards is purely professional. As an advertising executive whose company provides a mobile phone and thus has no good reason to use such public telecommunication facilities, I am nonetheless intrigued by the different styles of solicitation that can be found there. In their own way, they are new business pitches on the smallest scale. The amount of money at stake is not great—Caroline Archer gives a range from £20 ($36–$38) asked for the most basic services, to several hundred pounds to satisfy more sophisticated and exotic tastes—but what interests me is that in this microcosm of communications, the "pitches" of the prostitutes exhibit exactly the same strengths and weaknesses displayed by professional presenters in situations where millions, or even billions of dollars are at stake.

Thus, one day last year, in the midst of researching an upcoming conference presentation, I found myself in a telephone box in Berkeley Square, armed with a camera and hoping with all my heart that I wouldn't hear a tap on the glass and turn to see Sir Martin Sorrell, or Marie Capes, our company secretary, standing behind me with eyebrows raised. Before me the wall was papered with an array of cards similar to those shown in Figure 3.1. Pictured on neon pink, yellow, and blue backgrounds, white, black, Asian, and Latina women pouted in various states of undress. Some modeled lingerie; others burst forth from body-hugging rubber and leather; some wore nothing more than computer-generated starbursts to protect what little remained of their modesty. With the obvious exception of the girls' ethnicity, my overwhelming impression was one of sameness.

Being from a research background, I decided to level the playing field and compare the copy of those cards showing just blonde Caucasian women. In the further interests of decency I won't show them here, but let it suffice to say that they all looked vaguely like Pamela Anderson, only less so.

One woman wearing a nurse's outfit and a smile promised to make my "Dreams Come True." This was supported, in a variety of unfamiliar typefaces, by the following: "Sensual Body 2 Body Massage with

'Veronika.' Stunning German Blonde. V.I.P. and Fantasy Services Available. 5'8." 22 Yrs. 24 Hrs." The mention of 24 hours was especially highlighted.

To her right, a "Stunning Blonde Russian Model" offered "All Services. Very discreet. No Rush. All major credit cards accepted. Home/Hotel Visits. Local." And then in italics, *"Private Escort Available."* Whatever that means.

Another who didn't feel the need to reveal her nationality enticed me with "Hotel/Home visits available. All fantasies fulfilled. Open late," while a "Sexy Slim Blonde Beauty, 21 years old" offered "Exotic Massage, Hotel Visits, No Rush." That was the second time I had been promised there would be "no rush." It made me think of the builders working at that very moment on my kitchen at home, who were being paid by the hour and were therefore also in no rush. Having seen Fred the Stonemason and Pete the Skip Driver working the previous day without shirts, the image flashing through my mind wasn't quite the one that this Sexy Slim Beauty had intended.

On the right hand wall, "Busty Brigitte" listed "Toys, Video, Shower, Drinks, All Services, Hotel Visits" as attractions, beside a picture suggesting that spending the extra money to print the word "busty" had been really rather unnecessary. Her neighbor, meanwhile, eschewed the opportunity to show a picture, choosing instead to describe herself as a "Mature continental blond," and to focus on just one asset: her "Very comfortable apartment." Enough said.

That was all very interesting, but sadly reminiscent of those very bad car commercials in which clients insist on their agency forcing as many features as it is possible for a highly trained voiceover artist to read in the course of thirty seconds. Zero-to-sixty-in-eight-point-four seconds, dual overhead cam, six-cylinder, fuel injection, advanced braking system, leather seats, front and rear cup holders, front and rear cigarette lighters for the kids' electronic games, attractive styling, available in a wide range of stunning colors. . . . As the *Washington Post* said of Clinton's State of the Union Address, they say everything but end up telling you nothing.

The problems of the tart cards extended beyond sheer volume of information. Sure, each of these young ladies seemed to have adopted that age-old strategy that says, if you throw enough shit at the wall, some of it might stick. But they were also saying many things that I could see quite easily for myself from the picture, namely that they were blonde (well, from the roots up) and, in Brigitte's case, busty. And finally, many of them were committing that cardinal sin of trying to tell me what to think. Telling me that they are stunning, or sexy, or beautiful, next to a picture that suggests just the opposite, will not make me believe that they are any of those things. I can't imagine that anyone else would be fooled into believing it either. And as for making my dreams come true, how on earth was German Veronika going to make 2006 the year that England finally won the World Cup?

None of them appeared to be thinking about *me* as a potential customer. The only relevance to what I might be looking for was superficial. If I had a thing for blondes, then maybe I had come to the right phone box. If I was drawn to Russian or German women, then I might call those who had made their nationality a feature. But where was the benefit? You might say that the benefit is so obvious it doesn't need to be mentioned, but I don't believe that to be true.

The point is, I imagine that for every reason why a man might pick up the phone and call one of those women's numbers, there are at least five others why he might not. And these have nothing whatsoever to do with age, complexion, hair color, breast size, hours of operation, or willingness to travel. Instead, they reflect his concern that he might be making the wrong choice. The woman pictured on the card might not be the woman who answers the door. Even though she says, "no rush," she might not mean it. She'll just want to take his money, do only what she has to do, and get him out of the door as fast as she can.

This is why another printed card in the same telephone box really struck me. It had the same kind of colors, the same kind of picture as the others. A young, smiling blonde, she had chosen to tell me only three things about herself. The first was her name: Helen. Not Hungry Helen, or Hot Helen, or indeed any other seedy attempt at alliteration. Just Helen. The second thing was her age: 23. She had then made the choice to exclude all the other information that her competitors seemed bent on communicating; potential customers would probably take it for granted that she would be willing to visit their hotel, and if they were interested in the range of services offered, then they could simply ask. So far, so good. But the third and final point she made was the zinger: beneath her picture were the words, "Genuine Picture."

That's what I mean by *surprise*. Surprise means saying something different from everyone else, or saying the same thing in a way that they have never heard before. Those two words, "Genuine Picture," somehow made Helen appear just that little bit more attractive. But they also cast very grave doubts on the authenticity, not only of the others' pictures, but also of their claims. Helen's card was involving in that it invited me to participate in its communication. It was very simple. And it shook my perception of all of her competitors.

I saw the same thing happen once in a series of new business pitches that I judged on behalf of one of WPP's largest clients. In the course of one day, five agencies presented their credentials for handling this client's very large research needs (and in return receiving a very large fee.) The first agency arrived at 8 A.M. A group of four or five executives entered the room, spent at least ten minutes trying to connect a laptop to the client's projector, and then began their pitch. The most senior member of the group began by saying how much he wanted this particular client's business, and how wonderfully qualified his agency was to be the client's partner. Their presentation, he assured us, would demonstrate clearly how different his agency was from its competitors. And then, one by one, his colleagues reviewed the scope of the task, outlined their "core competencies," and proposed a differentiated, cost-effective research solution, burning through hundreds of extremely dull PowerPoint charts in the process. After answering a few questions, they left the room and the next team was invited to enter.

After fiddling with the computer for about ten minutes and making the same jokes as their predecessors about needing a child to make it work, the most senior member of the second group began by saying how much she wanted this particular client's business, and how wonderfully qualified her agency was to be the client's partner. Their presentation, she assured us, would demonstrate clearly how different they were from their competitors. And then, one by one, her colleagues reviewed the scope of the task, outlined their "core competencies," and proposed a differentiated, cost-effective research solution. After a few questions . . . okay, you get the picture. Lunchtime came, and after three such identical presentations, I was tired, confused, and actively considering running away to join the French Foreign Legion.

After lunch a fourth agency said exactly the same things, in exactly the same way. I resolved to give the fifth agency the benefit of the doubt, but faking a heart attack really seemed to be the only option.

The door opened and just one man entered. He greeted us warmly, and looked around the room. On top of the long table from behind which all the others had presented, the projector stood on standby, its fan whirring softly. He opened his bag and pulled out a laptop. This was the moment. I could almost feel the chest pains. My fingers were tingling.

Then he shook his head, and put the laptop back into his bag. He went to the back of the room and picked up a chair, bringing it over and placing it right in front of the five of us who comprised the review committee.

"Do you mind?" he asked. "I'd really like to just have a chat."

There is a God, I thought. For the next forty minutes he talked interestingly and knowledgeably about our business, appearing to know more than all of the others put together. The real *coup de grace* came when he said that he thought he was perhaps less well qualified than all of his competitors to handle our research, but that he wanted to meet us anyway and see whether there might be a role that he could handle with his limited experience and resources.

Of course there was a role. He had just played a very useful one by making all the others look like the grey, uninteresting people they really were. I wanted to kiss him.

The parallels between the world of escorting and business are not confined to presentations alone. In the week that I write this I have been involved in recruiting people to WPP's Marketing Fellowship program. Each year we hire about ten of the brightest graduates from universities around the world and put them through a three-year program, in the course of which they work in three different operating companies, on two continents. Our aim is to recruit future generations of management, and competition for places is fierce. In 2005–2006 we had more than 1,300 applicants, only 60 of whom were successful in obtaining a first interview.

When I am interviewing, I often ask the candidates to talk about brands. How would they define a brand? Do they have a strong affinity for any particular brands? This year, I was disappointed by the number of people who immediately started talking about Apple or Nike or Innocent (a U.K.-based beverage brand). That's not to say that these brands should not be admired. I admire them greatly myself, and talk about them a great deal with my clients. But that is the problem. Everyone in our business talks about Apple and Nike and Innocent, and it is therefore very confusing in an interview situation—again, it's a pitch in all but name, with the candidate as the product and getting hired as Point B—to talk about these brands originally. Never in any of those interviews did I hear a point of view about Apple that made me respond, "I've never thought of it that way."

One young woman did stand out. She stood out because when I asked her the question, she thought for a moment (which was good in itself), and said, "I'm not sure if this is what you're looking for." I smiled encouragingly. Try me. "Well," she said, "I love Marmite." And she went on to talk in the most engaging fashion about that quintessentially British vegetable extract that an American friend once described to me as "the closest food experience I ever had to eating toe-jam." While the others zigged, she zagged. And even though what she said was both very smart and very personal, the fact that she had the courage to think beyond the expected answer counted for a great deal.

The great advertising man Bill Bernbach once said of his craft: "You can say the right thing about a product and nobody will listen. You've got to say it in such a way that people will feel it in their gut. Because if they don't feel it, nothing will happen."

That is as true of presentations as it is of the advertising that an agency might produce. The members of the audience have to *feel* what you are saying. That means that they have to be involved on an individual level, as described above, but they also have to be personally moved. So even when you are presenting material with which audience members feel entirely familiar, you have to present it in a way that surprises them.

I'll give a brief example from an advertising pitch I made in the United States in the 1990s. This, and the work that resulted from it, is described in rather greater detail in my earlier book, *Truth, Lies, and Advertising*. Here I am concerned solely with the part of our presentation that brought to life the problem we needed to address.

When Porsche asked Goodby, Silverstein & Partners to pitch its North American advertising business in 1993, the company was experiencing serious problems. From selling more than 30,000 cars a year in the United States just seven years before, its annual sales were now below 4,000. Porsche executives offered many reasons for the decline: Porsche's model lineup had changed, with the cheaper 924 being discontinued; there was more competition from cheaper Japanese sports cars; Porsche's prices had increased by an average of 117 percent between 1986 and 1993, and this, in a time of recession, had left Porsche beyond the reach of many potential customers; finally, they talked of a decline in the brand's appeal. Their research (which was extensive) had shown that many people associated the brand with the so-called conspicuous consumption of the 1980s. At the briefing, declines in brand image on key dimensions were shown on countless graphs and tables. There was also, I recall, a fascinating study of the effect on Porsche's business of fluctuations in the dollar-deutschmark exchange rate.

Many of these problems were beyond our control. We couldn't stop the Japanese car manufacturers from talking about zero-to-sixty acceleration times that matched Porsche's at half the price. We couldn't persuade the German Chancellor to change his economic policy. And like it or not, we were still faced with the task of selling expensive cars in a recession. The only problem we could address was that of Porsche's brand image, but first we had to understand it ourselves and—maybe more important, have Porsche's executives understand it—in terms that were more human than numerical.

In one focus group, I had asked a group of non-Porsche owners to imagine that they were sitting in their car at a stoplight. A cartoon drawing showed them in their car, looking over as a Porsche 911 drew up alongside them. From their car emanated an empty thought bubble. What would cross their mind if they were in this situation? I asked them to write down their thoughts in the bubble. One respondent summed up the feelings of many more when he wrote just the one word (see Figure 3.2): ASSHOLE!

In our pitch we told the audience from Porsche that we had spent many hours sifting through their various research reports, as well as conducting primary research of our own. The reasons underlying Porsche's problems were, we had concluded, very complex. They could be summarized, though, on just one chart. Actually, they could be summarized in just one word. This word would provide a vivid demonstration of the problem our advertising and other communication needed to address. People leaned forward in their chairs. They were intrigued.

A few words of introduction were offered on the nature of the research exercise, and then I revealed the slide shown in Figure 3.2.

FIGURE 3.2 Cartoon showing the reaction of an ordinary American driver to the driver of a Porsche.

There was, as you can imagine, a sharp intake of breath from the assembled Porsche executives.

Porsche's communication, I explained, had in recent years been somewhat arrogant and Teutonic. It had fueled the image, held by the ordinary man, of Porsche drivers as rather arrogant people with more money than sense. I briefly described another simple exercise we had conducted in which we interviewed 1,000 people across the United States and asked them for their impressions—good and bad—of various brands and their users. When it came to Porsche, 200 of those interviewed had something bad to say about Porsche drivers.

"One in five people," I said. "That's a lot of people to pass on your way to work who don't like you."

Of course every member of our audience drove a Porsche. And they were beginning to look very uncomfortable.

"Your problem," I continued, "is that many people who really want to buy a Porsche, who really want to drive a Porsche, are embarrassed to do so. They do not want to buy one of your cars because they are scared by what their friends and perfect strangers alike will think of them. And *that* is the problem we need to address."

Several years later, in a conference room in Germany, I heard a group of senior Porsche executives still referring to the need to address "The Asshole Factor."

Simple. Personal. Surprising. Maybe even shocking. But it worked.

In any pitch you have to assume that many, if not all, of your competitors will be talking about the same things. So you either have to say something different, or say the same thing better—which may make this a good point to return to that telephone box in Mayfair, London.

Also in that telephone box was a card that had none of the production values of the others. It had no picture, and it had not been printed. All it contained was a name, a telephone number, and four words, all handwritten.

In my opinion, it represented a great deal of thought. It recognized not only the dull uniformity of the category in which the card's sponsor was operating, but also the hopes and fears of any man who might enter this telephone box with more than a simple phone call in mind. It

FIGURE 3.3 A photo of the tart card that made the author want to offer Amanda a job in an advertising agency.

left a very large gap in the communication for any such man to complete for himself. And what I really liked about it was that it used words that all of us would like to use about our own employment situation but seldom do. It put her offer in the context of the monotony of all our lives, and instantly demolished any fears that a potential customer might hold. Given the choice, wouldn't you want to visit the one woman in the phone box who felt this way about her work?

The card said quite simply, "I love my job." (See Figure 3.3.)

I was tempted to call her, but not for the reasons you might expect.

I wanted to offer her a job in an advertising agency.

Creating Belief

In a book about speechwriting called *The Sir Winston Method*, the former presidential speechwriter Jamie Humes writes, "It doesn't matter how many statistics or facts you rattle off, if the audience senses you aren't really committed." He goes on to quote an old saying, which is that "People don't care how much you know, unless they know how much you care."

Successful presenters exude enthusiasm and belief from every pore. Successful job candidates are passionate about the things they have done and intend to do. In the course of my WPP Fellowship interviews, a young man told me about his undergraduate history dissertation with such vigor that it was hard to imagine a business problem that he would not find exhilarating. When I spoke to the interviewees who hadn't made it to the last round, again and again I found myself explaining that, relative to the lucky 22 who would be coming back, they just didn't seem to have the passion we sought. Those who had made the cut might have shown this in very different ways, but it was always there, and it was irresistible.

Over the years I have spoken with many clients after they hired agencies where I was working, and asked them why they had made their decision in our favor. A common response was, "Because you wanted it more." They knew from the energy that we had put into preparing and delivering our presentation that we really cared, not just about booking more income, but about solving the particular problem that we had been set. We believed in our solution so passionately that it would have felt like a personal affront to be rejected. Our desire and confidence were contagious.

At the heart of all of the most persuasive presentations I have ever witnessed was a powerful belief on the part of the presenter that what he was saying was right, that *he* was right. When he stood before the Lincoln Memorial on August 28, 1963, Dr. Martin Luther King had a different way of showing his passion than Steve Jobs did in my meeting with him, and both were quite different in the way they communicated from, say, my parents on the night they persuaded me that I really didn't want to own a motor bike. Everyone is different, and no one way of being passionate is better than another. Dr. Martin Luther King was a speaker in the southern Baptist tradition. Steve Jobs is fiercely intelligent. Dr. Jane Goodall is one of the quietest speakers I have ever seen in public, but she has an intensity beneath the softness of her voice and manner that makes the hairs on the back of my neck stand on end. My parents had—and still have— an uncanny ability to make me agree with their point of view before they have even expressed it. With people like these there is no halfway point. When they believe in a position, giving any ground at all is tantamount to failure.

My favorite story about passion in a business setting comes from George Lois. In *What's the Big Idea?* he writes of the time the owner of New York's largest matzoh maker, A. Goodman & Sons, turned down a poster campaign whose headlines were all written in Hebrew. His concern about the campaign's ability to reach non-Hebrew speakers was not without foundation.

"There must be some way I can sell you this," Lois said. He then rolled up the poster and climbed out of the window. He stood on the outer ledge, gripping the raised sash with his left hand and waving the poster with his right as he screamed out across Long Island City, "You make the matzoh, I'll make the ads!"

The owner prevailed upon him to climb back in, with the promise that he would indeed run the campaign Lois had authored, headlines in Hebrew included. And as he left, he suggested that if Lois ever decided to give up the advertising business, then he would personally offer him a job as a matzoh salesman.

CHAPTER FOUR

- **Making Connections**

  – Planning the Perfect Pitch

Seeing Relationships

The job of the presenter involves far more than the ability to stand up in front of an audience and deliver the perfect presentation. First, as described in previous chapters, presenters have to understand the psychology of the audience. Second, they have to possess the philosophical abilities to take vast amounts of information, sort the relevant and important from the irrelevant and unnecessary, and distill the remaining material into a single, motivating idea. They then have to write a presentation with the skill of a playwright, creating a plot with enough drama, twists and turns, to hold the audience's attention as the central idea comes to life. Finally, in the presentation itself, they have to bring the skills of a performer. It's a lot to ask of one person. Researching, writing, producing, directing, performing. . . . Kevin Costner, eat your heart out.

I have already talked about audience psychology. In this chapter I focus on the second and third stages: those that involve the collection and interpretation of information, and the crafting of the story. Bringing those to life in the context of the presentation itself will be discussed in Chapters 6 and 7.

In *The Mind of the Strategist*, Kenichi Ohmae writes:

The best possible solutions come only from a combination of rational analysis based on the nature of things, and imaginative reintegration of all the different items into a new pattern, using non-linear brain power.

It's a wonderfully succinct description of a lengthy, work-intensive process that will take me possibly 30 more pages to outline in detail. Ohmae's summary, though, is important for two main reasons. First, you may be relieved to see that he's not talking about inventing anything from scratch. His process of problem solving involves bringing old elements into new combinations, which is, not surprisingly, easier than creating anything truly original. This may be obvious, but a key benefit of combining old elements in a new combination is to achieve that wonderful blend of familiarity and surprise described in Chapter 3, which makes ideas seem simultaneously more enticing and less risky to buy. Second, the ability to see relationships that is inherent to this process is without doubt easier for some people than for others. That reality may scare you. But don't worry: It can be learned, as I hope the description and some specific examples below will show.

The advice that follows is based in part on James Webb Young's *A Technique for Producing Ideas*. James Webb Young joined the J. Walter Thompson advertising agency in 1912 and retired in 1928 as vice president of creative work, but what he wrote based on experience almost a century old is as fresh and relevant today—arguably more so—than it has ever been. It's a slim book, only 60 small pages in length and very economically written, but it's intelligent and useful reading for anyone responsible for having ideas and, perhaps more important, training others in the best way to come up with them. In almost every respect it's similar to the method I have used myself in developing advertising ideas and presentations; the only difference is that, until now, I never got around to formalizing it, or even regarding it as a "process." The reason for doing so now is that today's business culture seems to make it more and more difficult for us to create the time and space necessary to think through problems effectively, let alone come up with the right solutions. Many of us spend our time inefficiently, and as a result the ideas and presentations we create and deliver are often not as well thought through as they should be. I'd like to suggest a process for thinking about and preparing presentations that can be adopted by anyone and should prove productive in almost any kind of business. But to be truly effective—for reasons that I hope will become clear and which I will explore further in Chapter 5—this process also has to become a part of our corporate culture. None of us will be able to prepare and craft a truly effective presentation if we are not able to remove at least some of the obstacles to thought that most modern business environments place in our way.

A Five-Step Program

The technique described here has five stages, each of which acts as an essential foundation for the next. In other words, you cannot move directly to the second without going through the first, and the fourth will not work unless the first, second, and third have each been completed. Of course there may be exceptions to this—everyone gets lucky once in a while—but you should know that if you take a short cut you are quite likely to compromise the quality of your final product. In this case, the final product is obviously a winning new business presentation, but it might just as well be an effective advertising campaign, the development of a successful product, or devising a winning election strategy. The same basic principles apply to all, and I urge you to try them out in different contexts.

When I have described this process to others in the past, I have generally encountered two reactions. The first is disappointment because, as several people have told me with ill-disguised chagrin, "It's so simple." Of course what they really mean by "simple" is that it is unsophisticated, not easily encapsulated on a PowerPoint slide, and therefore unimpressive. I say guilty on all charges except for maybe the last one. While the process itself may well be unimpressive, it should be judged not on its own merits but rather on the merits of the resulting presentations and ideas, and in turn on the results that the process yields. I regard the fact that it cannot easily be summarized and projected onto the wall of a conference room as a significant point in its favor. It has been developed according to beliefs about how people work best and create the best ideas together, and if this doesn't make for neat charts, zippy graphics, and the opportunity to stick a trademark sign on the title page, then too bad.

We are too often victims of a culture of post-rationalization, which probably has its roots in the scientific community but which is both widespread and virulent in the marketing world. When we report on our successes, we want people to be impressed, so we tell our stories not as they really happened, but rather in the form that we have been led to believe that intelligent, sophisticated people should tell them. Even when we have guessed at outcomes and made intellectual leaps on the basis of nothing more than gut feeling, we pretend that there was a clear logic to everything. In this kind of reporting, there is no place for intuition, common sense, or coincidence, but these are the words that we would use if we were really telling the truth.*

As noted in Chapter 3, simplicity is a quality to be admired in any form of communication, and simplicity of expression is much more likely to result from a process that is itself simple than from an approach that seeks to impress through its complexity.

The second common reaction I have encountered when describing this process is that I am somehow taking a risk by sharing it. Surely, people say to me, you are undermining your own competitive advantage by telling your rivals how to work? Yes, of course that's possible. But while my preferred working method is simple in form, it does require great intellectual rigor and intuitive skills on the part of its exponents, as well as a lot of hard work. Even if people accept its utility, if they understand what I'm saying and believe me to be right, they will not necessarily change their behavior. And that's okay. My purpose in writing this is to suggest that there might be a better way of spending our time at work, and if even a small proportion of those who read this change their ways for the better, I will have achieved what I set out to do. Some is much better than none, and at least I will die knowing that I tried.

---

*One notable exception is an article written by Paul Feldwick in the winter, 2005 issue of *Market Leader*, in which he tells the true story of BMP DDB Needham's campaign for the British credit card, Barclaycard. He tells of big ideas that got smaller and smaller, poor guidance from professional researchers, dismal creative work, and finally a famous campaign that grew from someone in a focus group saying, "Why don't you use Rowan Atkinson because he's funny." Perhaps when reading case histories as a guide to best practice, Feldwick suggests, "we should remind ourselves that in the real world of business there are no additional prizes for elegance, logic or neatness—only for ending up with something that works."

Step One: Grazing

The first of the five steps in preparing a presentation is to gather raw materials. As wildebeest roam across the Great Plains of Africa in search of water and new pastures, so too the presenter has to search for and graze upon raw materials to feed his or her mind.

This gathering of raw materials seems like such an essential and obvious step that it should scarcely need mentioning, except that grazing is a stage that many people ignore. They want to jump straight to the solution before they have really considered the facts, which may seem like a good way of saving time. Often, though, it results in nothing of the kind; the only discernible effect upon time is that the audience's is wasted. Important information is ignored, and that which remains tends to be unfiltered, unconnected.

In Chapter 1 I criticized the sizeable proportion of presenters who inflict too much unprocessed information upon their audience. It's what the presentation coach Jerry Weissman refers to as the "Data Dump," and it was one of the main reasons why Marcia Clark and her colleagues lost in the O.J. Simpson case. In *Presenting to Win*, Weissman expresses the hope that no presenters reading his book will ever inflict a Data Dump on their audiences. "But performing one," he continues, "is vital to the success of any presentation. The secret: The Data Dump must be part of your *preparation*, not the presentation. Do it backstage, not in the show itself."

On any project, I try to organize a Data Dump as soon as possible after the client has delivered the brief, and ideally even before. My colleague Craig Davis, who is the global creative director of JWT, often refers to a principle called the 5/15/80 rule. This says that we enter any given assignment knowing five percent of the relevant information. A further 15 percent of the information is that which we know we don't know. And the 80 represents the 80 percent of the relevant information that we don't even know we don't know. I happen to believe that it's quite an accurate model, and it scares me to think about it every time I receive a new brief from a client.

That's why it's dumb to try and jump straight to answers. You simply don't know enough to do so with any degree of confidence.

In Chapter 7 I will introduce the idea of the "Day One" exercise that is essential in getting any new business pitch off to a flying start. It involves bringing together the pitch leader, the core supporting team—including, if possible, the client—and a small number of individuals who will be invited based on specific experience (for example, they might bring intimate knowledge of a category or market, detailed technical knowledge, or be an expert on the psychology of a particular consumer). Indeed, they might be invited based on their *lack* of specific experience and more for their ability to look at problems from a fresh perspective, for their catalytic qualities. These people might spend an entire day together, sharing what they already know (if each shares the five percent that they know, they will very soon fill in many of the obvious gaps in their knowledge), and figuring out what they need to do to explore the mysterious 80 percent. In this chapter, however, I want to focus on the kind of raw materials that have to be gathered: the raw materials that will provide the content for such a Day One exercise and the essential foundation for effective ideas and presentations.

James Webb Young divides the type of information that needs to be collected into two kinds: materials that are *specific*, and those that are *general* in nature. In advertising, specific materials are those pertaining to a product or brand, its category and competitors, and the target audience with whom the brand's managers want to create or expand a relationship. The general materials are more about the relationship of the category to the lives of those who frequent it, and the social, economic, and cultural context in which they live. For the presenter in any other business, the specific materials are those relating directly to the client's brief, while the general materials are the things that add color, drama, and create connections to the lives of those in the audience.

Even though most of us would deny it, it's probably true that many of us rarely work hard enough at even the specific information gathering, and often we ignore the more general, contextual information altogether. But as Marcia Clark and her team showed us in the O.J. Simpson trial, we do this at our peril.

Of course all of us talk about getting an intimate knowledge of products, categories, and consumers, but very often we are simply going through the motions and checking boxes without really getting to the heart of the matter. It's possible to read reports, and study all the data that exists, and commission research to fill in at least some of the gaps, but still not really know or understand. Much research is too structured, failing to leave room for the unexpected human anecdotes and experiences that are truly revealing. Far too much of it takes place in environments that suit the sponsors but work against openness on the part of respondents. As an advertising agency planner or as a presenter, there is really no substitute for spending time with the people whose motivations you are trying to understand and represent—not just talking to them and asking questions, but observing them, listening to them interacting with each other and with the products, preferably in their "natural habitat."*

In this sense, developing specific knowledge of a category and its consumers is similar to the task of the novelist, painting a picture of a certain place and creating characters. In my own experience, researching an as-yet unpublished novel, *Parts Unknown*, which is based largely in the area of Uganda where Western tourists go to track mountain gorillas, I needed a lot of specific information about mountain gorillas and the terrain and vegetation of the Mount Gahinga National Park, which I could find in books and on the Internet. But I also spent weeks in East Central Africa myself (not too

---

*The shortcomings of traditional research and recommended alternatives to achieve a deeper, more genuine understanding of consumer attitudes and behavior are discussed in *Truth, Lies, and Advertising*, particularly in Chapters 3 ("The Blind Leading the Bland") and 4 ("Peeling the Onion").

arduous a task), tracking mountain gorillas and gaining an intimate knowledge of the places where my story would be set and the truth of my characters revealed.

To capture the truth of the people and place convincingly, however, I needed much more than this specific information. This brings me to the value of the more general material to which James Webb Young referred.

Writing about Uganda or Rwanda and mountain gorillas requires more than an intimate knowledge of the terrain on which the gorillas reside, or what they smell like (sweaty and musky, like a teenage boy's bedroom, if you're interested). I had to know about the historical and cultural context: Africa's colonial history and the way it affected Uganda; national and tribal rivalries; the dictatorships of Amin and Obote; the government of current president Museveni; the weather at certain times of the year; the difference between Congolese and Ugandan music; the AIDS crisis; fear of Ebola; the food that a Ugandan family might eat for breakfast, lunch and dinner; how a typical Ugandan five-shilling note feels when held between thumb and forefinger.

Such knowledge can be gained on a specific search, but more of it has been picked up randomly and indexed. In the months and years that I have spent planning, researching, writing, and rewriting *Parts Unknown*, I have been constantly on the lookout for such material, much as I do in my other life as an advertising professional.

There are certain subjects that I have to speak on again and again, and certain questions that I have been asked so many times that I couldn't even begin to count them. Over the years I have collected a vast library of information and references that allows me— I hope—to address these issues and questions in interesting ways. Many of the examples I have used in this book came from that library. The material I find and file is occasionally from professional publications, but more often it's not. If you read the bibliography at the end of this book, you will see more books and articles that are of general interest than of specific relevance to the subject of presentations.

To be a good presenter, a good source of ideas, and a good writer, you have to be a *collector*: a collector of general knowledge about life—drawn from published information and your own experience—which you can cross-reference with your specific knowledge of products and people. The more material you can store away in your mind, and in an easily accessible file if you don't trust your memory, the easier it will become. The most important thing about this process is that it has to happen constantly. Collecting specific material for a presentation is a job for now; collecting general information to give that presentation depth and breadth is a job for life.

In Chapter 3 I mentioned an incident that occurred when Goodby, Silverstein & Partners was pitching for the North American Porsche business in 1993. When asked in a focus group to imagine what a man might be thinking when he drew up next to a Porsche 911 and its driver at a stoplight, a respondent wrote a single word on the sheet we gave him: *Asshole!*

That was one item of information collected in the course of a fairly traditional research program. But it reminded many of us of a joke that we had heard, albeit in slightly different forms, in the past. Here it is the way an American might tell it. (In Britain the porcupine becomes a hedgehog.)

Question: What's the difference between a Porsche and a
   porcupine?
Answer: With a porcupine, the pricks are on the outside.

This joke could be viewed as a second piece of information. It's very general, but also very familiar. Like the first, it reflects Porsche's reputation in a particular cultural context.

Finally, here's a personal experience. When GS&P pitched the Porsche business I, like many others on the pitch team, had actually never driven a Porsche. Because we knew we were pitching against some Porsche enthusiasts in other agencies, and especially because the client expected to see real passion for the brand from those presenting, we decided to rent a convertible 911 for the duration of the pitch and have every team member drive it for a day or two leading up to the presentation. (Really, it was legitimate research, as my retelling of this particular anecdote more than a decade later confirms.) When my turn came, I arranged for my wife to meet me at my office in the afternoon and we took a drive out across the Golden Gate Bridge, over the mountains of Marin County and out to the rolling hills and spectacular coastline of Point Reyes. It was a beautiful sunny day, and with the roof down the ride was a lot of fun. In the early evening, still buzzing from the drive back from Limantour Beach, we drew into a parking lot near one of our favorite restaurants.

I spotted a space on the next row, but as I approached the turn, I noticed a large pickup truck and, beside it, a bunch of people holding beer bottles. Heads turned as they heard the deep rumble of our engine. I knew what was coming, but had no place to hide. A large, bearded man sitting on the back of the truck bed said something—obviously about us—to a young Tonya Harding look-alike standing nearby, and as we passed she said, loud enough for us—and probably everyone else in the parking lot—to hear, "Yeah. And he's *bald*, too!"

It hurt, but it was also educational.

So there you have the example of three separate pieces of information about Porsche, each from very different sources, but all basically saying the same thing.

"Now this gathering of general materials is important," says James Webb Young, "because this is where the previously-stated principle comes in—namely, that an idea is nothing more than a new combination of elements. In advertising an idea results from a new combination of specific knowledge about products and people with general knowledge about life and events." He draws the analogy of a kaleidoscope, in which the greater the number of pieces of glass in the instrument, the greater the possibilities for new and interesting combinations. So it is with the development of advertising ideas, or ideas for presentations. The more elements of the world around us that we can consider, the more likely we will be to create a striking idea.

When I start work on a presentation, I arm myself with a large board, a pad of Post-it notes, and a small marker pen. Every piece of information that might be relevant to my final presentation, I write on a Post-it note. Thus in preparing the Porsche pitch, I had one Post-it note that said, simply, *Asshole!* On another I wrote, *Porcupine joke.* On a third were the words, *Parking lot incident.* Each note was stuck on the board, along with others that said things like, *Product pricing graph, Quantitative image study, School interviews, Newspaper articles, Yankelovich study 1991, Competitive context, Emerging emphasis on value,* and many more. They were merely headlines—I had all the detail to back them up, but at this stage it is better to keep things at the thematic level. By the time I finished, I had perhaps 60 or 70 Post-it notes on the board. These represented all the material at my disposal: all the things that I *could* talk about if I had three hours at my disposal. (In fact I had 30 minutes to show Porsche's executives that my agency understood the key problems they had to overcome, and to propose an elegant solution.) About one-third represented our interpretation of information that Porsche had given us. A further third was information we had collected ourselves specific to the client's brief. And what remained was general cultural material about Americans' relationship with cars, with high-ticket purchases, with each other, and with their dreams.

The task now was to organize it. And that's why I write my key points on Post-It notes. They can be taken off and stuck back on in a different order. A better order. I usually put them on a board rather than a wall because I can take the board away with me.

Figure 4.1 shows a "Connection Board," like the one mentioned above, that I created when I was planning the structure and content of this book. I think of such a board as resembling the Lunar Module, depicted in a famous old Volkswagen print ad: "It's ugly. But it gets you there."

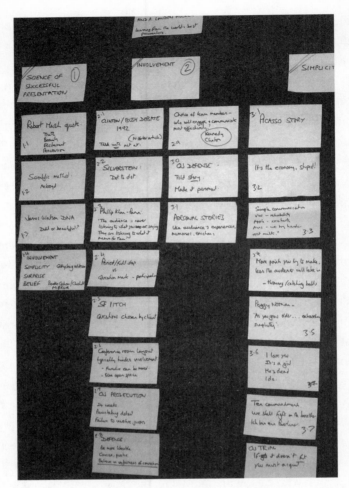

FIGURE 4.1 A "Connection Board," showing the author's Post-it notes used for planning the structure and content of this book.

Step Two: Looking for Meaning

As you are collecting raw materials, you should already be looking for connections. James Webb Young describes the process of feeling over your facts "with the tentacles of the mind. You take one fact, turn it this way and that, look at it in different lights, and feel for the meaning of it. You bring two facts together and see how they fit."

The connection between the three items of information collected for the Porsche pitch mentioned above—the drawing, the joke, and my first drive in a Porsche—is very clear. Each is a slightly different manifestation of the same problem, namely that many Americans regard Porsche drivers as arrogant assholes who have more money than sense. But how do these relate to the research conducted by Porsche that says the majority of Americans still regard Porsche, for want of a better phrase, as "the ultimate sports car?" How do they relate to pictures drawn by BMW and Mercedes owners in our research, showing their cars annotated with phrases like "reliable," "efficient," and "sophisticated?" And to pictures drawn by Porsche drivers of winding mountain roads, under a happily shining sun? What is the connection to the 117 percent average price increase for a Porsche car between 1986 and 1993? And how do all these diverse materials fit with, say, the national speed limit on American roads, arrogant Teutonic headlines on previous Porsche advertising, acceleration statistics for Mazda's new sports car, and the fact that on Porsche's production line in Germany, the engine does not move along a conveyor belt from technician to technician, but rather the technician—one technician—moves with the engine and builds the entire thing himself?

The links are not always so obvious. But they will be there.

Any ideas—however stupid they may seem—must be written down, ideally on Post-It notes that can be added to the board. Later on these attempts at summary might well create the links between different parts of the presentation, and even expressing your half-baked thought in words brings you a little closer to the logic, to the solution that you seek. There are always better words, but you can find those later.

(This reminds me of an interview I once read with George Martin, the legendary producer of The Beatles. He said that when George Harrison first started writing songs, he would agonize for hours over a single word. John Lennon suggested a solution. Just put in a word, John said. Any word. Just make sure that it scans, carry on with the next line, and come back to it later. The example Martin gave concerned the lyric for *Something*.

Harrison had the first line: *Something in the way she moves*. He also had the start of the second line. *Reminds me of*—. He wanted five sylla-bles. Nothing worked. Lennon completed the line for him: *Reminds me of—a cauliflower.* "Now get on with it," he said. George could con-tinue writing the song, even if it would take him a little longer to find the words to replace Lennon's favorite brassica. Eventually, *a cauli-flower* was replaced by *no other lover*.)

I should repeat that it's important not to be afraid of expressing an incomplete, and quite possibly incorrect, thought. Whether you are do-ing so in the company of other people, or sitting alone in a small room breathing in the hallucinogenic fumes of a marker pen, it makes no dif-ference. Let it out. Put it up on the wall. Even if a small part of it makes sense later, you have achieved something.

In *Bird by Bird*, the California writer Anne Lamott describes the es-sential process for the novelist of writing what she so disarmingly calls a "shitty first draft." Although she is talking about creating fiction, the basic requirement for exploration without fear is the same. And while *Bird by Bird* is essentially about the act of creating a novel (and even though Anne Lamott probably didn't know this as she was writing it), it's also a superb book about presentations.

"The first draft," she writes, "is essentially the child's draft, where you let it all pour out and then let it romp around all over the place, knowing that no one is going to see it and that you can shape it later."

Just get it down on paper and stick it on the wall. There may be something on the very last Post-It, at the bottom right-hand corner of the board, that tells you exactly the direction you should be heading, exactly what the higher theme of your presentation should be. But you couldn't have got there without writing the 32 other observa-tions first.

If you have done what I suggested above, by now you should have a board filled with separate items of information and with observations and important points you might want to make in your presentation. A good idea now might be to get another board of equal size and move your Post-It notes to this new board, this time in a different order. An-other way of doing this is to write your points on single sheets of paper and move them around on a large table or on the floor. The point is to see how two facts or observations that you would never naturally have placed together might fit.

This part of the process does require more than a few minutes and a few random changes. And it does require you to physically move points around. Believe me, I have tried to look at one point on one part of the board or table and imagine how it fits with one that is several Post-It notes removed, but it's just not the same as actually putting them together. Try all the different orders and combinations you have the energy for, and then hang in there a little longer and try some more. If something obviously doesn't fit, remove it and place it on a "no fixed abode" board. When you have two or three such vagrant items of information, see how *they* might fit together. I once wrote an entire presentation based on the juxtaposition between two pieces of material that wouldn't fit with anything else I had.

There may come a time—no, there *will* come a time—when despite a lot of moving around, a lot of maybe, perhaps, and not-quite, you are thoroughly confused. The board and the points affixed to it become a blur. Far from being closer to a solution, it seems as if you are further away than you were when you started. That may not exactly be true, for reasons I will explain, but it is probably time to move to the next stage.

Step Three: Drop It

This is the stage at which you are most at risk of people thinking you are abusing their trust, their confidence, and most important of all, the large amounts of money they pay you. This is where you leave your Post-It notes on their board or your sheets of paper scattered all over the floor and go do something completely different. You need to put the whole exasperating problem as far from your mind as you possibly can.

I admit that my last sentence is technically not altogether accurate. What I really mean to say is, put the whole exasperating problem as far from your conscious mind as possible. Because if you do this right, you will continue to think about it; you just won't know that you are doing so.

This may seem like a strange digression, but at my home I have one of those strange and wonderful English ovens known as an Aga. It's the traditional oven of farmhouse kitchens, filled with bricks that are heated by an internal furnace and which provide a constant heat source. In the old days these furnaces burned coal or wood; these days they are more likely to be run by gas or oil. My Aga has four ovens, which stay at constant temperatures ranging from the hottest, the roasting oven, to one that is merely warm enough to heat plates prior to eating. The way to cook meat or casseroles in an Aga is to give them a short time in the roasting oven, and then put them into one of the middle ovens—the simmering oven—for several hours. Once it's inside, you can forget all about the meat because you can't smell a thing. This can be a problem (as many a baking tray filled with small lumps of charcoal that used to be sausages will attest), but when you time it right you can do your preparation, nuke the meat in the roasting oven, then leave it in the simmering oven and forget all about it. Deep down you're looking forward to your lunch or dinner, but the thought isn't distracting or painful. You can do something completely different until several hours later you open the oven door, the aroma of beautifully cooked meat fills your kitchen, and you are ready to eat.

So it is with the unconscious consideration of an advertising or presentation conundrum. You have done your preparation: the meat of your presentation, if you will excuse the pun, is trimmed and seasoned. Now the simmering oven of your brain has to do its work. To do this, however, it requires the right stimulation or fuel.

I know people who swear, quite literally, by "sleeping on" a problem. They work until last thing at night, and then retire to bed with a notepad on their nightstand. When they wake—perhaps next morning, or maybe quite randomly in the middle of the night—they will have solved the problem. The main idea of the presentation is clear, they know the starting point and they know how the main elements of their story fit together. They write it down quickly before they forget it, and then go back to sleep.

I have experienced this myself, although because I have a deeply in-grained problem with taking a notepad to bed with me, I try to avoid it where possible. The one notable exception was in the process of writ-ing *Truth, Lies, and Advertising*, where I had struggled for three or four weeks to articulate the main idea of the book, and as a result—despite numerous shitty first drafts—could not find the right place to start. I was staying in Florida with my family at the time, and I remember waking up at 3 A.M. with the opening pages crystal clear in my mind. We were staying in a small suite that comprised a bedroom, a bath-room, and a living room. As my wife was fast asleep in the bedroom and our infant son was sleeping in the living room, the only place I could go to capture this unexpected solution was the bathroom. I snuck in with my laptop and typed the first ten pages sitting on the floor with my back against the bathtub, stopping only when my battery expired. I'm sure that you have experienced similar epiphanies, although one hopes in more salubrious surroundings.

I prefer to do my unconscious thinking during waking hours. Most of my best ideas have come to me while running. Now that my knees are too damaged from all that mobile thinking, I find that the act of mowing the lawn provides the perfect incubator. When I'm working from my home office I'll leave my notes and confusion behind, spend an hour going mindlessly up and down the lawn and, when I finally re-turn to the Post-It notes a new and different order will almost miracu-lously suggest itself. The important point is that I will deliberately take a break from work, and this is as discrete and necessary a part of prob-lem solving as either of the two previous steps (which seem more like "proper" work) or the two that are to come.

Take a break. Get away from it. Watch a movie. Listen to music. Whatever works. But be clear that what you are doing isn't negligent or taking advantage in any way. It's an essential part of the process, and anyhow, if it's good enough for Nobel Prize winners, then it's good enough for the rest of us.

In *The Double Helix*, James Watson writes of his own way of deal-ing with complex problems. This is an interesting example because it was somewhat at odds with the approach of his partner, Francis Crick.

While Watson spent *some* time in the laboratory and with their models, he couldn't be there all the time as Crick could. To think, he had to get away. Unfortunately Crick found Watson's recurrent absences and apparent failure to take the project seriously extremely irritating.

"The next few days," Watson writes, "saw Francis becoming increasingly agitated by my failure to stick close to the molecular models. It did not matter that before his ten-ish entrance I was usually in the lab. Almost every afternoon, knowing that I was on the tennis court, he would fretfully turn his head away from his work to see the polynucleotide backbone unattended. Moreover, after tea I would show up for only a few minutes of minor fiddling before dashing away to have sherry with the girls at Pop's. I went ahead spending most evenings at films, vaguely dreaming that at any moment the answer would suddenly hit me . . . hoping that an undergraduate party the next afternoon at Downing would be full of pretty girls."

How could anyone leave the polynucleotide backbone unattended? It's a crime. But every night when Watson returned to his lodgings he would make new sketches of the structure of DNA, doodling fused rings of adenine, his brain fueled by the tennis, the sherry, the movies, and the pretty girls. Only by removing himself from the chaos could he begin to make sense of it. And make sense of it he certainly did.

The Double Helix is a very personal story of scientific discovery; it contains a number of important lessons that stretch way beyond the boundaries of Watson and Crick's pioneering work, and indeed of science itself. In the preface to the book, Watson says:

> Here I relate my version of how the structure of DNA was discovered. In doing so I have tried to catch the atmosphere of the early postwar years in England, where most of the important events occurred. As I hope this book will show, science seldom proceeds in the straightforward logical manner imagined by outsiders. Instead, its steps forward (and sometimes backward) are often very human events in which personalities and cultural traditions play major roles.

In other words, the *specific* task of solving the DNA conundrum was affected by the *general* cultural climate in which their work was conducted, and by the interesting—some would say unlikely—power that surged from the combination of Watson's and Crick's divergent personalities and working methods.

Now we turn from Nobel Prize winners to an advertising agency in San Francisco.

About a week before Goodby, Silverstein & Partners' pitch to Porsche, I left my office at around 11:30 A.M. with the team's account director, Marty Wenzell, and media director Rob Kabus, and drove to a place that was in those days called Candlestick Park. It was the home of the San Francisco Giants, and we were going to a baseball game.

For the previous two or three weeks we had been working flat out, collecting the information referred to in previous sections. We knew we had a lot of great stuff, but so far had failed to make sense of it. We knew what we were going to talk about with the client but not how, or in what order. Our presentation still lacked a theme and narrative structure.

We settled into our first baseline seats, drank a couple of beers, and ate more than our fair share of hot dogs and pretzels. At no point did we talk about work, or even think about returning early to the agency. None of us would ever have contemplated leaving a ballgame early.

When the game was over, we walked to our car in one of the massive lots that bordered San Francisco Bay. We knew that we were in for quite a wait to get out of the lot; like all stadium complexes, Candlestick Park had a great system for getting you into parking spaces, but when it came to getting out it was every man for himself.

Marty, the account director, turned on the radio. "So," he said. "What the fuck are we going to do about this presentation?"

Neither of us responded. I was watching a man who must have weighed in excess of four hundred pounds, wearing slugger Will Clark's jersey. It made me wonder what it must be like for Will Clark, seeing a big old pile of blubber like this wearing a jersey with his name and number on the back.

Rob yawned. "Maybe we're talking to the wrong people," he said.

"What do you mean?" Marty asked.

"I don't know. We've been talking to all these Porsche people. But they're not the problem, are they?"

I turned around. He grinned. "You know," he continued, "the average number of Porsches a current Porsche owner has owned is about five, right?"

Right. The problem was, a lot of them were failing to buy the sixth.

"And all of the research says people believe there's no better sports car than Porsche?"

Absolutely, if you get them to look at a sports car as a holistic thing. But a lot of other manufacturers had been busy persuading people that a sports car was just about speed, in which case Porsche cars could be matched, a whole lot cheaper.

"So it's a waste of money trying to convince potential Porsche buyers that it's the best engineered car in the world. They know that already. The problem is getting them to buy one. They're scared that if they buy one the rest of the world will think they're just trying to compensate for their tiny little dick."

"Asshole," Marty growled, referring to our focus group research, not to Rob.

"He's bald, too," I added.

By the time we emerged from the lot and were heading north on highway 101, we had agreed on the central idea of our strategy and presentation: that we should aim our advertising at the people who would never even consider buying a Porsche but who would have opinions about those that might. The aim should be to persuade them to like Porsche more, or at least dislike it less. The campaign should not be, as previous Porsche campaigns had been, about the joy of owning a Porsche, but rather about the unique experience of *driving* one. (Bring on the drawings of those winding mountain roads and the amazing handling of the car.) That was more socially acceptable, we thought.

"When the heck did you think all that up?" Marty asked Rob as we finally drove into our agency's parking lot.

"I don't know," Rob said.

I'm sure he was right.

And whatever everyone else thought when we returned, bringing with us the sweet fragrance of beer and hot dogs—and in my case a fantastic sunburn—we had all worked very hard.

Step Four: Adapt and Distill

This is perhaps the hardest part of all, as it is the phase where you must have the patience to keep on working over your idea until it is right, the courage to share it with others, and the humility to recognize when more work needs to be done.

Once you have made some sense of all your information, found the critical connections, and arrived at the core idea and general outline of your presentation, you need to start work on the correct content and flow. It is the stage that James Webb Young describes as "shaping and developing to practical usefulness," editing mercilessly, throwing away the irrelevant, and crafting whatever you believe to be useful—useful to the successful communication of *that idea*.

The first thing to do is share your idea with others who are involved in the project or whose opinions you respect. This can be hard, but it's the only way to appreciate the basic principle that I outlined in the first chapter of this book: it's not what you say that counts, it's what other people *hear*.

When you describe your idea to people who have not heard it before, does it make sense? And—this is very important—does it make sense without having to show all the detail that you will use in the presentation itself?

When I first worked on new business at the London agency BMP in the 1980s, I remember going to show my boss, Chris Cowpe, the first draft of a presentation I was due to deliver two or three days later. On the day of the pitch itself I planned to use an overhead projector to show the thick pile of charts that I had prepared. For this discussion, though, I placed a hard copy on the desk between us, ready to take Chris through the entire deck if he wanted me to.

Chris reached out and took the charts from me, placing them out of sight below his desk. "I want you to imagine," he said, "that it's the morning of the presentation. I want you to imagine that we were late getting the documents together at the agency and in the panic you left your overheads on the roof of the car. They are now scattered all over Paddington and Bayswater, so you have no charts. And you thought you were speaking for 30 minutes, right?"

I nodded, already knowing that I wasn't going to like what he was about to say.

"Well," he said, smiling as he sensed my discomfort, "Chris Powell was supposed to talk for five minutes but instead went on for forty-five. Then the client's chairman came in unexpectedly and said he only had five minutes, but he'd like to hear what we have to say. So you've got two minutes to talk about the strategy. What are you going to say?"

On that occasion, nothing very useful, from what I can remember. But it was a very powerful lesson. Thereafter I learned to have a single sentence that described the idea, and then some key pieces of evidence that supported it. The presentation, Cowpe taught me, had to have a soul. Without a soul, it would be nothing more than a collection of facts. The soul was the idea, the unifying idea that drew its strength from some of those facts and in turn breathed life into the others. If you had to choose one thing for people to take away from your presentation, this would be it.

For Porsche, we would aim our advertising at the people who would never even consider buying a Porsche but who would have opinions about those who might.

For Unilever, the belief of a majority of those in our target group that getting dirty is an essential part of a child's development should be turned into *action*.

The U.S. economy under a Clinton administration will be better than the economy under four more years of George Bush.

To convict O.J. Simpson would be to convict the entire African-American community.

We are going to persuade people to buy more milk by reminding them of the horrors of running out of it.

This book exists to save the world from shitty presentations.

Those are the central ideas. They should be that simple, and subm. ted "to the criticism of the judicious," as James Webb Young puts it, in the same way that Hollywood executives pitch movie ideas to studio chiefs. If you can't write the ideas down in a space smaller than that afforded by the average postcard, then your presentation will have no focus, no direction, no soul, and consequently no great chance of succeeding.

If the idea does indeed intrigue, then you should explain how you intend to tell the story. What key points will you make? How will you illustrate them?

If all is well, you will return to your Post-It notes with a clear destination in mind. From merely representing all the information that you have at your disposal, the notes now have to be rearranged so that each symbolizes a scene in the presentation. I say "scene" rather than "point" because this is the stage at which you need to be thinking as much about the drama of what you have to say as about the content.

The author and screenwriter William Goldman says that "the key to all story endings is to give the audience what it wants, but not in the way it expects." Thus each part of the presentation needs to engage and surprise in equal measure. If the desired end point is the audience embracing one of the core ideas listed above, how can you use the information at your disposal to take them on the most interesting journey to that idea?

In *Story*, which many people regard as the bible of screenwriting, Robert McKee describes a story as "a design in five parts." The first is the *Inciting Incident*, which puts into motion the other four elements: *Progressive Complications*, *Crisis*, *Climax*, and *Resolution*. Just as most good movies and novels conform to this structure, so too do most of the best presentations.

Here is the basic design for my part of JWT's presentation to Unilever for its global laundry business. JWT and Lowe shared this account, each producing work for different parts of the world around the idea of "Dirt is Good" mentioned in Chapter 2. If you will allow that the existence of this campaign represents an Inciting Incident, it conforms very closely (although unconsciously at the time of writing it) to McKee's model.

1. The power of the "Dirt is Good" idea.

Like all great brand ideas, *Dirt is Good* can become a potent force in culture. It is based on a powerful human truth (all parents want the best for their children); it makes a clear promise (the dirtier we talk, the better people will assume we clean); and it resolves tension (between dirty and clean, between good and evil, between deeply ingrained cultural beliefs that dirt is bad, and our own knowledge that the things that get us dirty as kids are perhaps the things we benefit from the most).

2. The problem.

Just as it is universally true that parents want the best for their children, it is also true that what people say isn't necessarily what they do. The majority of mothers agree that getting dirty is helpful to their children's development, yet the majority of those same mothers get angry when their children come home with dirty clothes. "Dirt is Good" cannot succeed unless intellectual acceptance is translated into action.

3. An even bigger problem.

We believe that the only way for parents to appreciate the value of the developmental play that lies at the heart of *Dirt is Good* is not just to believe it but encourage it, as if they are able to experience it *with* their children. The problem is, parents across the world seem to have forgotten how to play with their children. Children are either left to their own devices, or play is hijacked in the interests of furthering their education. What time most parents spend with their children is not really time spent together at all. Parents are doing chores, talking on the phone, and checking their BlackBerries while the kids retreat to the TV or video games.

4. Catalyst for change.

We know that, contrary to what most parents believe, children actually want to spend more time with their parents. Psychologists tell us that children can benefit greatly, both psychologically and physically, from such play. We want to start a conversation that leads to parents putting down their phones and getting down on their hands and knees on the lawn, in shared messy play. And we want the kids to start that conversation for us.

5. How we know we're right.

This is an important cultural idea. It matters. We have already seen the effect it can have on families in China, India, Brazil, the U.S.A, and the U.K, when parents are encouraged to spend time with their children and given ideas about activities that both will enjoy. If parents play the way they are supposed to play—at the kids' level, supporting, helping them overcome the challenges and celebrating their successes—they will doubtless remember the good times from their own childhood. It will feel good. And it will be contagious.

In the final presentation, I talked for 40 minutes from the preceding outline, illustrating my points with a variety of visual aids ranging from charts from Unilever's own research, to newspaper articles about the lack of parental interaction with children, and children's drawings of typical time spent at home in which their activities were separate from those of their parents. I'll talk more about the design and theater of presentations in later chapters, but the key message here is that presentations have to be distilled before they are written in full. If I had needed to, I could have told the *Dirt is Good* story in less than two minutes. This is essential, not only to be able to deal with the kind of unforeseen circumstances that Chris Cowpe asked me to imagine almost 20 years ago (which I have indeed encountered several times over the years), but to understand—really understand—the story you intend to tell.

Step Five: Writing the Presentation

If you have followed the above steps, you have gathered your information, found the right connections, and after a period of both conscious and unconscious mastication you have arrived at the central idea you wish your audience to take away. This idea has been developed with the key supporting evidence and a two-minute summary written. You have shared your thinking with people whose opinions you respect, and made any necessary amendments to improve the logic and increase the drama inherent in the story. Now it's time to create the version for presentation.

The process I described above already differs from the most common method of presentation preparation in many significant ways. Perhaps most significant, however, is that up to this point I may not have gone anywhere near a computer keyboard, and I have definitely not produced any slides.

You won't need me to tell you that in today's business world, the default reaction of most people when asked to create a presentation is to fire up PowerPoint on their computer and start making slides. Lots of them. These people might say that they are doing with PowerPoint what I am doing with my Post-it notes or sheets of paper covering the floor of my office, but there's a key difference: my Post-it notes and handwritten headlines are a means to an end, a way of organizing, while a first-draft PowerPoint presentation is invariably an end in itself—a "Fire! Ready! Aim!" exercise in cutting corners and projecting solutions before the problem itself has been fully understood.

I don't want to get into what a presentation should look like right now, except to say that if you are producing slides too early, you are putting the cart before the horse. Anything that is projected onto a wall or mounted on a board for presentation should by rights be regarded as a visual aid, yet most people make the mistake of seeing it as the presentation itself.

A presentation is much, much more than its message. What you are seeking to communicate is just one of a number of factors that influence your ability to move an audience. What you say, and what they see and hear, should not be the same. Yet how many times have we sat in conference rooms and listened to a presenter reading the text of his PowerPoint slides verbatim? I will look at this and other unfortunate abuses of PowerPoint in Chapter 6, but for now let me say that what people see in your presentation should never take precedence over the essential idea you want them to take away.

I write a presentation as an author might write a children's book: the story comes first, and then I add the illustrations that help bring it to life.

I always write my presentation as a complete script. This obviously takes a very long time, but I have always believed it to be time well spent. It is without doubt easier to create a sequence of charts and write notes on the additional points that need to be made, but there's often a price to be paid later on. As the example of the London 2012 Olympic Bid presentation will show in Chapter 9, the difference between one word and another that (at least according to the thesaurus) means pretty much the same thing might seem insignificant, but in a situation where one person's vote on the fourth ballot might mean the difference between victory and defeat, the implications can be immense. Every single word needs to be carefully selected, and every transition planned, with the same precision as the ideas themselves.

Writing a script means writing a complete narrative, a complete story. Once finished, you can read it as such and judge it as such, without the temptation to say, or even think, "I'll figure that out later." This may seem like a minor point, but in reality it is also important to write it as you will say it. As I am typing, I tend to say the words inside my head, writing to the rhythm that I want my presentation to follow. Once it's written I read it out loud, finding the words and phrases that make me stumble, shortening the sentences that seem unwieldy, figuring out where I might need to repeat a point for emphasis or leave a thought hanging for a while. Reading out loud is for me a powerful test of the quality of my writing—as I have discovered from reading to my children, nothing exposes bad writing like hearing it spoken aloud—and it is also the first step in a disciplined rehearsal process.

A presentation is meant to be spoken, not e-mailed to all and sundry (an important consideration that I will return to later) but while Power-Point slides can rarely speak for themselves, a prose narrative can.

While I would never want to give the script of my presentation to a client, I often send an early draft of it to colleagues who might live and work thousands of miles away. I try to write so that the presentation stands without the help of any supporting slides; imagining that half your audience is blind is a pretty good starting point. Thus I have to think about a succinct way to describe a research chart showing market share, or a graph that illustrates the different levels of awareness of a campaign between older and younger target consumers. Because the point I am making will be amplified by the visual, I tend to use visuals only where particular emphasis is required and the old see-and-say rule works in my favor. In Chapter 9 you will see the entire script of the London 2012 presentation and none of the visuals. The script tells a complete story, a story that was subsequently enhanced by the use of very carefully selected pictures. I stress this because in my experience most presenters start with the visuals, and then treat what they are going to say simply as an exercise in linkage. The unfortunate consequence of this is that the presentation becomes little more than a series of visuals, with the presenter reduced to a mere supporting role. To all presenters I say this: *You* are the presentation, and nothing is more important than what you have to say. I truly believe that the time spent in crafting a presentation is directly proportional to the seriousness with which it will be received.

One common problem encountered by presenters is running out of time. In advertising agency pitches this always happens, and the consequence is invariably that the media director (who for some reason is always last) is forced to make a 20-minute presentation in a tenth of that time. The reason for the media director being so thoroughly shafted is that other presenters have taken longer than they should, and that is usually because they have not planned properly. If you write a full script, you can tell to within a few seconds how long it will take to deliver. This will make everyone involved more confident, and that has to be a good thing.

I first encountered one further benefit of writing out a script in full entirely by accident. On the eve of WPP's pitch to Samsung for the electronic giant's global communications business, I was asked to talk to the people who would provide simultaneous translation of our presentation to the non-English speakers in the audience. Could I please give them some advance warning of any unusual phrases or industry jargon that I intended to use? Now if you have ever seen the subtitles for the hard-of-hearing that appear at the bottom of your television screen during a live broadcast, you will know that the text the hard-of-hearing audience is reading is usually at least 30 seconds behind what has been said, and more often than not riddled with mistakes and omissions. And this is when the subtitles are being provided in the same language as the original spoken version.

With this in mind, it's perhaps not difficult to imagine the problems that can arise with the translation of one language into another, and where the specific subject—communications strategy—may be unfamiliar to the translators. Having written a complete script for my presentation, I was able to give them a copy the night before, double-spaced with room for their notes, and with clear guidance on how long I might be spending on any particular visual aid.

Detractors of this method of presentation preparation will say that it makes for robotic, spontaneity-free performance. I say, bollocks. While in my presentation to Samsung I chose not to improvise for the benefit of the translators, to safeguard the clarity of my message as it was being delivered in Korean, I usually do improvise. Having written, rewritten, read and reread my script so many times, I know it back-to-front and upside-down, and this allows me to deviate when I sense that the audience needs me to. I might cut out a section that has been rendered redundant by a previous question, or add more detail when the faces of my audience tell me that a little more explanation of a particular point is required. I always carry a copy of my script, but like an infant's blankie it is more for comfort than any practical purpose.

In general, the most important benefit of a script is that it gives you a feeling of control. Control over the message, control over time, and control over the vagaries of your own mind. I don't know about you, but I kind of like that feeling.

CHAPTER FIVE

- **Trevor's Sledgehammer**

  – Creating room for thought

Crushing a BlackBerry

A little over a year ago, on a warm July morning, I ran over my agency–provided BlackBerry with my car. After feeling a small but satisfying bump, I stopped. Then I shifted into reverse and ran over it once more, just to be certain.*

Upon inspection, I have to admit that the damage was disappointing. While the BlackBerry literature talked of "an exceptional wireless e-mail and data experience," and new levels of connectivity and connectedness to make any "mobile professional" salivate with desire, it had made no mention of durability. Yet even under the weight of more than a ton of German sheet metal, little more than the screen seemed to be damaged; not at all the effect that this particular mobile professional was looking for.

That's when I borrowed my neighbor Trevor's sledgehammer. And I'm happy to report that, despite some still-lingering damage sustained in my right shoulder from wielding the heavy weapon, it took just one blow to finally extinguish that nasty little red light. (See Figure 5.1.)

You may well be wondering at my wisdom in admitting so publicly to the destruction of company property. After all, Sir Martin Sorrell (who was kind enough to hire me and, at the time of writing, continues to employ me) is not renowned for his fondness for wasting money. But I reveal my transgression, at great personal risk, to make a serious point.

The day my BlackBerry died was a good day not only for me but also for my employer. In the months that have passed since its demise, I can confidently report that my productivity has been improved, my levels of creativity enhanced, and, as if that were not enough, some

*This chapter is adapted from an article I wrote in WPP's in-house newspaper, *The Wire*, in November 2005, "A Berry Personal Tale."

FIGURE 5.1 What a BlackBerry looks like after it has been struck hard by a sledgehammer.

people (my wife and work colleagues included) have suggested that I might also have become a nicer person. It's almost enough to make me wonder what could happen to WPP's stock and my children's college fund if I were to send Trevor and his sledgehammer on a tour of all our offices.

I know that this may sound a little extreme, but desperate situations require desperate measures. If I could describe any one chapter in this book as the most important for anyone to read and take notice of, this would be it. Because with the best will in the world, no one can follow the process described in Chapter 4 and create a great presentation if they do not have the right environment for analysis, interpretation, and writing. Crushing a mobile communication device may be a very satisfying first step in addressing the problem I am about to describe, but it is only the first step—the first of many that have to be taken if you are to take control of your life and create the time and space necessary to come up with better ideas and ways of bringing them alive.

The More Connected We Are, the Less Intelligent We Become

As I have traveled the WPP network, I have come to realize that many of my colleagues have a problem. These individual problems combine to create a bigger problem for the operating companies, and in turn for the Group itself. And it's not just WPP's problem. It's shared by virtually every other company in the business world, and you don't even have to come to the office to see it in action. I see it every time I board a train to travel from my home in Somerset to my office in London. I see it as I wait in airport departure lounges with my wife and children. I see it in hotel dining rooms, in restaurants, in the line at Starbucks, and even in the aisle at Safeway. It's everywhere.

This problem, in essence, is that our society's obsession with speed, and with being available 24/7, is reducing our intelligence, and thus our ability to come up with the best solutions for our colleagues and clients. "Always on" technology like a BlackBerry, mobile phone, or computer means that we are distracted when we should be concentrating on what we are paid to do, and even when the machine is not actually interrupting us, our minds are constantly ready for it to do so and cannot truly focus on the task at hand. In the old days, a person sitting down at a conference room table would lay out a notepad and a pen. Today, even if the notepad and pen survive, they are likely to be joined by one or more of the devices mentioned above. Once displayed, you know as well as I that it's rare for a user to ignore them.

A recent study commissioned by Hewlett-Packard suggested that frequent use of text messages and e-mails has a negative effect on the brain that is equivalent to smoking two joints of marijuana or having a sleepless night. Probably not as much fun, I suspect, but the same overall effect. Researchers at the University of London found that tapping away on a mobile phone, a BlackBerry, or a computer keyboard, or simply checking them constantly for electronic messages, may temporarily knock about ten points off a person's IQ.

These findings are corroborated in a paper in the *Harvard Business Review*, published in January 2005 by the psychiatrist Edward

Halliwell. He identifies a syndrome that he calls Attention Deficit Trait. This is not a neurological condition like the closely related and better known Attention Deficit Disorder; instead it is created by the way we work. According to Halliwell, the numbers afflicted by it are growing exponentially.

He argues that we—as humans, not just as businesspeople—are being crippled by two related delusions. The first is that it is a sign of weakness if we do not manage to create the time to do everything that is expected of us. Because there are not enough hours in the day for most of us to fulfill our own and others' unrealistic expectations in sequence, we feel we have to attack them simultaneously, to multitask. As heroic as that may make us feel (and appear in the eyes of our superiors) the human brain doesn't cope well with juggling lots of tasks at once, and consequently its effectiveness is reduced. (Remember the tennis ball analogy in Chapter 3?)

The second delusion identified by Halliwell in today's business world is that if we are not constantly connected, the world will come crashing down around us. The e-mail has to be answered, the presentation sent, the call made. Not later, not tomorrow, but now. Reply to all, copy everyone. A person's quality as an employee or a manager seems increasingly likely to be judged not by their wisdom, but rather by their response time. Never mind interrupting the research and writing for the $100 million new business presentation in order to respond to the e-mail; in this speed-addicted society, he who replies quickest shall be exalted, while he who actually takes the time to think is marked down for being inattentive.

The human brain has never been asked to track so many different data points. Never before has so much status been invested in being seen by others to be so much in demand. If left unchecked, this is a problem that will get much worse. Estimates of the volume of e-mails we receive vary, but the average per user in Britain, according to the Hewlett-Packard study, is 32 a day, increasing at a rate of 84 percent each year. I'm no mathematician, but if I generously assume that reading and responding to these e-mails takes an average of one minute each, and that the 84 percent rate of increase continues, then within four years we will all be spending about six hours a day dealing with e-mail. Within nine years, we will receive enough e-mails each day to keep us occupied for 128 hours, which if I'm not mistaken is more hours than even the most ambitious attorney would think of billing in a single day. My only hope is that between now and 2015 we can either stop the madness, or I will be able to find myself a job as a hair stylist for household pets.

The physiological problem is that when confronted by multiple and sometimes conflicting tasks, the frontal lobes of the human brain get overloaded. As Halliwell says, "When you are confronted with the sixth decision after the fifth interruption in the midst of the search for the ninth missing piece of information on the day that the third deal has collapsed and the twelfth impossible request has blipped unbidden across your computer screen, your brain begins to panic." Most people wouldn't know this was actually happening to them, but when the frontal lobes become overburdened, the lower, more primitive parts of the brain shift into survival mode, dimming intelligence. When ADT kicks in, people lose their perspective, their flexibility, and their sense of humor. They make impulsive judgments or sometimes avoid making any decisions at all. They drown in the details, becoming more and more irritable. Some people deal with the condition better than others, but regardless of how well they think they can cope, their performance will be impaired.

It is impossible to collect the large amounts of information required by the process outlined in Chapter 4 if you don't have the time or freedom to do so. It is impossible to sift through that information and find the necessary connections, the interesting relationships, if your train of thought is constantly being interrupted. And how can you develop a logical, compelling flow for an argument when you are constantly having to start over? The answer is simple: you can't.

I'm sure that much of this will feel familiar. I know it to be true because I have experienced it myself and seen it in the behavior of others close to me. But perhaps the most frightening aspect of the condition, beyond its direct impact upon a person's work performance, is the insidious way that it affects the so-called "personal" time of our lives.

This too has a profound effect upon our ability to collect information and to approach the process of interpretation, synthesis, and dramatization in an open, healthy state of mind.

Bringing Work to Bed Is Bad for Your Sex Life

Because most of us think that there are too few hours in the day and too many tasks to complete, we often take our work home with us. Thus unscheduled e-mails and calls can interrupt our social life too. There was a time, not so long ago, when we all went home to relax, took vacations to get away, and enjoyed the down time as we walked, drove, rode, or flew to work. Now we can be called on our mobile phones anywhere in the world, day or night. Airplanes have connections that allow e-mail access at 30,000 feet, all the way across the Atlantic. And in every restaurant, around every swimming pool, in every vacation spot around the world, you will find business men and women talking on mobile phones and tapping away on keyboards while supposedly spending "quality time" with their families.

The fact that a lot of people never switch off, relax, and recharge, despite their superficial devotion to duty, means that they are doing their employer few favors. I have always thought that the quality of the time a person spends away from work is the most significant influence on the quality of the time they actually spend working. It's simple: if an employee is happy, healthy, and relaxed, he or she will be much more productive than one who is not. Those who allow work to creep into their home lives are stepping onto a dangerously slippery slope. Checking e-mail before bed can make it difficult to sleep. Just one phone call can ruin a conversation and set off a chain of events that can destroy a vacation, a child's special day, even a marriage. And in the great journey of life, those are the only things that really matter.

When I arrived in San Francisco to take up my position as planning director at Goodby, Silverstein, I endeared myself to our then-director of human resources by unilaterally changing the agency's vacation policy as it pertained to members of my department. While a new employee at the agency might be entitled to one week of vacation time in their first year and two weeks after five, I insisted that all of my planners be given unlimited vacation. (Actually, I just told them that they could take it, which was a verbal contract the agency could not break.) You can imagine how that was received in certain quarters, but my rationale was simple. If I had two planners of similar intellect and experience, and one worked for me for 51 weeks each year, and the other for 48, I would bet that the one who worked less would be much more productive over the course of the year. All I asked of the planners was to treat the "unlimited" part of the plan with respect, and to promise me that they would do something useful with the extra time. In the ten years that I was with the agency, I doubt that anyone in my department took off more than four weeks in any given year. But when they were away, in the glorious days before everyone had mobile phones and remote access to e-mail, they were really away.

What my grandmother used to say about too much work making Jack a dull boy was, along with all her other sayings, quite astute. So every time the planners took time out from the agency they traveled, and read novels, and saw movies and art that gave them a broader, deeper cultural context against which to consider their business problems. They would bring back random pieces of the general information mentioned in Chapter 4, which could both inform and add color to their ideas and presentations. When they thought about work issues—which inevitably they did—their distance gave them the clarity of thought they needed to come up with new and interesting angles on problems that just a few days previously had seemed almost insoluble.

Of course the technology that allows us to turn once-enjoyable evenings, weekends, and vacations into unpaid extensions of our working hours is unlikely to go away anytime soon. Neither is the "I Want It Now" culture that pervades every sphere of human existence, from education to gardening, from the marketing of constipation medication to the management of soccer clubs. But if we allow ourselves to be subjugated by that technology, and compromised by the pressure to always be doing, delivering, on time and preferably sooner, we betray ourselves, and we betray our potential. We betray the wives, husbands, sons, and daughters who matter most to us, and—here's the real irony—we betray our employers and those clients who trust us to really be worth the fees we are paid.

Our obsession with connection and addiction to mobile phones and e-mail may never be completely curable. It can, however, be managed. And I don't necessarily mean managed with the assistance of an overweight German automobile or a visit to Trevor Walbridge's tool shed. It means taking a stand against other people who believe that speed is a more important quality than intelligence; it means sometimes disappointing them in the short term in the interests of longer-term satisfaction; it means really taking control (as opposed to the illusion of control offered by the BlackBerry) of your own life.

Taking Control

Taking control in the context of this book means carving out the time and space to think, and protecting your health and happiness so that at these times you are able to think freely and creatively.

Taking control means keeping your work and home life separate, so that when you are at home you can devote real time to your family and friends, do the things that you enjoy doing, and explore life and culture. Don't bring e-mail home with you or answer your mobile late at night unless you know it's a friend. There are very few business calls made at 9 P.M. that cannot wait until the next day. Just a few evenings spent talking to your family instead of Burland from sales, or Grogan from account management, and you may find yourself entering the office with a new spring in your stride. Presentations are much easier to prepare when you are relaxed and happy.

Taking control means looking after your brain. Sleep well, eat well, and try to get some exercise every day. There are very few problems that can't be worked out in a gym or when walking the dog. When I was in San Francisco I used to schedule meetings three lunchtimes a week with "JG," who happened to be Joseph Gannon, a trainer at my gym. If people had known that I was going to the gym, they would have assumed that this could be overridden, but if they saw a meeting on my calendar the time would be protected. I used to take these meetings very seriously. As described in Chapter 4, these times out of the office were often the ones when, having spent the morning sifting through piles of data and identifying the key components of a presentation, I would literally as well as figuratively "drop it." Running along the Embarcadero, with the Bay glistening to the east and the skyscrapers of downtown San Francisco shining white in the sunshine, the thickly knotted rope of my presentation would slowly, inexorably, start to unravel. Bigger ideas would begin to reveal themselves, and the first hints of a logical flow might emerge. On my return to the office, the Post-It notes that comprised the headlines for my presentation would move around their board as if by magic. The presentation would have been written with nothing more complicated than a stolen hour and a pair of ASICS running shoes. Or, in exceptional circumstances, a pair of baseball tickets.

Taking control means never taking work with you on vacation. Or giving work the opportunity to reach you on vacation. I once went away for a week on Maui, Hawaii, to chill out before a major new business pitch, and the vacation was ruined by an HR person from our agency calling to complain that someone else's car was in my parking space at the office. When I told her that I wouldn't give a flying fuck if little green men were parked in my space at the office, it set off a regrettable chain of events that left me on the telephone every day instead of in the hot tub on our *lanai.* Thereafter I allowed myself to be contactable only in an emergency, with the number left in the hands of someone who truly understood the definition of that word. Even receiving calls or e-mails from friends back home can be a drag—it just reminds you of the daily life the fantasy of your vacation is allowing you to escape. Ideally, the only communication between you and the folks back home should be in the form of a postcard, telling them that you're having a nice time and not missing them one bit.

Moving back to the office, *taking control means not allowing interruptions.* I do this by working from home when I need to write a presentation script, with my e-mail disconnected and mobile phone switched off. If I have to be in the office I find a room and post a polite notice on the outside asking not to be disturbed. The logic and content of a presentation can only be as good as your own discipline in creating it; if you allow constant interruptions during its preparation, the chances are that the presentation itself will be fragmented, and some of the more important connections will undoubtedly be missed. Of course, it would be unreasonable to suggest that other work responsibilities should be abandoned completely during preparation of a new business presentation. Such interruptions can, however, take place on your own terms. They can even be made to work for you.

Taking control thus means scheduling the interruptions you can't avoid. I try to restrict the number of times I check and respond to e-mail or voicemail messages to three a day. Once when I first get to my desk, once again just after lunch, and finally in the hour before I leave the office. I don't respond to all incoming messages immediately because some of them actually require some thought. This works for me in three ways. First, it allows me to focus on one thing at a time. When I'm checking e-mail, I'm checking e-mail, and when I'm writing a presentation I'm writing a presentation. Second, even the act of checking messages provides an opportunity to clear my mind from the work of preparing the presentation, and at the point of searching for meaning described in the previous chapter, any break is useful. Finally, the spacing that such discipline involves means that most of my responses to messages are better thought through than they might have been if I had gone straight to the "reply" button. I have learned to love the "Save as Draft" icon on my e-mail, because it has stopped me from making a fool of myself on numerous occasions.

Taking control means making space for thinking. A colleague at JWT, Ryan Lietaer, recently wrote to me expressing the wish that our business culture could be more geared towards creating ideas for clients, instead of the current model in which people seem more concerned with keeping on top of their in-tray. He's absolutely right—far too many of us spend far too much time doing, and not half enough thinking. It's important, particularly to the preparation of presentations, to recognize that thinking time does count as working. If this means spending a train journey drinking Earl Grey tea, eating bacon sandwiches, and reading *The Times* from cover to cover, so be it. That's how I spend most of my train journeys, and it's amazing how often I find a current story that's pertinent to the theme of a presentation I am about to give, a photograph that might be the perfect illustration for a point, or indeed an article that I think might be of use someday, even if I'm not sure how, or when, or where. (Regardless, it will be torn out and carried home to be filed for future consumption.) And when I'm not reading the newspaper or a good novel, I'm watching and listening to my fellow commuters. Sometimes the thinking I am doing is of the specific nature described in the previous chapter, but more often it is the general information I am discovering and processing, drawn from that most abundant source that we know as real life. Maybe I can't allocate the time easily to a particular box on the timesheet (there we are—more evidence of corporate pressure to always be *doing*, preferably at someone else's expense), but it all helps me in doing a better job for both my agency and clients.

Finally, *taking control means treating others as you would like to be treated yourself.* In addition to controlling our own time and space, remember that each one of us can exert a positive influence over others. We can send fewer e-mails, and therefore reduce the time that it takes others to deal with them. I regard the "reply to all" and "cc" buttons as inherently evil. I can see the point of replying to everyone on a very short mailing list about a subject that is relevant to all of them, but most people use the device at best indiscriminately (do I really want to read replies from 43 people to the all-agency e-mail asking if anyone would like to order a cab home after the Christmas party?) and at worst, politically (look how clever I am, look how hard I'm working, see how I kicked his sorry ass). Such deliberate—as opposed to unthinking—use of multiple replies and copies is generally the hallmark of an insecure and unpleasant person.

Other people should be given the time and space to do their thinking. If they ask for peace and quiet in which to work on their ideas and presentations, it should be given. If they want to work from home or a table in Starbucks, they should have the flexibility to do so. And if they want to take a break at the gym, remember that it's not only their own interests they're thinking of.

Every time one person resolves not to make business calls in the evening or at the weekend, or not to send an e-mail on a Sunday morning, the effect is felt by many more. You have probably heard the scientists' cause-and-effect story of the butterfly beating its wings in the Amazon and starting a storm over Europe. And maybe every decision to not disturb a colleague at home, not copy the boss, not insist on a vacation contact number, is the equivalent of one tiny beat of that butterfly's wings.

It's up to us.

If we want that storm to break, we know what to do.

And I suspect that if we do, and when it does, the rain will feel good. Very good.

CHAPTER SIX

- **We Will Fight Them in the Boardroom**

  – How to ruin a great idea by presenting it badly

Imagine This

It's June 4, 1940, and Prime Minister Winston Churchill stands before the British House of Commons, ready to report on the successful evacuation of Allied troops from Dunkirk. The nation is euphoric: despite terrible losses of both men and equipment, more than 300,000 Allied troops have been rescued from the jaws of the advancing Germans. But Churchill's task is not to celebrate this unexpected deliverance. He needs to prepare the British people for darker days ahead, as the army licks its wounds, as factory workers strain to replace lost planes, vehicles, and weapons, and as Hitler's army readies itself for an invasion. Maybe most important of all, he has to issue a clear appeal to the United States: Europe needs help.

He's made some important presentations in his time, but probably none as important as this one.

He clears his throat, jingling the keys and loose change in his pocket as he consults his notes one last time. Then he hits the advance button on his laptop. A title spirals onto the screen, halting at the top and leaving a large, teasing expanse of white space below.

DUNKIRK: WHAT WENT WRONG?

Now he speaks. "Dunkirk," he says. "What went wrong?"

All eyes are on the screen, drawn inexorably by the strength, the rugged self-assurance, of his 40-point Helvetica Neue Bold typeface. Churchill's finger hovers expectantly over the lower right-hand corner of his keyboard, before the lightest of touches brings three bullet points spiraling in to fill the space below the question.

DUNKIRK: WHAT WENT WRONG?

- **Reasons**
- **Implications**
- **Recommendations**

–A Presentation by the Prime Minister

He turns toward the screen, nodding in silent appreciation of his words, before turning back once more to face his audience. "I have a lot of charts to get through," he says. "So I'd be grateful if you could keep your questions until the end." With another deft touch of his index finger, the opening page is pushed aside by a new, bouncing title.

MILITARY OPERATIONS IN FRANCE AND BELGIUM REVIEWED

"I would like to start with a review of the military operations in France and Belgium leading up to the Dunkirk evacuations."

The Prime Minister starts to build. Each new word spins onto the screen to the sound of an electronic bursting bubble, taking its place in line in the way, he fancies, that a platoon of soldiers might fall in. He wonders whether the assembled Members of Parliament will appreciate the symbolism.

**MILITARY OPERATIONS IN FRANCE
AND BELGIUM REVIEWED**

- British and French armies entered Belgium at request of Belgian king
- German advance cuts communication between British and French armies
  - Mechanized divisions
  - Rapid deployment force
  - Infantry
- Valiant Defense of Calais
- Retreat to Dunkirk
  - Evacuation by Royal Navy and Merchant Navy
- Untimely Nature of King Leopold's Surrender
  - No warning
  - Not cricket

"You're all familiar with the chronology," Churchill says. "The Belgian king asked us to help, and at very short notice both we and the French obliged. Unfortunately we underestimated the strength and power of the German advance . . ."

He's starting to find his rhythm. More electronic bubbles burst as the screen fills with bullets and sub-bullets, the density of the slide a testament to his hours of preparation, his knowledge, and his mastery of all that PowerPoint can offer the data-rich, time-poor executive.

More slides follow: a table showing the performance of RAF fighters against their Luftwaffe counterparts; an organization chart to remind the members of the Allied Forces' command structure; a series of mixed text/graph slides comparing English and German losses; a spreadsheet of which he is particularly proud, analyzing the loading and unloading time of Royal Navy ships versus those of the Merchant Navy; and the highlights of a continuous tracking study measuring British consumer confidence through the critical period of the retreat of the British Expeditionary Force. Pie charts thrust skywards, tables fill, and images from the Clip Gallery add color and dimension. It's a shame, he thinks, that there's no suitable image of an airplane for his slide about air power, but the hot air balloon has probably made the point.

He pauses, wiping his brow with a handkerchief. His timepiece, placed carefully on the lectern beside the state-of-the-art laser pointer, indicates that he has overrun his allotted time by more than half an hour, but he only has three more slides to share. Electronic copies will be available for everyone to take away and analyze at their leisure. This time not even the Leader of the Opposition could accuse him of lack of attention to detail.

"And finally," he says, "I'd like to deal with the issue of a potential Nazi invasion. In particular I would like to make some suggestions for ways in which we might try to stop such an invasion." A Clip Art picture of a policeman on traffic duty dissolves onto the screen. He's holding up his palm, next to a headline that reads simply: Stop the Nazis!

"There are lots of places where an advance might be arrested," he says. "We've been kicking around a few thoughts. Maybe you could do the same and e-mail me any other suggestions. The 'etcetera,' if you like." He presses the advance button once more, and nine bullets shake simultaneously to the screen, accompanied by a rumble of thunder. He had wanted ten but could only come up with nine. The "etc." doesn't really count. Nevertheless, the slide remains powerful. Very powerful.

STOP THE NAZIS!

- France
- Seas / Oceans
- Coastline
- Bridgeheads
- In the country
- In the city
- Urban / rural confluence
- If necessary, around the Empire
- Etc.

"Obviously it's a little late for the first item on the list. That particular horse has left the stable. But we can at least try to stop them from getting any further." Or should he have said "farther?" The spell check on his computer provides no help whatsoever where such subtleties of the English language are concerned.

"I think these are pretty self-explanatory," he says. "So all that remains is to mention that we could probably do with some help from our friends in America, so let's hope for that sooner rather than later. There will be an electronic copy of this document for everyone, but right now I'm happy to take any questions." He reads the last line of his notes, as he touches the advance button for the final time. "Thank you for listening."

**THANK YOU
FOR LISTENING**

Raising a Nation

How would our world be today if Prime Minister Churchill had really delivered his famous "We Shall Fight on the Beaches" speech using a laptop, PowerPoint, and a distinct lack of imagination? Would I be writing this book in English? Would you be allowed to read it? Would you and I have even been born?

Of course we'll never know. Alone, and even in the face of hierarchically confused bullet points, poor typeface selection, and inappropriate Clip Art, it's possible that the British stand against Nazi tyranny could have continued. It's possible, but I doubt it. And if Churchill had e-mailed a copy of his presentation to President Roosevelt with a note saying, "F.D.R.—w8ing 4 u—W.," it might not have kept America from entering the war, but I question whether it would have tipped the balance toward intervention.

Some might say that soldiers and firepower win wars, not speeches. They may argue that whatever Churchill said on June 4th was irrelevant to the final outcome of the Second World War; compared to Hitler's mistakes, Russian winters, and American military and economic power, Britain's resistance may have been relatively insignificant. But after the Dunkirk debacle Britain fought on alone for more than a year before Hitler invaded Russia. Its cities were bombed night and day, its ships were sunk, its armies driven back in the few remaining overseas theaters of war. It was a full 18 months before the United States entered the war. Yet against overwhelming odds the British hung on and eventually prevailed.

The British prevailed because Churchill refused to believe that defeat was inevitable or victory impossible. On that day in 1940 he succeeded in persuading his people to believe in him, in the possibility of success, and in their own power to fight on. Though it may not have seemed like it at the time, that well-crafted speech was worth at least as much as several highly trained regiments of soldiers, squadrons of Spitfires, or brand new battleships. It was probably worth much, much more, because in a speech lasting no more than a few minutes, with absolutely no visual aids, Churchill rallied a nation. (See Figure 6.1.)

The reason I turned Churchill's speech into PowerPoint was not to make fun of him or his speech. On the contrary, I believe he was one of the greatest speakers the world has ever heard, and that particular speech was one of his finest. While running workshops across the world on presentation techniques, I have asked people to consider what might have been if, in the hot summer of 1963, Dr. Martin Luther King Jr. had faced his audience in Washington, D.C. and said, instead of "I have a dream," "I have a . . . PowerPoint Presentation." Dr. King's speech is perhaps the finest I have *ever* heard. Yet even the greatest

Turning once again, and this time more generally, to the question of invasion, I would observe that there has never been a period in all these long centuries of which we boast when an absolute guarantee against invasion, still less against serious raids, could have been given to our people. In the days of Napoleon the same wind which would have carried his transports across the Channel might have driven away the blockading fleet. There was always the chance, and it is that chance which has excited and befooled the imaginations of many Continental tyrants. Many are the tales that are told. We are assured that novel methods will be adopted, and when we see the originality of malice, the ingenuity of aggression, which our enemy displays, we may certainly prepare ourselves for every kind of novel stratagem and every kind of brutal and treacherous maneuver. I think that no idea is so outlandish that it should not be considered and viewed with a searching, but at the same time, I hope, with a steady eye. We must never forget the solid assurances of sea power and those which belong to air power if it can be locally exercised.

I have, myself, full confidence that if all do their duty, if nothing is neglected, and if the best arrangements are made, as they are being made, we shall prove ourselves once again able to defend our Island home, to ride out the storm of war, and to outlive the menace of tyranny, if necessary for years, if necessary alone. At any rate, that is what we are going to try to do. That is the resolve of His Majesty's Government-every man of them. That is the will of Parliament and the nation. The British Empire and the French Republic, linked together in their cause and in their need, will defend to the death their native soil, aiding each other like good comrades to the utmost of their strength. Even though large tracts of Europe and many old and famous States have fallen or may fall into the grip of the Gestapo and all the odious apparatus of Nazi rule, we shall not flag or fail. We shall go on to the end, we shall fight in France, we shall fight on the seas and oceans, we shall fight with growing confidence and growing strength in the air, we shall defend our Island, whatever the cost may be, we shall fight on the beaches, we shall fight on the landing grounds, we shall fight in the fields and in the streets, we shall fight in the hills; we shall never surrender, and even if, which I do not for a moment believe, this Island or a large part of it were subjugated and starving, then our Empire beyond the seas, armed and guarded by the British Fleet, would carry on the struggle, until, in God's good time, the New World, with all its power and might, steps forth to the rescue and the liberation of the old.

FIGURE 6.1 **An excerpt from Churchill's speech to the British House of Commons, June 4th, 1940. This speech was notable for its lack of technological sophistication and complete absence of visual aids.**

ideals, the most intelligent thinking, will fail to create belief, will fail to win over the people who really matter, if they are presented badly.

If at this point you are expecting me to make an all-out attack on PowerPoint, you will not be far wrong. Of course there is an argument that says it is not the fault of PowerPoint that it is the medium for so many shitty presentations; rather it is the *presenter* who is at fault, for using it badly. But I have heard the same argument used to defend ownership of assault weapons and the keeping of pit bull terriers as family pets, and quite frankly it doesn't hold up for PowerPoint any more than it does for AK-47s or fighting dogs. Yes, I accept that presenters are often to blame for using it badly, and I will discuss ways in which it can at least be used to better effect. But in the form most often used for presentations, PowerPoint represents intellectual lethargy on the part of the presenter, and generally induces something similar in its audience. It undermines good thinking by forcing the imprecise use of language, by fragmenting information, and by encouraging the triumph of order over content. These inherent problems are then compounded by slavish devotion to an array of tools that are supposed to help (constraining templates, ridiculous Clip Art, and goofy transitions, to name but three), use of inappropriate materials, and a widely embraced presentation style that involves reading every last word on the slide. As Edward Tufte observes in his wonderful short book, *The Cognitive Style of PowerPoint:*

> Imagine a widely used and expensive prescription drug that claimed to make us beautiful but didn't. Instead the drug had frequent, serious side effects: making us stupid, degrading the quality and credibility of our communication, turning us into bores, wasting our colleagues' time. These side effects, and the resulting unsatisfactory cost/benefit ratio, would rightly lead us to a worldwide product recall.

As desirable as a worldwide recall might be, I somehow can't see Microsoft supporting it. But if that's not an option, how can we make the best of a bad situation?

Many Slides Do Not a Presentation Make

More than ten years ago, I made a pitch presentation to Adobe Systems, the creator of graphics software that may well reside on your computer. At the time it was one of Silicon Valley's up-and-coming companies. Goodby, Silverstein & Partners had worked with hi-tech clients before (Electronic Arts had been the agency's founding client), but not for some time. Our reputation had been built in the world of consumer products and sports franchises, and the general feeling in Silicon Valley was that we "didn't get" hi-tech.

We thus felt that in our presentation we had to do everything we could to prove our technological credentials. We decided that for the first time in the agency's history we would make our presentation using a computer and slide projector. Our normal approach was simply to talk, and if we needed to show anything we would do so using large boards. This time, however, we felt that this approach would merely accentuate our Luddite credentials. On the two previous occasions that we had met the client, we had been treated to PowerPoint presentations; if that was the way the Silicon Valley players did things, we thought, then that's how we would do them too.

On the day of the presentation we arrived, laptop and slide projector in hand. We also brought a large art bag containing a boarded version of our presentation, just in case.

We were the last agency to present, and we entered a conference room containing a large table with all the chairs oriented towards a pull-down screen. On the table was a projector, its blue umbilical cord only recently severed from the previous presenters' computer.

"Just hook up to our projector," we were told, as one might be told to remove one's shoes before entering a Japanese restaurant. Thank goodness we had taken the hi-tech pledge.

The computer was duly connected and fired up. For the next half hour, we struggled in vain to make our presentation work. I still don't entirely understand the nature of the problem, but words like "software," "compatibility," and "operating system" were uttered with knowing nods by the Adobe technical people who had been sent to help us. On our side of the table, we were whispering nontechnical words like "shit" and "fuck," and phrases like "I told you it was a stupid idea" and "I'm going to kill Harold." (Harold was the technical consultant whose unenviable job was to bring our agency and its management into the late twentieth century.) No amount of tweaking, rebooting, reloading could solve the problem. Prayer did not help. We had lost the pitch before we even started.

"I'm very sorry," Jeff Goodby said when the Adobe marketing executives arrived a few minutes later, to find their screen retracted and a large open space on the table where for as long as any of them could remember a projector had stood. Behind Jeff, stacked face-in against a wall, was a pile of boards. As he tried to explain our technological misfortune, the expressions on their faces suggested that he might as well have been wearing furs and a Davy Crockett hat. I began to think that what was to come might prove even more disagreeable than the time I presented to David Stern at the National Basketball Association.

But whatever our misgivings, we pushed on. Jeff was delightfully self-deprecating, and optimistically suggested that in fact our inadequacies might be useful as Adobe sought to expand its franchise and embrace those who were similarly technically challenged. The rest of us picked up on his theme, and as board followed board, as we spoke for long periods with no visual aids whatsoever, and as our low-tech standards got progressively lower, we started to sense a change in our audience. Their initial surprise and suspicion had lifted, and most, if not all, seemed genuinely engaged.

As we brought our presentation to a close, giving each of them a beautifully bound book that showcased our love of design, one of them said, "That was deliberate, right?"

What did he mean?

"The whole computer problem thing. That was just theater." He gave us one of those Rachel-from-*Friends* "You *guys!*" looks.

No, really, we insisted. We absolutely *were* that incompetent.

"Well," he said, shaking his head. "I've gotta say, that was one of the most refreshing presentations I've seen in a long time." His colleagues nodded in agreement.

"You bet!"

"No computer!"

"No slides!"

"You guys really get it!"

We were awarded the Adobe advertising account the next day. And in the rest of my time at the agency, we never attempted to give another presentation using a computer.

A large part of the reason why we succeeded was that our presentation was so different from those of our competitors. We *felt* different, and that was appealing to Adobe executives who were reaching out into markets where they had previously not ventured. The other key difference, several members of the Adobe audience told us later, was that our low-tech approach really focused their attention on us, and on what we were saying to them. During the other presentations, they had done what audiences always do in PowerPoint presentations—they read the slides instead of listening to the presenters. The other agencies' presentations might as well have been sent via e-mail.

Quite by accident, we had achieved what Steve Jobs was to do in our dim and distant future, and what the owner of the final research company did in his presentation to my client described in Chapter 3. By adopting a completely different approach, by focusing the audience's attention on us rather than on our slides, and by making our presentation more of a two-way conversation, we had highlighted our ideas, and made presentations that may well have contained similar material seem quite deficient by comparison.

With other audiences, whether deliberate or not, this approach might have been less successful. But at least it caused us to think about it in every future presentation we gave. What was the best way of engaging this particular client, and what was the best way to present and sell the idea we were recommending?

In the course of my day job with WPP, I work on countless presentations with others. Sometimes I am cast in the role of author, but more often I am a sounding board for their ideas. I am guessing that more than 90 percent of the time, the first draft of any presentation I am sent and—perhaps even more worrying—the first draft of even a point of view on an important issue, will arrive in the form of a PowerPoint deck. It is a default reaction, a natural assumption, that this is what the audience expects, and this is the way that intelligent people in the twenty-first century should exchange information.

I beg to differ, on both counts.

First, if you agree with me that surprise is an important—indeed vital—element of any good story, it should follow that to present all of your stories in exactly the same way is to admit your inadequacy as a storyteller. Audiences expect PowerPoint only because they have been beaten into submission by it, and because no one has ever had the courage to question their judgment.

Second, PowerPoint might be the simplest, most efficient way to prepare and deliver a presentation, but to regard that as a positive attribute is to say that laziness is a more admirable attribute than intelligence. The mindset that values PowerPoint as a means of sharing information confuses efficiency with effectiveness, and of course the latter is the only meaningful measure of quality. The problem is that PowerPoint is not designed for the benefit of the message a presentation is meant to convey, or even for the benefit of the audience, but rather *for the sole benefit of the presenter*. Its very reason for being is therefore at odds with the basic principles of communication outlined earlier in this book.

One Size Does Not Fit All

There's a word that up until a few years ago I had never heard in regular conversation, or even in irregular conversation. In fact, it probably didn't even exist. That word is "deliverable," and it has come to govern many of our lives, not necessarily for the better.

Today as we finish one meeting and turn our attention to the next, talk inevitably turns to deadlines and to deliverables. By a certain date we promise to deliver a presentation, slides, a leave-behind, an electronic leave-behind. At the touch of a button these deliverables can be delivered anywhere in the world; you no longer have to be present, or awake, or even alive, to be the recipient. And when the last slide has been projected, the document mailed, the disc handed over, everyone can breathe a huge sigh of relief and think, "job done."

That is the beauty of PowerPoint. With one set of slides you have your presentation materials, a leave-behind for those who were present, and a virtual experience for those unfortunate enough not to be there in person. How convenient is that?

Very. But just as with wine that comes in boxes and some of those meals that can be cooked in 30 seconds in a microwave, such convenience comes at a price. My opinion on this is very simple: for a presentation, visuals should be created that will assist in delivering the message (that is why they are called visual *aids*); for a leave-behind, if you must share these visual aids, they should be accompanied by a prose summary of the key points; if the task is to share the information with someone important who couldn't be there, then ideally they or you should buy a plane ticket and the presentation should be repeated. If this last scenario proves impossible, then a well-written prose summary augmented by live discussion is the only acceptable alternative. The most important point is that PowerPoint is generally unsuitable for every one of these tasks. It can fulfill multiple functions simultaneously, but perform none of them very well.

I will talk more about leave-behind documents in Chapter 8, when I will look more closely at the day of the presentation and fulfilling the aim of leaving the client wanting more. For now, let us focus on the presentation itself and explore in a little more detail why PowerPoint is far from being the ideal tool for connecting to and influencing an audience.

Too Much Information

In the fifth century B.C., Plato shared his concerns that the growing art of writing was a threat to the oral tradition of Greek civilization. Writing, he feared, would make many people "trust to the external written characters and not remember of themselves . . . they will be hearers of many things and will have learned nothing."

Clever man that he was, I doubt that even Plato could have imagined the volume of words that could be crammed into a single PowerPoint slide and projected on the wall for us to enjoy. The simple fact is that in confusing the role of presentation visuals with the requirements for a leave-behind document, people try to tell their entire story and project it word for word onto the wall of the conference room. This means that most slides contain far too many words, and these words appear in a landscape format that still feels unnatural for many of us to read. But once they are there on the wall, we feel compelled to read them, whatever the presenter happens to be saying at the time. On the rare occasions that a presenter elaborates on a point, or takes an unscripted diversion, what they are saying is generally lost as the audience continues to read the words on the screen.

Consider that the next slide might have been part of my "Dirt is Good" presentation to Unilever, but thankfully was not.

Dirt is Good resolves tension

- All great brands resolve cultural tensions
  - Virgin is antidote to unpleasant flying experience
  - Apple brings humanity to computing
  - Nike attacks gender and race limits
- Tension is the active ingredient, energy source
- In *Dirt is Good* tension lies between clean and dirty, good and evil. Tension resolved by cleaning
- But there is a problem
  - Must be resolved to optimize *Dirt is Good* potential

In fact, as PowerPoint slides go, its word count is fairly modest. A mere 67 words, if my counting is correct. It is, however, slightly painful to read, for reasons of both layout and typeface selection, and no doubt if I had shown that particular slide I would have encountered great difficulty in holding my audience.

What I did instead was to show a large board, on which the "Dirt is Good" logo was shown, alongside the logos of Virgin, Apple, and

Nike. Above the logos were four words, in caps: GREAT BRANDS RESOLVE TENSIONS.

I had talked about this before with some of the clients in the audience, but not all. As I exposed the board, I paused for a moment to let them take it in. The clear message was that we saw the "Dirt is Good" brand idea in exalted company. We weren't just trying to ingratiate ourselves here—at the heart of the *Dirt is Good* idea we saw a powerful connection between the brand promise and a cultural truth relating to dirt.

So what, the audience members were thinking, are they going to say about our relationship to these brands? And what do they mean by "resolve tensions"?

This is what I said: "Finally, as well as representing the high ground of a category, all great brands succeed in resolving underlying tensions between individuals and the culture in which they live. Virgin was the antidote for people who thought that flying was an experience to be endured, rather than enjoyed. Apple brought humanity to computing. Nike didn't just compete with Adidas—it attacked the limits placed on people by their race and gender. We believe that this cultural tension is the active ingredient in any great brand. The other things I have mentioned give the brand its reason for being; its *energy* comes from this inherent conflict.

"In "Dirt is Good" there is tension: a dilemma between clean and dirty, between good and evil. The brand resolves this tension by cleaning.

"But there is a problem. And this problem has to be resolved before 'Dirt is Good' can achieve its full potential."

On my board I said very little: simply that "Dirt is Good" has something in common with brands that any marketer would admire. This image remained in front of them—with me physically holding onto the visual—with their attention focused firmly on me as I explained this common feature. The news was all good, until the end, when I changed direction and told them that there was a problem. The problem was the one I mentioned in an earlier section of this book, namely that what people say isn't necessarily what people do, and that while it is good for people to tell us they agree that getting dirty is a positive force in a child's development, it's not very helpful to our business if they still get mad at their own kids when they come home dirty. But I didn't want to tell them that right away. I wanted to introduce the point using three or four pieces of evidence that they could add up and interpret for themselves. Right now, all I wanted to do was plant the idea that while they were doing most things right, the news was not all good.

Coming back to the fictitious "Dirt is Good" slide for a moment, I hope it's clear that for presentation purposes it says too much. I happen to think that a presentation visual should communicate in much the same way as a billboard, which means that it should be able to make its point to a person passing at 50 miles per hour. I was always told that any more than seven words on a billboard created problems for communication, and while seven may not exactly be the magic number (as I think about it, that suggests that the legendary "Refreshes the parts that other beers cannot reach" campaign for Heineken should never have run), it's certainly in the right ballpark. Presentation slides should be the physical manifestation of the KISS principle ("Keep it Simple, Stupid!"), and there is no rule that says you can't be this simple when using PowerPoint. I used PowerPoint to create my charts for the "Dirt is Good" presentation, but chose not to use any of the offered templates or stupid cartoons. I also chose to mount the images on boards instead of projecting them, so that I could put my arm around them, and thus physically possess the ideas.

Of course my chart with a simple headline and four brand logos would not have been suitable for a leave-behind document. But it was never intended to be. Our leave-behind was a prose document, which happened to include the three paragraphs shown above in their entirety. If instead I had used the fictitious PowerPoint chart and others like it, I would have raised the next problem of the software: that for certain purposes it cannot capture *enough* information.

Not Enough Information

The low resolution of PowerPoint compared to the possibilities offered by even a page like this, means that shortcuts often have to be taken.

When writing the fictitious "Dirt is Good" slide, I had to choose between including all the information pertaining to other brands and cultural tensions on one slide and risk overcrowding, or splitting it between two or more slides and facing the danger of fragmenting my message.

The choice made by most PowerPoint presenters is to put everything onto one slide, which is exactly what I did. The result? What Edward Tufte describes as "Over-generalizations, imprecise statements, slogans, lightweight evidence, abrupt and thinly-argued claims." The difference between the 67 words of the "Dirt is Good" PowerPoint slide and the 149 words of its prose version may not seem like much, but in fact it is quite significant. Even at the micro-level, compare the following:

Nike attacks gender and race limits

with: "Nike didn't just compete with Adidas—it attacked the limits placed on people by their race and gender."

You could say that the first, taken from the PowerPoint slide, is simpler. I would agree, if simplicity were defined solely by word count, but of course it is not. The second statement is, in fact, the simpler of the two, because it is written in generally correct English, and even if it might require some further explanation, it makes more sense than its abbreviated version. The reason it couldn't be written that way on the slide is twofold: first, because of the strange convention that says full sentences represent superfluity on PowerPoint; and second, because it just plain didn't fit in.

There are several other examples within those two different versions of the same point where meaning is lost through the editing process demanded by PowerPoint. To look at just one of those, compare:

Tension is the active ingredient, energy source

with: "We believe that this cultural tension is the active ingredient in any great brand. The other things I have mentioned give the brand its reason for being; its *energy* comes from this inherent conflict."

Now imagine that you are a person who was not present at the presentation (which, unless you are one of about 30 JWT and Unilever executives, should be pretty easy). Looking only at this one small part of the presentation, which would you rather read? Which would give you the better sense of what we were trying to say? Now imagine the above multiplied by 50 PowerPoint slides, and you will see the size of the gap in meaning that can open up between the presenter and an absentee audience.

Bullet Points Dilute Thought

The use of bullet points predates the introduction of PowerPoint by some time, since it was the favored method of language compression in the days when presentations were delivered on 35 mm slides and overhead projectors.

On the surface, bullet points (so-named for the bulletlike marks that signify the start of each new phrase or point) might appear to represent economy of language and well-ordered structure. In fact, as the above examples and the imagined version of Churchill's "We Shall Fight on the Beaches" speech show, this generally accepted bullet structure encourages laziness that undermines meaning. Converting sentences into truncated, grammatically incorrect form so that they will fit the page is an exercise in obfuscation; bullets very often become like shopping lists, where fruits, canned foods, and laundry powder are written down in the order in which their absence is noted, rather than the order in which they might be found in the store; and the precise relationship between different points in the list is not only often unstated but also unconsciously misleading.

In the Churchill example shown earlier in this chapter, the bullets broadly reflect chronological order. In the first slide, the bullets show that Churchill will divide his speech into three parts: reasons for the disaster, implications of the disaster, and recommendations for what is to follow. The same is true on the second slide, the review of military operations, where the events are simply listed in the order in which they occurred. This is at least logical, although without the accompanying commentary, most of the points would make little sense, and there is no suggestion of hierarchy. What were the most important lessons learned? What has to change to avoid a similar defeat happening in the future?

This problem is perhaps most obvious in what our twenty-first century, PowerPoint-enabled Churchill does with the climax of his presentation: the slide that shows his ideas for stopping a Nazi invasion. To see where it goes wrong, turn back to page 120.

Again, the intention is to list the places where meaningful resistance might be mounted in a logical order. The invaders would have to be engaged in the act of invading (i.e., as they attempt to cross the English Channel and land on our shores) before they can be engaged "in the country" or "in the city." But the list—which is no more or less uncertain and insipid in its language than most PowerPoint slides I have seen—gives no indication of relative importance. The fact that we all remember Churchill's "We Shall Fight on the Beaches" speech rather than his "We Shall Fight in the Hills" speech is a fair indication of what really mattered, although even that is perhaps not the key. The real statement of Churchill's intent as seen in the actual text of his speech, lies in phrases like, "We shall not flag or fail . . . We shall defend our Island . . . We shall never surrender." Whatever it takes, he was saying, whatever it costs, we will defend what is ours.

Compare that to a woolly list of places where we might or might not care to stand up and fight (urban/rural confluence?), and tell me which would be most likely to raise *you* to arms.

Clip Art Is Nature's Way of Saying You Have No Imagination

Perhaps the most ludicrous part of the "Stop the Nazis" slide is the Clip Art visual of an American traffic cop. It's stupid because he's a cop, it's stupid because he's American, and it's also stupid because he's grinning. But it's the only visual I could find that fitted with the theme of halting someone's progress. All of which is to say that I must be pretty stupid too.

If you have seen more than a few PowerPoint presentations you will know that such stupidity is hardly a rare occurrence. The Clip Art gallery on my PowerPoint program gave me access to all the ridiculous visuals I used at the start of each chapter of this book. There are many more that I could have used, but these are the ones that amused me the most. I hope you realized they were meant as a joke, because my editor continues to be convinced that people will see them as serious expressions of my craft.

THIS IS A SLIDE ABOUT TEAMWORK

- The Clip Art visual shows a man in a blue suit with swollen glands and extremely small hands, giving a box of radioactive material to a woman in a purple suit who has borrowed her hands from a newt.

The reason they are all ridiculous is that they never exactly make the point. If they don't, there's really no purpose to their being there. At best they add nothing, and at worst they detract from what will be said. The teamwork example shown is a classic case in point. Because the Clip Art index says this is a visual about teamwork, the unimaginative among us might well be tempted to use it to illustrate a point about, yes, teamwork. The fact that both of the characters depicted appear to have been exposed to levels of radiation so strong that they have started to turn into amphibians might just get in the way of the message, but that seldom seems to hold the user back. PowerPoint does give you the option of inserting your own photograph, which is generally a better option if you can devote the necessary time to finding the right one. But sometimes it's better to use no picture at all. On the occasions that I use

PowerPoint, my slides tend to be a mixture of headlines and photographs. I also use a great number of blank slides: a simple black screen allows me to talk with no visual distraction whatsoever.

If I were making Churchill's presentation and thought that visuals were necessary to assist me in the part covered by the "Stop the Nazis" slide, I would do one of two things. The first option would be to use a single headline to summarize what I am talking about. Everything that I say for as long as this line is on screen will be related to that single thought.

WE SHALL DEFEND OUR ISLAND

The second option, and this is the one that I would normally choose, would be to show either a beautiful antique map of Great Britain (to emphasize the point that the country has successfully repelled invaders for almost a thousand years since the Norman conquest), or a picture of quintessential British countryside. *That* is what we are defending. I would often choose a picture over words because it captures interest without hijacking attention, but this is a decision that has to be made slide by slide. Headlines can be used as signposts and to summarize key points. But headline after headline after headline can be dull. A little imagination, and a lot of time spent searching for the right images, can go a very long way.

Transition Should Be Invisible

Finally, a word about transitions.

Don't.

Don't allow transitions to distract from your message or from you as the presenter. PowerPoint allows you to do all sorts of magical things with your words, from appearing on the screen as if being typed live, to whirling in as if from outer space with, if required, whirling-in-from-outer-space sound effects.

Such transitions are the PowerPoint equivalent of a fussy referee in a soccer match. The job of a referee is to ensure the smooth progress of the game, and the best ones allow it to flow with the minimum of interruption. Indeed, the very best become almost invisible. But those who are driven more by the ratings that drive their career advancement than by a genuine love of the game, tend to use the rules as an opportunity to draw attention to themselves: every sound of the whistle is accompanied by extravagant hand gestures and an attitude that suggests the referee is much more important than the 22 players on the field.

Fancy transitions call attention to themselves in exactly the same way, and like all of the other "presenter aids" noted above, they undermine the integrity of the presentation.

Enough said.

Improving Presentation Style

"In day-to-day practice," Edward Tufte writes in *The Cognitive Style of PowerPoint*, "PowerPoint presentations may improve 10% or 20% of all presentations by organizing inept, extremely disorganized speakers." He then adds that the use of PowerPoint inflicts "detectable intellectual damage" on the remaining 80 to 90 percent.

As he rightly points out, the best way to improve any presentation is by improving its content, in the ways outlined in previous chapters. By making the material more relevant to the audience, by eliciting their participation, by making simple points that are highlighted and augmented visually, by telling a story with dramatic twists and turns, you will increase your chances of success.

What you *show* to an audience (as distinct from what you say) should be judged as an attorney would judge the inclusion of an item of evidence. If it helps to support the case, then it should be used. If it is simply another item of information that does not help to build an argument, then it should not. As we will see in Chapter 9, David Magliano and his team spent hours, days, even weeks selecting visuals to accompany the London 2012 Bid presentation. To some observers these visuals might have appeared as little more than decoration, as a way of making the presentation more pleasing to the eye. Yet every single slide had a purpose, every one carried a message to specific members of the audience.

Of course David and his colleagues would be the first to admit that the precise impact of these sometimes subtle messages was almost impossible to gauge. But one thing was clear. Their visuals worked for them, rather than against them. And in these days of unquestioning devotion to PowerPoint templates, that is sadly all too rare.

CHAPTER SEVEN

- Benign Dictatorship
  - Leading the perfect team pitch

Wine Talks

In the ten years that I worked for Goodby, Silverstein & Partners, we pitched several times against the same agency. In the interests of decency I won't name it, but it was also based on the U.S. West Coast and had a very strong creative reputation.

Every time we pitched against this agency, we won. It was weird, because the law of averages alone should have ensured that we lost at least once or twice. But each time the same thing happened. We would be named on the same pitch list, along with maybe two or three other agencies—a cast of extras that seemed to change each time—and at the end we would be awarded the business.

Of course we liked to think that it was because of the brilliance of our strategic insights and the excellence of our creative solutions—in other words, the quality of our answers to the task we had been set. It was a good assumption, so good in fact that we didn't want to spoil it by actually asking a new client if it were true.

One day, however, we held a dinner to consummate a relationship with a client who had just hired us in preference to, among others, our near neighbors. It was, if my memory serves me correctly, an extremely good dinner held in a private dining room at *Boulevard* in San Francisco. By some strange and welcome twist of fate, our new client shared our enthusiasm for big California cabernets, and he seemed more than happy to take an extended tour around the restaurant's impressive wine list. I was driving, which is why my memory still serves me correctly, but our client, whom I shall call Eric, was not. And thus, at some point after we had finished our entrée but before dessert arrived, he leaned across the table and said, or maybe slurred, "Wanna know why I hired you instead of those other guys?"

The silence seemed to last a very long time. I had dropped my napkin, and it needed to be retrieved. My partner Harold seemed to have found some breadcrumbs in his wine glass and was signaling to a waiter to bring him a new glass. Jeff and Robert looked at each other with eyebrows raised. Did we really want to know this?

"Oh, you don't have to tell us that," Colin Probert said. I remember thinking, That's Why He's The President.

"Who, Wieden?" Rich Silverstein piped up from the other side of the table, referring to Portland advertising agency Wieden & Kennedy. Wieden was the agency for Nike and ESPN, and apparently there was great rivalry between us, except that we didn't know it.

"No," Eric said, with a dismissive wave of his hand. "Their TV was great. But Dan Wieden hates research. That wouldn't work for my board. And it's a real pain in the ass getting flights to Portland."

"Fallon?" Rich was desperate to hear that we were better creatively than at least one of those great agencies. Fallon was Fallon McElligott, the agency from whom we had inherited the Porsche business. In my opinion, over the last decade they had consistently produced the best print advertising in the world.

"No." Eric dismissed the question once more, like a pitcher shaking off the catcher's suggestion of a fastball inside. Too obvious. "Great strategy. Great print. Maybe better than yours—we should talk about that. The TV wasn't so great. But on the day we went to Minneapolis," he continued, "It was as cold as *fuck*. They were saying on the TV that if you were outside for more than ten minutes you could die. I thought I was going into cardiac arrest just stepping into the cab." He looked around the table as if to say, what do you expect?

I nodded. I too had been to Minneapolis in January, and chose unwisely to walk just a few blocks to my meeting. When I arrived in the lobby, my face had been so frozen that I was unable even to pronounce my own name.

"No," Eric said again, certainly not in response to Colin's offer of a top up from the bottle of 1991 Caymus. "When I say *those other guys*, I mean those other guys in town." He held out his glass. "They told me—they pitch against you all the time."

"Really?" Colin said innocently. If he hadn't meant Fallon, and hadn't meant Wieden, then we all knew exactly who he did mean.

"Right," Rich said, clearly hurt by the discovery that his victory over Weiden and Fallon owed more to flight schedules and wind chill factor than to any demonstration of creative superiority on our part. Indeed, Eric had said that Wieden's TV campaign and Fallon's print were better than ours. "Yes," he said forlornly, "We do pitch against them a lot."

"You guys were a *team*," Eric said, thumping his left fist on the table for added emphasis. "And they were a bunch of individuals."

"Ah," Colin said. That was the only encouragement any of us provided.

"Your presentation felt like the same presentation from start to finish," Eric said, warming to his subject. "And each of you seemed to enjoy what your colleagues were saying as much as I did." He went on to tell us that in the other agency's presentation, each of the speakers seemed to be working from a brief that was different from each of the others. When one was presenting, the others would be looking away, or reading their own notes, or on two occasions which he noted, actually exchanging eye-rolling glances. "It was as if they didn't even like each other," he said. "So if you were me, who would you want to work with?"

We agreed that he had made the right decision.

I guess we were pleased to know that we were likeable people, and that our meetings with the client—especially the one where we had made our final presentation—had been fun. But it really would have been nice if he had mentioned that our strategy was just a little bit interesting, or maybe that he had liked one or two of our ads.

Teamwork

Even though many of the examples I have given thus far are about individuals who excel in particular aspects of presentation and persuasion, any lessons that might be drawn from them apply equally to situations where presentations are being prepared and delivered by a team. The philosophy and practice of effective presentation described in the preceding chapters simply needs to be embraced by the team as a whole and manifested in the preparation and execution of individual team members.

My personal experiences of pitching have been, with only one notable exception, as a member of a team. (I will talk in a moment about the one time that I pitched alone.) In the majority of these team pitches, another person had the role of team leader. More recently, in my time with Berlin Cameron in New York, I took on the leadership role myself. While I can't say that I particularly enjoyed the experience, the agency did win all of those pitches. At the very least, I can claim that I didn't screw it up.

So what follows is drawn mostly from my own observations of pitches that have worked and pitches that have not, and also of pitches that resulted in wins *in spite* of the agency's process, and at great cost further down the line. Such lessons, particularly those relating to wins that perhaps did the victorious agency more harm than good, are relevant way beyond the agency business. In years to come every one of us—whether we are in the advertising, construction, or missile business—will be able to remember a time when we were made miserable by a relationship that never should have been allowed to start.

This may sound like a cliché, but in the pursuit of new business I would rather describe it as an irrefutable truth: A happy team is a winning team. It doesn't take a degree in psychology to know that when people are happy they have more energy, they find it easier to think creatively, and they will be prepared to go that extra mile because it matters not just to the agency, but to *them*. It's personal. So everything that a team leader does in organizing a pitch should be done with the happiness of the team as the first priority. If that can be achieved, everything else should follow naturally.

The first and most significant factor in creating a happy and productive team is ensuring that you are pitching the right business in the first place.

Knowing When to Say "No"

It may seem like a weird place to start, but I'll begin by telling you about the aforementioned and only time that I made an important pitch on my own. It was on May 23, 1987, and it took place on a beach in Wales. In case you haven't guessed, it was the day that I proposed to my wife, and I'd like to think that my pitch had all the hallmarks of good presentation mentioned thus far in this book. I had done my background work carefully: From various meandering, nonspecific conversations, I had concluded that Lynda Caroline Webb did not regard the idea as completely ridiculous. I thus planned a weekend away in Pembrokeshire, on the west coast of Wales, where I intended to pop the question. Alone on windswept Marloes Sands, we sat in the shelter of some rocks to eat our lunch. We ate in companionable silence, and while she noted that I wasn't eating with my usual enthusiasm, she still swears that she didn't suspect a thing. When we had finished, I excused myself and walked back behind the rock, ostensibly to answer a call of nature. A few minutes later I appeared at the top of the rock and asked her to climb up and join me. Below us, in the sand, I had written the five words that I hoped might change our lives (see Figure 7.1). My message was simple, and from Lynda's point of view it was certainly surprising. (Her first words were, "I thought you were taking a long

FIGURE 7.1 Pitching the business on a beach in Wales, May 1987. Yes, I did once have hair.

:e.") Thankfully she didn't make me wait too long before
o appoint me.

ason I mention this has nothing whatsoever to do with presentation technique. My point is this: I asked Lynda Webb to marry me because I was in love with her, I wanted to spend the rest of my life with
her, and I believed that she might want to spend the rest of her life with
me. But if only the first two of those three reasons had applied I might
not have asked her—at least not then or there—because I would not
have wanted to be rejected. And not just because it would have ruined a
good weekend.

One of the most important lessons I have learned in my career is
that a critical component of any successful new business strategy is
to pitch only business that you want (*really* want), and believe you
have a reasonable chance of winning. Pitching new business in any
context is time-consuming, expensive, and exhausting, and it would
be irresponsible, not to mention self-destructive, to pursue an impossible or inappropriate cause at all costs. My marriage proposal wasn't
just about wanting to be married: I wanted to be married to the right
woman, and I didn't want to mess up an enjoyable relationship by
having her say no. The combination may well be why we are still
married.

Of course many businesses do not think this way. If yours is one of
them, and you are concerned only with the chase and with the short-
term income that potential clients represent, then you might not want to
read the rest of this section. If, however, you look at every potential relationship through the filter of the caliber of work and quality of the
personal relationships it might offer, as well as its potential for future
growth, then I invite you to read on.

The first pitch I ever made with Goodby, Berlin & Silverstein, in
1989, was to Pioneer Electronics. The agency was invited into the pitch
about two months before I was due to join, but because my previous
employer, BMP, was affiliated with Goodby I was allowed to fly out
from England to make the pitch.

I remember thinking that the atmosphere in the pitch was very
strange, but attributed it to the difference between British and Ameri-

can business culture. Some of the clients seemed quite aggressive in the way they asked questions, and there was some weird chemistry between different groups on their side of the room. Having not been part of most of the previous meetings, and seriously jet-lagged, it was hard for me to judge.

About two weeks before I was scheduled to make my permanent move, I got a call saying that we had been awarded the business. On my first day in the new job I was to fly down to Los Angeles and attend a briefing with the Pioneer Laser Disc division.

Fourteen days later, I was sitting in a conference room at Pioneer's L.A. offices. A senior executive entered and his first words were, "Well, of the four agencies who pitched, you were fourth on my list. But I guess we'd better try and make it work."

A little later that same morning, I accompanied one of our creative directors as he presented a concept for a newspaper ad to a Japanese client from another part of the company. The man gave a pretty good impression of sleeping throughout the presentation, but after the visual had been explained and the copy read out for a second time, he finally opened his eyes and said, "I want it blue."

"Excuse me?" the creative director said.

"Blue! Words in blue!" the man said, banging his fist upon the table. He then stood up and left the room without another word.

Welcome to America, I thought.

After only six weeks as Pioneer's Agency of Record, Goodby, Berlin & Silverstein was fired in the course of a single phone call. The laser disc division ("The laser dicks," as they came to be known in our corridors) simply hated us, because we were not their choice. They had been steamrolled over by other divisions in the decision process, and set out to make life as unpleasant for us as they possibly could. Their aim was for us to either fail so miserably that the others had to see our unsuitability for the task, or be so unhappy that we resigned the business. They must have made life equally miserable for their colleagues in other divisions, because the support for us that had resulted in our hiring seemed to evaporate even more rapidly than it had built. If someone had walked into a room at

Pioneer a mere two weeks into the relationship and said, "Okay, who likes this agency?" I'm sure that not a single hand would have been raised.

We should have known. Apparently all the signs were there in the early meetings: dissonance between representatives of the different divisions; not-so-subtle comments from the laser dicks that they really liked BBDO; comments about our work for other clients that implied a radically different philosophy about what constituted effective communication. But we were so driven to win this important national account that we chose not to listen. We were like the women who think they can change the bad boys, the men who take trophy wives to impress their friends, the men and women who marry first and ask those difficult questions—about previous relationships or the desire to have children—too late for the answers to make a difference.

We should have said "no" when we were first asked to pitch. But we didn't, and we lived to regret it. Not only were we made to look ridiculous in front of our peers and other potential clients, but a very large proportion of our agency's staff—myself included—were made to feel very, very unhappy. It was only for a few weeks, but trust me, it felt like a whole lot longer.

Thereafter, we were much more careful in evaluating the opportunities that came our way. We would always meet with a client who expressed interest in working with our agency, but when we did, in addition to trying to project a good impression of ourselves, we would attempt to answer the following questions:

- **Why is this client here?**

  Are they really interested in us and in the kind of work we do, or have they asked for a meeting because someone has told them they should?

- **How strong is their brand?**

  Is it a brand that we admire and will be proud to say we work on? Does it have a genuine place in the world? If it disappeared tomorrow, would anyone notice?

- **Is the client the right fit for this agency?**

  Will they bring good ideas to the table? Will they be prepared to listen to ours? Will we enjoy working with them?

- **Will we be able to produce our best work together?**

  Do they want this as much as we do?

- **Who does this client really want to hire?**

  If it's not us, do we really have a chance of persuading them otherwise?

Addressing these questions led us to decline the opportunity to pursue a number of new business prospects.* We met marketing directors who were there only because a search consultant told them that they couldn't claim to be looking for a creative agency if GS&P wasn't on the list. In the dizzy years of the dotcom boom, we met countless groups of young entrepreneurs, pockets bulging with investors' dollars and bringing with them business ideas that were truly sphincter-puckering in their absurdity. When we asked one young Stanford MBA about his business strategy, he told us proudly that it was to get as rich as he could, as fast as he could, and then get out. We met smart people who didn't know how to listen, and nice people who didn't seem smart enough to be able to survive. We met people who said that if we wanted to be creative, they would give us five seconds at the end of the ad, but they would dictate the previous 25 seconds. And when we met Steve Jobs, however brilliant he was, it was clear that he didn't really care much for our work and really wanted to rekindle his old relationship with Lee Clow and Chiat\Day.

---

*You may have noticed that "How much will this client pay us?" is not among the key questions. While I won't attempt to pretend that size of billings and agency fees are not important, we always regarded them as lower in priority. The agency's belief was that in most cases an amicable balance could be reached between what the client demanded of us and what they would be willing to pay in return. In the time that I was with the agency we turned down more opportunities with big-spending clients on the basis that the quality of our work would be compromised than we did with small spenders on the basis of inadequate income projections.

To all of these people, we said a gracious "no." Even if we had been awarded their business, we just couldn't envisage being able to produce work we would have been really proud of. And because we knew that the single most persuasive new business tool in our armory was the quality of work we produced for existing clients, we had no great desire to compromise our principles, or dilute the time we were spending on that existing business.

This leads to two more very important questions that have to be answered by agency management before a pitch team is created.

Do our existing client commitments leave us with the time we need to devote to this new project? The first loyalty of any company should be to its existing clients, and it is a betrayal of their trust to pursue new business to the detriment of the work that is being done for them. If the answer to this question is "no," then there is really very little to be gained by pursuing a new client or accepting the invitation to pitch. The chances are that if you're too busy on other things, you won't win the pitch *and* you will piss off existing clients.

Can we put our "A" team on the pitch? The concept of available time isn't a question to be asked only of the company in general. In an advertising agency it is important to know whether people in the various support roles—IT, TV and print production, design and interactive, for example—will be available to put into some physical form the ideas that are generated, just as a builder must know that his electricians, plasterers, and plumbers will have the time to devote to a new project. The most important question, though, must be asked of the people who would in an ideal world play the key roles in the preparation and delivery of the pitch: the living examples of the agency putting its very best foot forward. I know that it is often tempting to proceed with a pitch even when the best people are not available to work on it, because I have sometimes supported such a decision myself. But invariably such an approach will fail. If the best people cannot be involved, cannot commit themselves totally, then the chances of the agency creating its best work and performing at its best in the final presentation are severely limited.

So decisions have to be made, and as hard as it may seem at the time, the success of an agency's new business performance may indeed be directly proportional to the number of opportunities that it rejects. (It reminds me of the old John West salmon line, which went something like, "It's the ones we throw away that make John West the best.") Rejecting opportunities for the reasons outlined above is not arrogant, but rather it is pragmatic. If a client hears you say that you cannot pursue his or her business because of commitments that you have made to an existing client, they cannot help but respect you for it. Indeed, it may make them want you more.

Andy Berlin used to say that the single most powerful word in new business is "no." Sometimes its use can remove problems that might otherwise have seemed insurmountable. When Hewlett-Packard first asked Goodby, Silverstein & Partners to pitch its business in the mid-1990s, the agency accepted the invitation. As the pitch progressed, however (perhaps as a result of the Pioneer experience), we became nervous about the politics that existed between different divisions on the client side, and we doubted our chances of success. These concerns resulted in our withdrawing from the pitch, but the client's reaction was immediate and visceral. No, they did not want us to withdraw from the pitch. They liked us very much, and if we saw problems on their side that might prevent us from doing the kind of work we wanted to do and which they, by the way, expected of us, then they would make the necessary changes. We invited the client into the agency to discuss these issues with our pitch team—everyone on the pitch team, not just the ones with big titles—and everyone seemed persuaded. We left the final decision to the pitch team, the people who were doing the work, and they decided unanimously to continue. We thus recommitted ourselves, and we won the business. Today H-P is among GS&P's largest clients, with its work running all around the globe.

Giving Real Responsibility

Once the decision has been made to pitch, the right people have to be selected to do the work and make the presentation. The first and most important choice is that of the team leader, who does not necessarily have to be an agency manager. As noted above, leaders need to have time to devote themselves fully to the task and also the ability to create a strong, shared sense of energy and possibility.

A few years ago I visited Porsche's production facility in Zuffenhausen, Germany. Porsche has a production line like most other car factories, but theirs is a production line with a difference. Instead of an engine rolling along a line of people, each of whom adds a different part, one individual follows the engine from the start of its journey to the end. He or she is responsible for the quality of that engine and, if you know what to look for, on any Porsche engine you will find some mark identifying the technician who made it. The people who make Porsche's engines are very proud of what they do, and Porsche's engines are correspondingly very, very good.

I share Porsche's belief that the best work results when real responsibility is given for a project from beginning to end. Thus, on any new business assignment, a small, tight team is most likely to succeed. In an advertising agency, that probably means an account director running the pitch, a planner as their strategic partner, a communications planner to represent the media perspective, and a creative director to inspire and oversee the creation of work. All these people should be committed to work on the business if it is won.* This team should also, if possible, include the client. Many clients won't want to get involved in a new business situation—in the interests of fairness if nothing else—but if they can be made to feel a part of the core team their input will be very useful.

The ideal situation is for a client to be involved enough in a pitch

---

*On this point there should be no negotiation. Clients do not want to work with and see presentations from a new business team. They want the people they will actually be working with. This is why, incidentally, I believe that the role of agency "new business director" is an anathema. It seems right to me for someone to organize the agency's new business efforts from a logistic point of view, and to coordinate the pursuit of new clients, but anyone with the words "new business" on their business cards should be prohibited from playing a direct, client-facing role in a pitch.

to feel by the end that not appointing your company is tantamount to firing you. Any more people than this in a core team will result in lengthier discussions, longer e-mail trails, elongated decision processes and, inevitably, more politics; in other words, lots of barriers to effectiveness. Remove those barriers, and you free the core team members to do what they do best. A similar approach seems to have been adopted in recent years by the military in the United States and the U.K., whereby the traditional model of larger, more unwieldy groups has been replaced by a system of smaller, more flexible and mobile, multidisciplinary units. While recent evidence in Iraq might suggest that it has not been an outstanding success, at least they seem to have the right idea.

I don't have a lot of time for so-called management tools, or marketing acronyms, but there's one that may be helpful in this context of selecting and defining roles for a new business team. It's called RASCI, and you may well be familiar with it because you have used it. More likely it will *feel* familiar because you've used it without knowing it; for a management tool, it does represent a higher-than-expected dose of common sense. The acronym breaks down as follows:

- **R is for Responsible.**

  Every pitch team has a leader who is responsible for the agency fulfilling its own and the client's objectives. This leader decides on the resources that will be required, the corresponding budget, and timing. The leader selects the team on the basis of individual expertise and, perhaps most important, the likelihood of the people being able to work well together. In turn the leader gives these core team members responsibility for their own parts of the presentation.

- **A is for Approve.**

  On every project a person should be clearly identified who has final sign-off. This person is also there to provide encouragement and ensure that the leader has the back-up necessary to complete the assignment.

- **S is for Support.**

  These are the people the leader needs to get the job done. They include the core team members identified above, who will be present at every stage of the process, and others who might be called in for shorter periods to provide specific expertise. A producer might be needed to edit video taken in research or to create a mood video. Someone else may be tasked with creating an interesting treatment for the brand logo at the end of commercials. Such single-task people are not involved in discussions on pitch direction.

- **C is for Consult.**

  Of course some outside expertise will be necessary at different stages of the project. Perhaps a psychologist might be engaged to give a clinical perspective on a particular human need or relationship. Maybe an engineer will be required to explain a complex technological advance. These people will be engaged as needed to provide information, and maybe used later as a sounding board for ideas.

- **I is for Inform.**

  Beyond the immediate team members and the person approving decisions, others might need to be kept informed. There's always a chance that senior executives will run into potential clients or pitch consultants at industry events, and even if they are not directly involved in the pitch, it's good for them to know the key issues that are being explored, and what progress is being made. These people should not be asked or expected to make decisions; they are involved simply for the influence they might wield in the background, and for the counsel that they might offer individual team members.

  Wherever I work I have sought out people whose opinions I value (see Chapter 4) to seek their perspective on ideas, on problems, and on the details of my presentations. They are able to comment without the encumbrance of specific knowledge, and if I listen with an open mind I find that they always help me to improve my work.

Better Ideas, Faster

The underlying principle of RASCI is that it improves clarity, account-ability, and teamwork, and through this combination allows the pro-duction of better work, faster.

In itself, speed is not to be valued, but as I look back at the projects I have worked on—in both new business and client contexts—an inverse relationship does seem to exist between the amount of time taken to complete a project and the quality of thinking that resulted. It seems to be a truth of most businesses—or indeed of most areas of human en-deavor—that the most exciting, groundbreaking ideas happen when people are working under extreme time pressure. It's why a lot of tech-nological advances happen during times of war, and why advertising agencies generally produce their best work under the severe time con-straints of a new business pitch.

So, based on the principle of a small, flexible team, my preference has always been for an accelerated, open process based not on endless meetings and lists of deliverables but instead on energy and ideas—on the energy that is created when small groups of people bounce off each other in confined space and time, and through ideas that are not con-strained by traditional industry definitions and divisions.

The approach to new business I am about to describe depends on people interacting with each other, and by that I mean *in person*. As lamented in Chapter 5, today's technology allows the illusion of con-nection but little more. In an age where people at adjoining desks e-mail each other and leave messages at midnight instead of speaking, we have to break bad habits and create teams who will sit together, eat together, drink coffee together, take walks together, and go to lunchtime baseball games together. (Anything else they choose to do together is up to them and we don't want to know about it.) There's a reason why copywriters and art directors work in pairs, and it's not because writers can't draw and art directors are illiterate. Ideas get uncovered more quickly when people dig together. And the ideas get better much more quickly when they are shared and debated by a small group of people who like and respect each other. Whatever any-one says, this kind of relationship cannot happen by voicemail, e-mail, or fax. It cannot happen across oceans and time zones or via telephone or videoconference. Teams work well together only when they are breathing the same air, so if it's a global pitch the first and best investment you can make is to decide on one location and fly the key people to it. If it's any kind of pitch, the best team will be one that has worked together before. You only have to watch an All-Star game in the States to see that individual brilliance does not a good performance make; I would take a team of people who know each other and have worked together so well that they can finish each other's sentences over a team of individual stars any time.

Day One: Hit the Ground Running

Because every project has different time constraints, I'm not going to say that a certain part of the process should take ten days, another part fourteen, and so on. What should be achieved, though, is a consistent spacing between the key milestones.

Far too often, I have observed pitches where weeks have been spent arguing over a brief, leaving mere days for creative people to actually come up with an idea. That's ridiculous. The maximum amount of time is needed not only to come up with a great idea, but also to execute it in every form possible.

The key is to start the way you mean to continue: fast.

On the day I receive a brief from a client (and preferably even be-fore) I like to organize a meeting to which each of the core team mem-bers and some carefully selected guests are invited. I referred to this in Chapter 4 as "Day One," and according to Craig Davis's 5/15/80 per-cent rule, it's the day when the selected individuals bring the 5 percent that they know they know, learn the 15 percent that they know they don't know, and open their minds to the 80 percent that they don't know they don't know. Their collective task is to identify the precise problem that has to be addressed if they are to successfully compete for the business, and to suggest some possible solutions. They do this by bringing information of both the specific and general kinds referred to in Chapter 4, and discussing the implications of this information not necessarily as clients, or agency mangers, or as psychologists, but as people. People who have lived, loved, laughed, cried, traveled, consumed, listened, watched, dreamed, and feared. People who bring with them both timeless human experience and an appreciation of the culture that surrounds them every day. If they are encouraged to bring that kind of experience with them, and some opinions, the connections they seek will generally start to make themselves.

People outside of the core team are invited to this meeting on the basis of their experience, their perspective, or their catalytic qualities. For example, expert consultants might be asked to provide insight on technology, audience psychology, or new media opportunities. If the pitch relates to an Olympic sponsorship project, the man you know who worked on London's successful 2012 bid might be invited, or the graduate trainee who happened to swim for Germany in the Athens Games. Others might be included simply for their enthusiasm or their ability to suggest unexpected solutions.

The way I like to run such sessions is to start by asking the client to give his or her point of view on the project and express an opinion on what the answer might be. Others then make presentations that are kept very short (no more than 10 to 15 minutes) to force the inclusion of only material that might be useful. In between the presentations are longer periods of discussion. I sometimes have people split up into teams and imagine how they would be launching this project if they were the marketing team at Nike or Apple. (We often talk about breaking rules, but it's important to force the issue. What does a particular idea really mean? There's nothing like imagining presenting to Phil Knight or Steve Jobs to make a shitty idea look *really* shitty.) The job of the moderator is to keep everyone's energy levels up, identify and exploit richer veins of conversation, and move swiftly to a new subject if the present one is not working.

The aim of this "Day One" exercise should be to crawl all over the problem and potential solutions so that by the day's end the participants have been forced to articulate (and agree) on the precise nature of the problem to be solved, and what in their considered (and now much better informed) opinion might constitute an interesting solution. The leader and core team should also have a clear appreciation of the scale of the task to be addressed, the time available to complete it, and the resources that will be required.

Day Two and Beyond

The approach to idea preparation described in Chapter 4 is given a head start by the successful execution of a Day One exercise, but much work inevitably remains to be done. One outcome of the initial information sharing and idea generation session will be to highlight areas where more information needs to be collected, first to fill in gaps in existing knowledge, but second and most important to provide evidence for the agency's final recommendations.

Different members of the core team will be charged with collecting information relevant to their particular area of expertise. While I don't want to go back over the same ground covered in *Truth, Lies, and Advertising* on the subject of consumer research and better ways to get to the truth, I do want to make three important points about its application to new business.

Research with a Purpose

First, I know that in a new business situation there's always a very strong temptation to spend as little money as possible. (While many agencies still have a deeply ingrained suspicion of client research, it does have one great advantage in that the client pays for it. In a new business situation, the agency always foots the bill.) Of course it's sensible to limit expenditure based on a clear understanding of the future income that a new business prospect might represent, but research is perhaps not the most sensible place to cut corners.

When a client sees an agency's final presentation, they will want to know that the recommendations being offered result from more than the agency's own thinking. To make a pitch without including consumer research of some kind would be like a prosecuting attorney asking a jury to convict on the basis of no evidence but rather on his very strong belief that the accused is "as guilty as hell." Without the nuggets of information that can be collected from carefully conducted consumer research, the connections described in Chapter 4 will be much harder to make.

A more sensible way to view pitch research is to recognize that it will take time and cost money, and therefore it must be very carefully thought through before it is conducted. For every agency that balks at spending money on research, there is another that spends almost for the sake of spending. ("Look how much we have spent on research—gosh, we must really want your business.") All too often, even in fiscally responsible agencies, new business teams emerge from an initial briefing and rush to set up consumer interviews and focus groups before they have really considered what that research is meant to achieve. A great deal of energy and momentum is thus wasted on an exercise that may have to be repeated because the first attempt was not focused on the right areas. In an ideal world, the Day One exercise will raise a number of questions that need to be answered, and many of these may be answered using existing information—if only the team knows where to look.

When primary research is commissioned, it has to be designed to answer very specific questions. In the example of the Porsche pitch discussed in previous chapters, our team knew from the earliest stage that the general public's perception of Porsche drivers would be a significant issue. We just didn't know *how* significant. In our research we therefore set out to give dimension to the problem (asking people to write down their feelings) and also to quantify it (conducting a poll to elicit positive or negative feelings toward a number of brands, including Porsche). I have already talked about the visceral impact generated by the drawing that gave birth to the infamous "Asshole Factor," but ultimately that impact would not have been sustained had we not been able to prove that such feelings were evident on a much broader scale. The quantitative study was expensive, but in the end it was money well spent.

Research for Presentation

The Porsche example leads me to the second major point about pitch research, which is that while it needs to have a purpose in a strategic sense, you must also remember its purpose in the final presentation. Research done well can be very persuasive, but this can happen only if it yields more than interesting information. Any pitch research project consequently has to be planned on the basis not only of the data it will yield but how that data might finally be presented.

My old partner Colin Probert used to make fun of what he referred to as the "box of tricks" I typically used in new business meetings. This unkind description applied to the procession of visuals that I presented to illustrate and bring to life key points. Whenever we conducted consumer or trade focus groups or interviews, I would have them filmed, but not as most research is filmed, to assist in the writing of reports. I would film it with a view to presentation, using a professional cameraman instead of a locked-off camera, and if necessary giving respondents their own microphones to guarantee sound quality. I could thus be able to show members of the target audience making, or supporting, key points of our presentation in their own words.

When people described their feelings in interviews or focus groups I had them draw pictures. If we asked them to complete activities for us before attending our research they were asked to keep diaries. When they reacted to new advertising ideas, they wrote down what the advertising was saying and how it made them feel. We had them take pictures of their homes, fridges, closets, and workbenches with disposable cameras. We took pictures of these people to project onto screens in our final presentation. In other words we did anything and everything we could to create materials that would help us dramatize our message. This all had to be carefully planned because we couldn't go back and do any of the work again. We didn't necessarily use everything in our presentation, but it was there if we needed it. When I prepared my strategic presentation in the manner described in Chapter 4, each of the exhibits was represented on its own Post-It note.

Sometimes it was interesting to have the audience experience the research and go through the same kind of thought process as our respondents had done. In a pitch for Isuzu's North American business in 1991, I commissioned a study that sought to quantify the strength of the Isuzu brand relative to some key competitors—Honda, Toyota, Nissan—and, because the assignment we had been given was for small cars rather than Isuzu's sport utility vehicles, Geo. The Geo Storm was actually the Isuzu Impulse, manufactured by Isuzu but sold by General Motors under the Geo brand name.

We took a picture of the Isuzu Impulse and mounted it on a board, along with five lines of description. We named the vehicle, gave its vital statistics (horsepower, acceleration, and fuel consumption), and pointed out that its handling had been designed in conjunction with Lotus. We then asked 200 people representative of Isuzu's target to tell us how appealing the vehicle was on certain dimensions.

We then took the same picture, and the same description, but changed the name of the vehicle: two hundred more people saw it as the "Honda DRX," another two hundred as the "Toyota CR2," and so on.

In the presentation I showed the Isuzu version. "Is this a fair description of your vehicle?" I asked the Isuzu executives. They agreed that it was. I then explained that people were asked to rate the car, based purely on what they saw on the board, on dimensions of quality, safety, reliability, and overall desirability. Heads nodded.

I then introduced the second board. "Gentlemen, please meet the Honda DRX." And the third. "The Toyota CR2." They looked confused.

"But that's our car," one said. "And Geo is the same car, but –"

"But people out there don't know that," I said. "We showed these to different groups, so no one saw all five as you have done. They just took it at face value, that Honda had this vehicle, or Nissan, or Isuzu. What's the only difference between the boards?"

The brand name.

The penny dropped, and a few of them were looking concerned.

Deep down they all knew. What they didn't know was how much difference it made. Our test was a little naughty, but it did allow us—in a manner that they had never seen before—to isolate the influence of the brand name. As a Honda, the Isuzu Impulse scored around 80 percent on all dimensions. As a Toyota it scored around 70. As a Nissan and as a Geo Storm, around 60. And as an Isuzu? Around 40 percent. The Isuzu brand name made people less likely to want to buy the exact same vehicle. And that defined the problem that our agency and Isuzu would have to overcome.

That particular piece of research was far from being the only reason why Isuzu hired us, but it sure helped.

Box of tricks? Call it what you like, Colin. It paid for your swimming pool.

Research as a Catalyst for Discussion

From Day Two onward, the core team should meet and talk every day. Although everyone will have their own tasks to complete, there are always issues that require everyone to contribute. These meetings should be meetings of equals; even if the leader has the casting vote, it's better if he or she is never compelled to exercise it. Perhaps most important of all, people should feel free to say whatever they like without fear of being ridiculed. Some of the best ideas I ever had started out sounding pretty stupid, but as Anne Lamott says in describing her "shitty first draft," I never would have got to the good version without first expressing the stupid one. Fortunately I was usually lucky enough to be working with people who recognized half a good idea when they heard it, and who had the patience to work with me until the half became whole.

If research is being conducted in a facility that allows viewing, it's often productive for all core team members—including the client if they will come—to observe and, with consumer opinion as a catalyst, discuss key issues. Although no one can ever predict exactly when the breakthrough will come in the search for a big idea, in my experience it very often comes out of the mouths of real people in focus groups. Like the time in a milk focus group when someone said, "The only time I really think about milk is when I haven't got any," and everyone in the viewing room—planner, account director, creative director, and client—simultaneously said, "Did you hear that?" This person had just articulated the idea we had been circling around but had thus far been unable to describe succinctly. Or the time when Berlin Cameron was working on a pitch for Pfizer's Zyrtec allergy medication, and we heard a woman talk of the frustration she and her children felt at having to come home early from a vacation because of her husband's allergies. Her husband, she said, always insisted that he could cope and refused to go see a doctor. He didn't seem to realize that as a result of his "I'm tough, I can handle it" stance, the lives of those closest to him were being ruined. Just a few minutes later we had figured out a strategy for Zyrtec that asked spouses and children to hold the allergy equivalent of an intervention—to force the allergy sufferer in their life to stop being an unmedicated martyr, and to think of the effect their allergies had on the lives of those around them. "If you won't do it for you," we decided to say, "do it for them."

That idea once again formed the soul of a winning pitch, a story of opportunities lost, of relationships compromised, of beautiful moments missed (see the Chapter 8 section called "What to Leave Behind").

Turning a Big Idea into a Big Presentation

I have always thought that about a third of the time available for a pitch assignment should be devoted to the creation of the brief, in which the core brand idea or point of view is agreed upon. Another third should be given to the development of a creative idea that best expresses this point of view. The final third is the time when this idea is executed in as many different forms as possible to show its potential breadth and longevity. This is also the time when the presentation itself should be prepared.

For Berlin Cameron's Zyrtec pitch, the idea of allergies affecting more than the sufferer came very early in the process, and when I lead a pitch it is always my aim to find and agree upon such an idea as soon as possible. That way creative and media people have the maximum possible time to work on advertising and through-the-line executions, and those responsible for making the final pitch can conduct research to provide evidence for their recommendations, create the materials they need to illustrate their points, and spend the necessary time writing and honing their parts of the presentation. Again, this works best when core team members share their work with each other, and it's incumbent upon the team leader to ensure that this happens. If a presentation is to be made based on the insight that allergy sufferers are not the only ones who are afflicted by their allergies, everyone who speaks should contribute to that idea, even if only by laying out items of information that might not be connected until later. In the case of the Zyrtec pitch I wrote a short document that synthesized the idea to give everyone common ground to work from; it also subsequently formed the basis of the prose summary of our presentation included in the leave-behind. Here is the document:

THE IDEA

In the world of the allergy sufferer, inertia is a very powerful force. Rational evidence that another medication might do a better job seems to fall on deaf ears as people prefer to "deal with" their symptoms rather than visit a doctor or discuss more appropriate treatment.

We want to plant the seed of doubt that their current medication might not be good enough.

If these people won't listen to rational argument, then we will try to engage them emotionally. We intend to do this by asking them to look at their allergies not from the perspective of their own suffering, as all other allergy medication advertising does (and which has so far failed to persuade them to take decisive action), but rather from the point of view of others who also have to endure their symptoms.

The idea is that it is not only the person with the allergic reaction who suffers. Others suffer too. In other words we are in-

troducing the concept, like secondary smoking, of secondary allergies.

We want to ask, "If you won't do something for yourself, will you consider doing it for everyone else affected by your allergies?"

Think of your family, who are forced to put up with your cranky moods. Have you spared a thought for the poor dog, who can't be walked because you can't go out in ragweed season? Have you considered your colleagues, in the open plan office, who have to spend all day listening to your sniffing, blowing, wheezing and sneezing? How do you think the kids feel when you tell them that you can't take them to the park, and that instead of the cuddly kitten they really want, they have to make do with a boring old goldfish? And have you ever paused to think about those lost romantic moments, gone in the time it took to sneeze or cough?

It's unfair. But you can do something about it. Ask your doctor about Zyrtec.

You may notice that I have referred several times to "the idea," "the big idea," and "the core idea," each time in the singular. I have touched on this before, but I cannot stress how important it is to focus on a single idea. It's the only way of building a strong body of work that has really been thought through (because with multiple ideas efforts are obviously diluted), creating and keeping a linear, logical flow to a presentation, and making sure that every important point is backed up.

In the Zyrtec pitch we thus had interviews with allergy sufferers talking about how they cope, intercut with interviews with the partners and children of those sufferers, talking about the effect that their spouse's or parents' allergies had upon their lives. Pictures of these people covered the room, along with pictures that some of us might look at and see as examples of beauty (a tree in blossom), companionship (a dog), or fun (a baseball park or kids' playground), but which allergy sufferers and their families would immediately see as threatening, as being off limits. We had drawings created by allergy sufferers to show how their allergies made them feel (see Figure 7.2), and others created by members of their families to show the secondary impact (Figure 7.3). We also had lots of other things, which I won't go into because I want to keep at least a few of them to myself. Let it suffice to say that they all gave shape, dimension, and color to our central idea.

We knew that at least some of our audience from Pfizer were either allergy sufferers themselves or lived with people who were. We wanted to use every opportunity to appeal to their own experience, and we decided to do that by sharing some of our own, by having members of our own team who had experienced allergy problems first- or second-hand talk about them as part of their presentation. The aim was to show that we didn't just relish this opportunity as a business challenge, but that we also saw it as important in human, personal terms.

Collecting the information and producing the materials, writing and illustrating the story, and having everyone sing from the same hymn sheet is at the best of times a difficult undertaking. That's why the

FIGURE 7.2 "How my allergies make me feel," by Kirsten, age 35.

FIGURE 7.3 "Mom, can we go to the park?" by Chelsea (Kirsten's daughter), age 8.

choice of team members up front is so important, and why it is vital that if responsibility is given, it is given unconditionally, from the very beginning of a project to the very end. And by the end, I mean the end.

Here's why I say that.

I know an agency where the senior managers have been known to bring four or five specially selected individuals into a room and say, "Guys, we believe in you. You go and win this business. You don't need us. We'll stay out of it."

The team members, emboldened by this dramatic gesture of confidence, go off and prepare the pitch. They gather their information, together they create the necessary connections, and they come up with the required big idea. They execute it in every way they can, from TV commercials to bar mats, pavement art, and lines of dialogue written into episodes of popular situation comedies. On several occasions they ask their managers if they would like to be brought up to date on their progress, if they would like to see the ideas in their embryonic form. "No, no, no," they hear back. "It's your pitch."

They write their presentation, and a day or two before the pitch, they invite their managers to survey the fruits of their labors. "It's really your pitch," they are told. "But if our feedback would help, then we will make ourselves available."

So they bring the managers into a conference room, and take them through a simplified version of the presentation. They expose the idea. They show the campaign.

"That's total shit!" the managers exclaim. "You're going to be responsible for us losing this pitch! If we don't come up with a better idea and write a better campaign by tomorrow, we're all completely screwed!"

They leave and retire to their corner offices with much huffing and puffing and slamming of doors. The team is left with little idea of what to do. Their confidence is shattered.

The next day, a watered-down version of the idea is presented to the client, a version that will fit with both the shitty idea that the team originally thought up and the new, improved idea with which the agency managers will save the day. In fact, their work has little connection with any of the analysis that precedes it, but it should be obvious that it is The Answer The Client Has Been Looking For.

The client feels that the presentation lacks a clear point of view. While one of the creative directions (the original idea) seems to have a logical connection to the strategy, the other—while undoubtedly striking—does not.

The agency does not win the business, the managers blame the team, and the team members blame their managers. But that's not all.

When the agency is next asked to participate in a pitch, a new member of the management team is asked to act as leader. He finds it difficult to motivate the members of his team and can't understand why. After a great deal of cajoling, he finally gets one of his team to admit that there's hardly any point in working hard to come up with an idea, because the guys from the corner offices will come down the night before the pitch and change it all whatever they do.

It's a true story. And I'm sure that there are many more like it, from many more agencies than I dare to imagine.

I've said it before and I will say it again. A new business team's chances of success rest in large part on the quality of the content they are presenting, but equally—and while many clients would not admit it, maybe more so—on their confidence, on their spirit, and on their belief in what they are presenting. The minute a senior executive does what is described above, all the confidence and spirit and belief that had been pumping through the veins of the supposedly "responsible" team will disappear. The people who, just a few minutes before, were actually looking forward to presenting their ideas, will now be demotivated, nervous, even fearful. And when they get into the room the audience will smell it.

One of the most important roles I have played as leader of new business pitches, if not the most important, is to ensure that situations like the one just described do not happen. I make sure of this by insisting that my partners or senior managers from our parent company or affiliate operating companies are either involved from the start and consistently thereafter, or not involved at all. It's my job to keep them informed of developments, and if the worst happens and they freak out, it's also my job to keep them away from the people whose energy and enthusiasm I am relying on to win the pitch. I have had to fly 5,000 miles to physically prevent someone from removing a creative director from a pitch one week before a presentation, and I have had to argue on the night before a final presentation that a campaign personally created in the last 24 hours by the chairman does not fit with our presentation and will not be shown. On both occasions, the manager concerned eventually played a supporting role in the presentation, supporting our ideas enthusiastically. And on both occasions, the client, on hiring us, commented on both the singularity of our message and the great spirit and cohesion of our team. If only they knew.

If such traumas can be avoided, then the countdown to the presentation itself begins.

I won't waste any time talking about the planning that is necessary to ensure all the different components of the presentation are ready in time for the presentation, except to say that in every successful agency pitch in which I have participated, someone has always played the role that Andy Berlin named "The Catcher." Their responsibility, as the name implies, is to catch all the balls before they drop to the floor.

They make sure that hotels are booked and plane tickets purchased, they organize rehearsal rooms and food, they make sure that boards are produced in time for rehearsal and shipping if necessary, and if someone is needed to spend hours in an editing studio putting together consumer reactions to the agency's campaign or a film to announce the proposed line, then they do that too. They cajole, they take care of the detail, they keep the leader informed. Such a person is worth his or her weight in gold. Yes, Abi, Jessica, and Natalie (to name but three), I'm talking about you.

I know that everyone who has ever been involved in new business looks back with pride on those nights before a presentation where the rehearsal didn't start until 11pm, and then everything had to be rewritten and no one got to bed before 6 A.M. with the presentation starting at nine. I have experienced that kind of pitch myself on several occasions and we did win a few of them. But we lost a few too, and I put those losses down to sheer exhaustion. Our presenters were so tired—and, as a result of the rewriting, so unprepared—that the presentation lacked energy and polish, we failed to make our points as clearly as we should, and invariably we overran on time.

As heroic as those late and awful nights might seem, I would like to suggest an alternative approach, an approach that is much more likely to result in success.

Rehearse, Rehearse, and Rehearse Again

A new business director once told me that his agency didn't like to rehearse for big presentations, because the senior people preferred to be spontaneous.

As he spoke, I wondered whether the clients who were the lucky recipients of this spontaneity interpreted it as such, or whether they might instead have seen the agency's pitch as disorganized, long-winded, ill-prepared, illogical?

I asked him how many of their last six pitches they had won. None, he said. But there were good reasons for each of those defeats. As my American friends would say, Yeah, right.

If the president of the United States rehearses for his State of the Union Address, so can we. If Michael Jordan shoots free throws for three hours a day and cellist Yo-Yo Ma practices for eight, and soccer star David Beckham takes free kicks on his own long after his teammates have left the training ground, then it's not inconceivable to think that we should practice our presentations. And I mean *really* practice— several times, including two full dress rehearsals in the room where the final presentation will be made (or in one selected for its identical size and layout), with all the equipment and visuals that will be used, in the precise form that they will be used. Practice doesn't kill spontaneity. On the contrary, the familiarity and confidence it brings free a presenter to be *more* spontaneous.

The final countdown to a pitch is obviously affected by whether the fixture is being played at home or away. While the majority of my pitches have been delivered on home ground, I have also had to fly from San Francisco to New York, San Antonio, and Portland, Maine, and from New York to Denver and Seoul. The only difference that such long distance pitches should make is to bring forward the deadline for finished scripts and materials by a day or two (or in the case of Seoul, three or four). Right from Day One, a line has to be drawn in the sand, over which tardy presenters, producers, room dressers, and senior executives alike should be prohibited from crossing.

Let me give you an example. If a pitch is in the agency's own office on a Wednesday afternoon, I will generally arrange a series of rehearsals that gradually increase in intensity toward the day of the presentation. They are spaced to allow sufficient time between for individuals to rewrite, practice, and improve, and they are timed so that by the final day the presenters are as well rested as possible.

Although this rehearsal schedule may vary, here's something approaching the ideal.

The Previous Friday: First Walk-Through

This is a critical—and generally quite unpleasant—stage. It should involve all of the presenters plus any people whose opinions on content and style might be helpful. In the theater, this would be the point where the actors read from a script as the director tells them where to stand and what they might want to do with their hands. In an agency, it's not very different. The session might start with the leader explaining the schedule for the last few days to everyone, and making sure that everyone knows what is required of them. The format for the pitch will be explained, and a timing plan drawn up: 10 minutes for the Chief Executive, 15 minutes for the business overview, 30 minutes for the strategic discussion, and so on.

It's then up to everyone who will be making those individual presentations to tell the others what they intend to say and what they intend to show. Some may have already written scripts, in which case they should read them as if they were presenting. Others inevitably will not have got that far. Even without precise presentation detail, this process is important because it gives each presenter an idea of how his or her part fits with the others; any glaring areas of overlap or omission should be obvious; opportunities to tie different parts of the presentation together more clearly should be identified; and each presenter can gain general feedback on areas that may need more explanation, better illustration, or the assistance of a very sharp knife.

One fact that we all need to remind ourselves of regularly is that rehearsals of any kind are nut-shrinkingly embarrassing. Exposing one's presentation for the first time in front of others really is like standing naked before them on a very cold day: If they don't like what you have to say, then it means they don't like *you*. While the group needs the opportunity to offer feedback, good and bad, some people aren't too good at receiving criticism in public and may need to be handled carefully. Criticism has to be constructive and the general atmosphere one of support and encouragement, but if changes need to be made, they can't be ignored for fear of upsetting someone. Someone has to be in the room who can be relied upon to ask the difficult questions and speak up when something doesn't make sense. They won't always be the most popular people in the neighborhood, but their role is invaluable if carried out with sensitivity. The rule governing such feedback is, of course, that what the presenters say is not as important as what the audience hears. I can think of only one or two occasions when following the advice of such rehearsal audiences and making changes has not improved the quality of my own final presentation.

If I'm leading a pitch I'll listen to the criticism and try to move on, but once the run-through is finished I will talk separately to those who need to make changes and let them know what exactly they need to do, offering direct assistance if necessary.

Monday Morning: Walk-Through with Full Scripts and Visual Aids

Some of the presenters will have been in good shape on Friday, and with the exception of work they may have had to do on visual aids, like video editing or creating presentation slides or boards, they could have enjoyed a relatively relaxing weekend. Others with more work to do as a result of Friday's first walk-through may have been rewriting furiously. In effect, this is the first serious rehearsal, where the stopwatch is run from the moment the first presenter stands, and everyone says exactly what they intend to say in the meeting, working with charts (or at least paper representations of them), videos, and other visual aids (the team has to see these to ensure that they are making the right point). At this time it's unacceptable to say, "Well, I'll say some stuff about how allergy sufferers feel about themselves, and then I'll stick in the video." What video? "Oh, we're still putting that together, but it will be kind of about how allergy sufferers' families have to deal with those allergies too."

Some people might say that it's impossible to have all their senior people commit to the detail of their presentations "so early." What? A massive 48 hours before the pitch? If so, maybe the wrong senior people are involved in new business. While in this world almost anything seems possible (I have worked on pitches where bleary-eyed account executives arrived on the red-eye from San Francisco in time to deliver revised leave-behind documents for a morning pitch in New York), it is better for any uncertainty to be removed. The story can be set in stone in the leave-behind, and the last two days can be devoted to taking care of the last 4 or 5 percent that will make the difference between a good and a great presentation. If people have the time to practice their presentation, it will become second nature. Jeff Goodby and Rich Silverstein were masters of "prepared spontaneity," often making apparently off-the-cuff comments during other people's presentations. While some of these were genuinely spontaneous (and we were all comfortable enough in each other's company not to mind), most had in fact been thought through over several days. Rich might say, "You know, the more I hear Colin talk about that, the more important it seems to me . . ." Rich and Colin would then have a quick exchange, before Colin continued with his presentation. The effect upon the audience? It was clear that Rich and Colin liked each other because they were both comfortable with the interruption. It was also clear that they had been talking a lot (what, a creative director and account guy actually talking to each other?), and were continuing to think about the client's problem even as they were making their final presentation. And perhaps most important of all, when Rich came to make his own part of the presentation, he could refer back to that important point of Colin's and show how it had guided some of his creative decisions.

These are the kinds of connections that need time to be thought through and built into different parts of the presentation. Some are as simple as one person saying, "As Craig said earlier on," or "Tim will talk about this in a much more interesting way later," but where opportunities become apparent for creative people to contribute to strategic points and vice versa, they should be taken. Obviously they should be limited to only those where the greatest possible impact might be made but, if carefully developed, these are the connections that give clients like Eric the sense of singularity of message, common purpose, and mutual liking and respect.

Tuesday Afternoon: Dress Rehearsal

With less than a day to go before the final presentation, it's time for a dress rehearsal. By now everything should be ready: charts/slides, boards, videos, leave-behind documents. Everyone will have had a day to gather their own final materials, to tweak their presentations, to discuss certain questions with each other, and to practice. Now it's time to put the whole show together.

Ideally this rehearsal will take place in the room where the final presentation is to take place. If the pitch is happening in the agency's own offices, that's easily accomplished. It may be harder if the pitch is taking place at the client's offices or at a neutral venue, but in that case it is essential that someone has seen the room, measured and photographed it, and is thus able to replicate that space for rehearsal.

By this stage, the key questions relating to dressing the room— where agency and client personnel will sit, and where presenters should stand—will have been addressed. (These are discussed in detail in Chapter 8, in the section on "Owning the Room.") Here the task is to choreograph each part of the presentation so that presenters are comfortable with issues such as where their materials will be, on which side they will deposit their boards after they have shown them, and who operates the television equipment. These might sound like minor points, but believe me, they can make a massive difference.

In the first pitch I ever made at BMP, for the Australian Tourist Commission, I was told that I would be presenting using boards, not the overhead projector that I was used to using in those ancient times. I had never presented from boards before, and unfortunately the production department had not produced mine in time for our one and only rehearsal. On the morning of the pitch, I arranged the boards from first to last, and placed them facing the wall so that my first point was hidden. What I should have done was to place my last board facing the wall, and then the next-to-last, and so on, so that I started at the back of the pile and worked towards the wall. If you're confused reading that, imagine how confused I was when the first board I revealed was in fact the climax of my presentation. It's a miracle that I was ever allowed anywhere near another pitch.

The dress rehearsal is all about identifying and removing such pitfalls at a time when they really don't matter. It's also a time for building energy and confidence, and hopefully having some fun.

On the eve of Berlin Cameron's pitch to White Wave for its *Silk* soymilk account, our team flew to Denver and met in a hotel conference room to rehearse. Before running through our presentation we ate dinner, and a few bottles of our lucky cabernet were consumed. When the creative director, Izzy Debellis, stood up to present his work, for some reason that now escapes me we all started laughing. For probably 15 minutes none of us could speak. Yes, it was disruptive to the rehearsal, but everyone left feeling completely relaxed. The next morning we made a great presentation and won the business.

Perhaps the most important point to be made about any rehearsal on the eve of a pitch is that it shouldn't run too late. People who haven't slept tend to look as if they haven't slept, and tiredness obviously makes it harder to generate energy and to think straight. Very often, when given the choice between one more run through of the presentation or everyone going to bed, I have almost always chosen a good night's sleep.

Wednesday Morning: Final Dress Rehearsal

If the pitch is in the afternoon, it may be wise to have one more run through at say, 8 A.M., leaving time for presenters to go away and have some quiet time on their own before the client arrives. It may be that the first dress rehearsal went so well that everyone agrees a further rehearsal is not necessary, but even if it is agreed that everyone need not rehearse again, there will be some presenters who want to and who will benefit from it. I am one of those presenters, because I find that every time I present my material I gain a little more control over it. I have written it out, read it aloud, and now every time I go through the script I am learning it so that when I make my final presentation I might talk for half an hour or 45 minutes without really consulting my notes. The simple act of standing before a picture to the audience's left and starting my presentation, moving gradually across the room until I have reached the last picture on their right, helps in this learning process, as physical actions and words become inextricably linked.

If the whole team rehearses, the aim is to take the energy levels up a notch but to ensure that everyone retains something in reserve. By now they should know their—and each other's—material back to front. It's now up to them to support each other, and to draw out those extra few degrees of performance to make the ideas really sing.

The people who say that rehearsal isn't necessary because they know what they are going to say and how they are going to say it are really missing the point. Rehearsal is about practice, sure. But most of all it is about team spirit and confidence. Everyone will see the presentation improving every time they go through it. They will feel themselves improving. But most important of all, once they go away and run through their material alone for the umpteenth time, they will not be doing it for themselves. They will be doing it for each other.

Superstition

Before moving to the pitch itself, let me say a few brief words on the subject of superstition. I am a superstitious person, and over the years I have developed a personal routine for new business that works for me. I won't share it because if I did it might not work any more, and anyhow, it's a little embarrassing.

Certain team rituals, however, do help to create the kind of spirit mentioned above. When a team from Berlin Cameron left the agency to make a new business presentation, it was always to the sound of the same piece of music played from the reception desk. At Goodby, Silverstein we always drank a certain California cabernet on the night before the pitch. (This dated from the time that Jeff Goodby was unable to fly to Maine for our pitch to Unum insurance because his wife was about to give birth, and he sent some bottles to our hotel to wish us luck. We won the pitch, and thereafter went to great lengths to ensure its availability in some pretty far-flung places.) At other agencies I have introduced other wines that will hopefully become a part of the tradition.

If they don't work, I'll just have to experiment until I find one that does.

CHAPTER EIGHT

- **The Pitch and Beyond**

  – How to leave the client wanting more

The End of the Beginning

It's the day of the final presentation.

For several weeks, and maybe even for several months, the agency has been working toward this day. By 5 P.M. it will be over and the presenters and all those who have assisted in the preparation of the pitch will be in the bar. Or, as often seems to happen to me, all those who have helped with the presentation and many more who haven't will be in the bar around the corner from our office, while I and the other weary presenters sit in an airport departure lounge, waiting for the long flight home.

It's almost over. Or is it?

It's very rare in the advertising business—and I suspect in other businesses too—for a client to award the business on the spot after even a spectacularly good presentation. I have never experienced what David Magliano and his London 2012 Olympic bid team did in July of 2005 when, just a few hours after the end of their presentation, they learned that London had been awarded the 2012 Games. Generally such decisions take time, and sometimes extended periods of complex negotiation. Politics may play a part, as might issues of remuneration. Because the politics will vary so much from case to case, it's hard for me to talk with any confidence about how to deal with them. All I will say is that if an agency has correctly identified the key problems that its presentation must address and overcome, and has done the required homework in understanding the motivations, prejudices, and desires of each member of the audience who will make or influence the decision, then most potential political issues should have been removed along the way. So too any financial considerations that might threaten to undo any of the good strategic and creative work that has been done. Discussions about staffing and remuneration should always happen in the background before the final pitch is delivered, so that any great gaps in expectations on either side can be identified before too much time is wasted and either side is put into an embarrassing or difficult situation.

In this chapter I want to talk about the day of the pitch, and ways in which the company pitching a client's business might create the kind of momentum necessary to carry it through even an extended decision-making process. This requires a display of energy, desire, and both individual and collective problem-solving abilities that exceed those of the agency's competitors. It has to be manifested in every part of the client's experience, from the way the agency feels to the client upon arrival (or the way their own conference room has been transformed), to the chemistry of the presentation, the ideas presented, and the way that these ideas might be packaged for future scrutiny. And it requires a carefully considered follow-up plan.

Welcome to the Next Level

In 1992, Goodby, Berlin & Silverstein was rocked by the departure of cofounder Andy Berlin. The agency had been on a tear: In the last year both American Isuzu Motors and the Carl's Jr. restaurant chain had hired the agency, and the general perception from the outside was that Andy Berlin was the person most responsible for driving this growth. The general sentiment in the advertising industry trade press was that, with Andy's departure, the agency's growth would come to a grinding halt.

Those of us left behind begged to differ. It didn't matter to us what people thought about Andy's role in putting the agency under the national spotlight; what bothered us was the notion that without him we had no future.

"Do you want to prove these people wrong?" Jeff Goodby asked an all-agency meeting a few days after Andy's departure had been confirmed. Heads were still nodding when he said that we had precisely the opportunity we needed to do so. We had been invited to pitch Sega's North American business against current U.S. Agency of the Year FCB, and West Coast Agency of the Year Wieden & Kennedy. If we won this pitch, he said, people would realize that our agency was bigger than any of its founders. If we lost, he said with a typical chuckle, "we really are screwed."

Six weeks later, a group of Sega executives arrived at the hotel in Foster City, California, not far from their own offices, where both FCB and Wieden & Kennedy had already made their presentations. Coming to the same room that had been hired for all three presentations, they found just a single executive from Goodby, Berlin (his name hadn't yet been removed from the door) and Silverstein. Unfortunately, they were told, the agency had been forced to change the venue for a slightly larger room just along the corridor. The executive hoped that this would be okay, since there were some things the agency wanted to share that required a little more space. The difference in price had been taken care of.

The doors of the new room were opened, and the Sega team stepped into a small ballroom that had been transformed into an indoor stadium. On three sides of the room were banks of bleacher seating, which were filled by every one of the agency's employees. On the fourth side, directly in front of them, was a low stage, with a huge wall of video monitors behind. The screens had been synched so that they acted as one: The combined screen was filled with live action from Sega's Sonic the Hedgehog game, being played at an advanced level by one of the agency's TV producers. (An obvious sign of both his misspent youth and our broadminded hiring policy.)

The clients took their seats before the stage, and Jeff Goodby introduced the team of presenters who faced them. He also explained why we had been joined by all of the other agency staff. He recognized that it was unusual, but the reality was that every one of them had worked on our pitch in some capacity. Each one of us, he said, had taken responsibility for mastering at least one of Sega's games. The Sega audience would see evidence of that throughout the presentation, but if at any point they wanted to challenge us and ask to see someone playing a particular game, or find out exactly what we thought of it, we would be happy to oblige.

For the next three hours we presented our vision of Sega as the "next level" of video gaming. Our strategy was to position new 16-bit

Sega hardware and games as the fastest, most colorful, most challenging form of video gaming—the major leagues to Nintendo's minors. Sega was loud, hip, and current; Nintendo was what you gave to your kid brother when you moved up. "Welcome to the Next Level" was the tagline on our campaign, and the big idea was that with Nintendo outspending us three to one, we would cram the information that would normally fill a 30-second commercial into 10-second spots. The pace would be manic, the volume unpleasant to adults, the message almost indecipherable to anyone over the age of thirty. But kids would get it. By excluding their parents through an impenetrable message, our implicit message to the kids was one of involvement. Come on inside, we were saying, we know what you *really* want. It was both an invitation and a challenge.

The presentation had all the drama of that idea. We moved at a furious pace, with presenters wearing wireless microphone headsets looking more like Madonna in concert than a group of agency professionals. Our voices boomed through an A-V system that had most recently been used by the Grateful Dead (I kid you not), and behind us the screens filled with wall-to-wall and floor-to-ceiling visuals and videos. We took the Sega executives inside the kids' bedrooms where we had conducted our research (including footage of the incident where a young planner was bitten by a small child dressed as Superman), into our agency where a team of kids had worked with us throughout our pitch, and into the very idea that we were recommending. We showed videos of individual creative teams presenting in the style of MTV v-jays, and we had also shot the commercials themselves. Altogether, in the course of the meeting we showed more than an hour and a quarter of video, with barely a pause for breath in between each element.

But that was the point. Sega was a video entertainment brand, and we wanted our pitch to represent the same kind of video entertainment. It was fast, it was fun, and the clients couldn't help but see the same kind of passion in us that we talked about relative to gamers' relationships with characters like Sonic or Taz. At the end we gave each of them a video of every one of the commercial ideas we had recommended, and asked them to take the videos home and show them to their kids. It's kids' opinion that really counts, we said. However much we like what we have presented doesn't really count. Ask your kids and their friends before you make up your minds.

The momentum carried Sega's marketing executives all the way to their decision.

Two or three days later, the senior Sega client visited our agency and asked, if he were to hire us, whether it might be possible to get two or three of the commercials we had presented shot, edited, and on TV by the following Friday. Maybe it had been a mistake to produce all that material for the pitch that quickly.

"I don't know," Jeff told him. "But I don't see why not." This in a world where agencies generally take at least three months to get a commercial on air.

By the following Friday, a mere two weeks from our pitch, Sega's "Welcome to the Next Level" campaign aired for the first time. Within a few months, riding the wave of hot games and an anarchic advertising campaign that made them even hotter, Sega had overtaken Nintendo and taken the number one spot in the expanding video game market.

Owning the Room

What our Sega pitch demonstrated more vividly than any previous experience was the importance, particularly when the pitch is being made away from the agency's offices, of "owning" the room—not just in a physical sense, but emotionally too. The room in which a pitch is delivered should be a physical manifestation of both the agency and its idea.

When clients enter their own conference room, or a hotel room that they have entered many times before, it has to feel different. Similarly, if the pitch is held at the agency's offices, the client must feel that the room is welcoming *them*, that it's not that way for everyone.

When traveling for a new business presentation, my list of essential equipment always includes those portable felt walls onto which the agency's work can be pinned, and easels that can be used to display boards in the presentation itself. While most agency conference rooms are designed with walls onto which pictures can be stuck or pinned, that is generally not the case in client or hotel conference rooms. There, fancy furniture and corporate art are *de rigeur*, and people tend to get upset if you start banging pins into the mahogany walls or taping ads over paintings of the chairman's favorite racehorse.

While everyone's preference for these things will vary, I like to cover every wall, so that when the clients enter they immediately sense a great volume of work and effort. Often I pin up all the visual aids I intend to use in my presentation—consumer drawings, graphs representing quantitative research, covers from *Time* magazine, pictures of respondents, competitive advertising—whatever. It doesn't matter whether the clients can see them, because until I deliver my presentation and tell the story that binds them and gives them meaning, they will be visually interesting but no more. It also doesn't matter if things like drawings or pages from consumer diaries are not really clear from a distance. If the audience is small in number, I will often ask them to stand up and join me to look at certain exhibits; sometimes I will refer to the originals and invite them to browse them at the next break, while projecting detail onto a big screen.

With presentations like mine, which often take the form of a journey through a series of visual exhibits, a dress rehearsal in the right space with the finished boards, slides, videos, and whatever else I might intend to show is vitally important to iron out any logistic difficulties that might emerge—like not being able to walk from one side of the room to another, or not having anywhere to deposit boards once they have been shown. It can, incidentally, be good to have other team members help out with handling large items such as boards or operating video equipment. There's something pleasantly self-deprecating about senior people doing such menial tasks, and it certainly helps build an aura of team spirit and cooperation.

The most important point about room dressing is that it needs to be done with a purpose, and that purpose has to extend beyond simply looking good. Even if the purpose might not be apparent to clients on entering the room, the way it has been prepared needs to reflect key elements of the core idea, and by the end of the presentation it has to tell the story as a wall of hieroglyphics in an Egyptian tomb might tell the story of a Pharaoh's life.

For Porsche, I remember filling a whole wall with pictures that young children had drawn of their dream cars, many of which looked remarkably like red Porsche 911s. "These kids dream of owning a sports car," I said later. "And in particular, many dream of Porsches. Where did it all go wrong?" On another wall were pictures drawn by adults of their relationship with their current vehicle—looking nice on the driveway, having comfortable seats and large, economical gas tanks. How did that childhood dream become this kind of car? As we told the story, we showed how the dream still burned bright for many; if only we could overcome the emotional barrier of what others might think of them for buying one, a Porsche still represented what a sports car should really be.

For the Unilever "Dirt is Good" pitch, we took a large open space in JWT's offices in Knightsbridge and divided it into five sections: an area where we welcomed the clients and discussed the key business issues around a large round table; an open space that I used for the strategic presentation; a kids' locker room in which we presented the creative ideas designed to persuade parents to participate in sports with their children; an entire supermarket laundry aisle for the part of the presentation in which we discussed bringing the idea to life at point of purchase; and finally another open area for questions and discussion. In this case, figuring out how to move people from one part of the presentation to the next required much thought and planning. Did we set up the room so we moved clockwise or counterclockwise around it? Originally we decided counterclockwise, but that meant me moving from the audience's right to their left as I traveled the breadth of my display of visual materials. As Craig Davis noted, that might have been okay if we had been presenting in a part of the world where people are used to reading from right to left, but here it simply felt unnatural. Overnight we rebuilt the entire room, and the next day the left-to-right flow worked much better for us.

Managing the Room

On issues of interior design and layout, I think it's fair to say that the majority of people do not have a great deal of imagination. When buying a house, most people tend to use rooms in the same way that the previous owners used them; they even arrange their furniture in the same manner. If a television was situated in the northwestern corner of the room under the previous regime, the chances are that the new owners will install their own TV in the same corner and position their sofas just as their predecessors had done.

The same phenomenon applies, I'm sad to say, even in the allegedly more creative surroundings of an advertising agency. If an agency team enters a hotel or client conference room and finds it set up with a long table running down the middle, chairs along either side, and a lectern and projector plug-in at the end of the table, they will often not even question that layout. They will sit on one side of the table, their clients will sit on the other, and the presenters will dutifully stand at the lectern. And in so doing, they lose a significant opportunity to influence the outcome of the meeting.

While there are obviously circumstances under which furniture cannot be moved, the only ones I can think of relate to strict rules governing clients' own conference rooms or cases where conference tables are so heavy that walls would have to be knocked down and cranes brought in to move them. In such situations, consideration should at least be given to changing the expected pattern of seating, or presenting from one of the long sides of the conference table rather than from one end.

The aim of such a minor change where restrictions apply, or a more major change of the type I will describe below, is to reduce the distance between the presenter and the audience. From years of moderating focus groups I learned that changing the default setup, in which the moderator sits at the end of a table, to one where he or she sits at the side, changes the chemistry dramatically. With respondents to his or her immediate right and left instead of psychologically "below" at the table, the moderator is now a part of the group rather than being in charge, and it makes a huge difference. When a presentation is given similarly "in the round," it encourages more audience participation and discussion. The same effect can be created at certain points of the presentation by having the presenter remain seated at the table with the client audience and agency team. Sitting down doesn't suit me, because my presentation style involves moving around and creating (and expending) a lot of energy; for others, though, it can work very well. While some people are legendary for being good on their feet, I would risk the wrath of my ex-partner Colin Probert by saying that he was equally good on his ass. He had a manner of opening a table-bound presentation that suggested this was to be a meeting rather than a presentation, that our intent was to talk with our audience rather than at them. As he often said, it felt weird to be standing to present at a table when everyone else was sitting down, and even if I and other presenters were later to roam around the table pointing at pictures on the wall, by remaining seated he set a tone that seemed to continue throughout the meeting.

Where conference tables can be taken apart and moved, I prefer to have them situated along the side of a room where I can use them to display presentation materials, arrange leave-behind documents, or position refreshments. For me the ideal arrangement involves seating without tables. A number of easels are the backdrop to an agency team sitting in a rough semicircle on either side of a large screen. The screen will certainly be used for showing video and possibly for slides (of the simple headline or picture variety). The persons presenting will start to one side of the screen and move around according to where they want to display their visuals. Between them and the audience, whose chairs are arranged in another rough semicircle to mirror the agency team, there is an open space, which can and should be used.

Some presenters are uncomfortable standing without any kind of barrier in between them and their audience, but they are not soccer players lining up to protect the goal against a firmly struck free kick and should not behave as such. Standing between the agency and client teams creates an implicit connection; it imparts confidence and openness, although its successful outcome does rely also on attention to details like polished shoes and buttons and zippers fastened in the way that both their designers intended and polite society expects.

Encouraging and Handling Questions

Another reason why careful planning and rehearsal are so necessary is that they are vital for any new business presentation to run on time. It may be that that the members of your audience are enjoying themselves so much when you exceed your allotted three hours that they will invite you to continue, but it is unlikely. Three hours is a very long time to exceed, and it would be a fair bet that if you have gone past that and not finished, you have either bored the pants off them or shown a disquieting level of disorganization—maybe both. When the London team made their presentation for the 2012 Olympics, they had 45 minutes and were told that if they exceeded that they would be cut off and allowed to go no further. As they were rather keen to get to Sebastian Coe's emotional closing statements, they timed each presenter to the second. David Magliano, the pitch leader, told me that during rehearsals he monitored whether speakers were over or under their allotted minutes as a coach might record split times in a race. Even 30 seconds too long might have seriously undermined the impact of London's bid. A super was removed from one film because it saved four seconds. Attention to such detail, and discipline in the presentation itself, are vital.

Planning for any presentation should have extra time built in for the inevitable departures from the script or changes of pace that result whenever people are nervous. This planning should also embrace worst-case scenarios, as described in Chapter 4. If the time available is unexpectedly reduced, or if the chief executive has rambled on for longer than any of you thought humanly possible, there must be a backup plan for communicating the key points in less time. Someone—usually the pitch leader—needs to run a stopwatch and have prearranged signals for telling team members to hurry up or slow down. (I have always had a signal for "slow down" but it has never been used.) And the presenters need to pay attention to those signals, because if they ignore them they run the risk of letting everyone down.

Timing is important because in any presentation there has to be time available, either throughout or at the end, for questions from members of the audience. However good a presentation might be, it is often the question and discussion time that makes the difference between good and great. By its very nature it allows a client to participate in the presentation rather than having it just thrown at them, and it gives the agency the first clear signs of how its communication is being processed. (Note that I said *processed*, not merely received.) If the ideas presented have been clear, the questions will often be geared toward development of those ideas. Any concerns raised will give both the excuse and valuable direction for following up with the client in the days immediately following the pitch. (See "How to Follow Up" later in this chapter.)

I usually prefer to encourage clients to stop me and ask questions whenever they occur to them, but this can be dangerously destructive to a timing plan, and there is always the risk that a series of follow-up questions will derail the presentation so completely that all sense of flow and memories of previous points made will be lost. Maybe better for the sanity of the timekeeper is the approach that invites comment and questions on burning issues as they arise, but asks for less important and more general questions to be kept back until the end. It's then the presenters' collective responsibility to ensure that the end is reached in time for that period of discussion to occur.

While the precise nature of a client's questions can never be known, many of them can be predicted with some certainty. It's thus the task of those planning and editing the presentation to spend time figuring out what those major questions might be and endeavoring to address them first in the course of the presentation. Several examples of this will be seen in the story of the London Olympic bid (Chapter 9). But when it comes to the question and discussion part of the presentation, there has to be a clear plan about who will lead the response from the agency, and who might answer a particular type of question. Thus, if a question is asked about an execution in the proposed campaign, the obvious person to answer is the creative director. Other, less obvious questions will be directed by the team leader to a particular member of his team.

Very occasionally, a comment from another team member in support of the first can be useful. For example, if I have answered a question about the impact of creative development research on the work we have presented, it can be quite powerful for the creative director to say what he learned from that and how useful it was in developing a new generation of work. On the whole, though, such secondary answers are not terribly helpful. When a second person opens his or her mouth, it's not too difficult to translate their meaning as, "What Bill would have said if he were as intelligent as me is . . ." or "You're probably too thick to understand what Bill just said, so I'm going to say it again in smaller words." For obvious reasons, neither interpretation is particularly desirable.

So, some organization and economy in the way the agency deals with questions is required. What the client is generally looking for at this stage is some indication of how much the agency believes in the point of view it has just presented, and how prepared the agency people are to listen to points of view that might be different from their own. Of course it's a delicate balance. An agency that presents an idea, hears a couple of critical comments, and says, "You're right, it sucks," may score high on the listening dimension but fare rather less well in the belief stakes. But an agency that says, "How about if this detail were to change? What did we learn about that in research? Let's look back at some response we got to a commercial we didn't show today and let you know how it might help overcome your concerns." That agency might do well on both. So too might an agency that disagrees with a client point of view on the basis of solid evidence to the contrary, but that also indicates a willingness to work through any differences of opinion if they are lucky enough to be hired and therefore able to work together.

On only one occasion can I remember something totally unexpected happening in the question and discussion part of a new business presentation. The surprise came not from a client's question, but from a completely spontaneous question on the part of one of the agency team.

Goodby, Berlin & Silverstein was pitching the Carl's Jr. hamburger business. Based in Orange County, California, Carl's Jr. was at the time still being run by its founder, Carl Karcher. Carl was a larger-than-life American entrepreneur who had built his empire from a single hamburger cart on the streets of Los Angeles. He was both a staunch Republican (a member of Ronald Reagan's so-called "Kitchen Cabinet") and a devout Catholic, and when we first met him, he gave each of us a voucher for a sandwich at his restaurant and a prayer card. His office walls were covered in pictures of Carl with world leaders—Reagan, Nixon, Margaret Thatcher, Pope John Paul II—and every meeting began with a prayer and the Pledge of Allegiance. Maybe you can imagine that our pitch to Carl and his team was not the most freewheeling of affairs. At a table as round as that favored by Arthur and his Knights, flanked by the flags of the United States and the State of California, we delivered our presentation as seriously and professionally as we knew how. The presentation itself was not without controversy: Carl himself had traditionally appeared in his company's advertising, and we were proposing that he appear as a cartoon alongside an animated version of his logo, Happy Star. This didn't seem to upset him too much, and by the time we invited questions from Carl and his colleagues, things appeared to be going pretty well.

When the last question was answered, Carl thanked us for our efforts and asked if there was anything else we wanted to say before leaving. Around the table we shook our heads. "No, thank *you*, Carl. It's been a pleasure."

"Could I say something?" A quiet voice came from the back of the room, where Chris Routh, a member of our TV production department, had been operating the video equipment. Although he had been introduced at the start of the meeting, Chris had faded into the background and, with the exception of an occasional nod to show that now was the time to roll a video, everyone had forgotten he was there.

"Sure," Carl said.

We all turned to Chris, with fixed smiles. Colin had gone quite pale. I saw Berlin's lips move. "What the f –?"

Chris stood. "You know, in meetings like this you always hear from the senior people who make the presentation," he said. "But a lot of other people worked on this presentation, and I'd just like to say how much it would mean to all of us to work on your business. If they were here I know they'd want to say that, so I thought I'd take it on myself to be their representative. And—you know. Thank you very much."

He sat down, and Berlin exhaled.

Although Andy and others later pointed out to Chris that *we* were the representatives of all those other people, and that such a comment could create the impression that we lacked discipline, no harm was done. In fact it was indicative of the freedom we encouraged in the agency and of the way that people seemed to take on responsibility beyond what their job description said.

Most important of all, Carl and his colleagues thought it was charming. And they hired us shortly afterward.

I mention this because one of the most important aims of any presentation should be to give the client's key decision makers a sense not just of how well you make presentations but of what it would be like to work with you. A feature of many of the best pitches I have been involved in was a comfort level between the presenters that allowed them to make fun of each other and even to disagree on important strategic and creative issues. (Such disagreement should be handled with care, but most good clients would rather work with people who challenge each other than with those who simply agree on an agency "line" in the interests of a quiet life.) Chris Routh's famous interruption in the Carl's Jr. meeting gave our audience a glimpse inside our agency culture that they probably would not otherwise have seen. Indirectly, it led to a number of subsequent decisions to open ourselves up to potential clients, and maybe even to the decision to have everyone come to the Sega pitch. It certainly exercised a powerful influence over the kind of materials we subsequently left behind to summarize our recommendations and leave our audience with a sense of who we were, not just as advertising professionals but also as people.

What to Leave Behind

It's traditional at the end of any presentation to give the client a document (usually in the form of a book, but electronic versions are becoming increasingly popular) to provide a reminder of the presentation to
assist in making their decision. Because it is left behind at the end of
the presentation, it is commonly referred to as a "leave-behind."

In the same way that many agencies choose to ignore the possibilities presented by a room that could be rearranged to their benefit, too
few take advantage of the opportunities presented by the leave-behind.
The default version—and I have probably seen hundreds of these piled
up in clients' offices over the years—is a bound document that includes
copies of all the slides presented in the pitch (which, if they are the
kind of PowerPoint slides described in the early part of Chapter 6,
means that the agency will be boring the client not once, but twice).
Sometimes a management summary is included, plus biographies of
everyone on the agency team and copies of any creative work that was
presented.

Yes, such a document is a reminder. To some extent it does the job
that has been asked of it. But in the form I described above it's a reminder of the content of the presentation, not of its spirit. It adds nothing to what has already been said.

I'm going to share two examples of leave-behinds that offer much
more. In very simple terms, they tell the story of the presentation. In
clear, concise prose, they summarize the main idea that the agency has
presented. They then demonstrate the relationship between the people
who work in the agency—not just the pitch team but the entire staff—
and that idea. Both were in the form of books and each, in its own way,
was beautiful. The aim was to create something that recipients would
not want to throw away but instead would want to spend time with. In
that time they would gain a unique insight into the agency and the people who work there. The agency and its staff were opening themselves
up to a group of strangers, but in so doing they hoped to make a connection to the common human ground on which the pitch idea had been
constructed.

The first is a book created by Goodby, Silverstein & Partners for Nikon in the spring of 1994. The first page read:

To shoot a picture:

One person sets the ASA, checks the light meter, sets the aperture, then the exposure, takes three steps back, squats, frames the shot, focuses, resets the aperture, focuses again, and shoots.

Another person aims and shoots.

So, who really takes the world's greatest pictures?

This book attempts to answer that.

On April 18th, the employees of Goodby, Silverstein & Partners were asked to bring to the office the one photograph that means the most to them. They were also asked to explain why they chose that particular picture.

We learned some things about photography that day.

We learned that what matters most to people is a picture's emotional content, and not its technique.

We learned that a picture can be poorly composed, blurry, underexposed—and still be considered "great." If not by most of the world, at least by whoever shot it. Or inherited it.

We learned that a photograph doesn't merely capture an image, but also a moment. And that it can trigger a flood of memories and details from that moment: the name of your aunt's basset hound, the smell of the steam rising from a Cape Cod clambake, the way your dad used to tickle your mom on the living room couch, the best man's toast at your wedding.

And because none of the pictures presented here were shot by a professional, we also learned that photography is probably the most democratic of art forms.

Anyone can shoot the world's—their world's—best pictures.

And everyone does.

On every following page was a photograph contributed by each person employed by GS&P, stuck to the page with an old-fashioned picture corner. Some were in color, others in grainy black and white.

There were pictures of grandmothers we had never met, of friends jumping on beds, of mothers so beautiful and fathers so handsome on their wedding day, of long lost but fondly remembered family pets, of moments of madness, and moments of perfection. My contribution was the picture in Figure 8.1 that I had taken the previous year on a visit to Rwanda. The accompanying text described why it meant so much to me.

This was the first mountain gorilla I saw in the wild. Not a care in the world, he just sat back against a tree, methodically stripping bark from a branch with his teeth. What's particular about this picture is that as I took it, another gorilla came up behind me on the trail. I wasn't aware of any of this, but others tell me that he paused, waited for me to move out of his way, and when I didn't, he simply shoved me to the side and into a patch of nettles. He paused once more, as if to gauge my reaction, then ambled slowly by. As I write, six months later, the civil war in Rwanda threatens the lives of these and all other mountain gorillas in the Parc National des Volcans. I hope that my experience was not the last of its kind.

FIGURE 8.1 The World's Best Picture: Mine.

"Everyone else had pictures of their wives and husbands," my wife complained when I showed it to her later. "And you used a gorilla?"

A second example comes from Berlin Cameron's pitch for Pfizer's Zyrtec business, in which the idea (as previously described) was to precipitate the equivalent of an alcoholic intervention. We sought to persuade allergy sufferers that they were not the only ones suffering from their allergies, and one particularly plaintive story from our leave-behind captured the essence of the idea as perfectly as any advertising ideas we had presented. In a large leave-behind book entitled "Opportunities Lost," the agency's general manager said:

> My mom is allergic to cats and dogs but we still had a cat as a family pet. Only the cat stayed in the basement and was never allowed upstairs. So I never actually got to watch TV with Sammy or sleep with him or chase him around the house. I had to visit him in the basement.

Everyone else told stories of times when others' allergies had affected them, or when others had been distressed by their own allergies. A picture of the person accompanied the story, so it was an opportunity for the Pfizer clients to meet those staff members to whom they had not previously been introduced and to be invited into the lives of those they had already met.

It's important when conducting an exercise such as this that everyone participates, which after the first or second time is really not difficult since the books become prized possessions—unique snapshots of an agency's culture at a particular point of time, to which people love to contribute. It's also important that the work be entirely the employees' own. We made a decision early on at Goodby that we would never edit the contributions of our staff: The memories were theirs so the words should be theirs too.

Everyone has these stories. By bringing yours to life in a leave-behind, you invite the client to contribute theirs, which will give your idea power through its relevance to those who sit in judgment upon it.

At the very least, it sure beats PowerPoint slides and chest-beating bios.

Of course, leave-behinds should also include copies of the creative work that has been presented and perhaps a video or DVD containing work the agency has produced for other clients. Ideally, the client will watch this not at the office in the role of a marketing person but at home with family, where the real work of advertising and other marketing communication gets done. They should be encouraged to do this: It shows great confidence on the part of the agency to submit its work to the criticism of those harshest of critics—the client's spouse and children.

Oh, one last thing. It's also not a bad idea to include a number where you might be contacted in the event that they decide to hire you.

How to Follow Up

I won't say too much about this, on the basis that how and when to follow up with a client after a pitch depends very much on their reaction to what you have presented and on any explicit instructions they may have given on what not to do.

Whatever they have said, you have to follow up in some form. A phone call or note the next day thanking them for coming, or for their hospitality, is the very least you can offer. In the course of this note or call, the core messages that you want to be remembered might be repeated, and any concerns raised by the client in the course of the meeting might be addressed. If the client would like to discuss any of this further, you will naturally be happy to do so.

On the day after Goodby, Berlin & Silverstein pitched the Isuzu business, Andy Berlin hired one of those large moving billboards and parked a message about how much we wanted their business in their parking lot. I seem to recall that all this did was block the exit to the lot and piss everyone off; even though we were eventually hired, I certainly don't remember him pulling a stunt like that again. It's a certain truth that "clever" stuff can and will backfire; when we were hired by Unum Insurance in Portland, Maine, our new client told us that one of our competitors had followed up a very good pitch with a picture of the entire team dressed as Maine fishermen. It felt like a bunch of slick New Yorkers making fun of people they regarded as hicks, and they were immediately discounted.

Such ideas need to be passed through a filter of common sense, and while it is important for a client to see how much an agency wants their business, too much desire can easily be interpreted as desperation.

In my view, follow-up conversations should always be substantive in nature, reflecting the desire of an agency to give the client all the information they might need to make an intelligent decision. It's necessary to adopt a constant state of readiness; invariably an uncertain client will ask for an audience with one or two senior agency representatives at the last possible minute, often requiring them to fly thousands of miles in order to answer some outstanding questions. Almost every major pitch I ever won has ended this way, with clients requesting further meetings at a level of secrecy so high that even some members of the agency pitch team were not allowed to know. Some of these meetings were about money, or for clarification of strategic and creative ideas presented, but most were for reassurance. The client wanted to meet some of us, or all of us, one last time to make sure that he or she was doing the right thing—to sit down with us as people as we might once we were working together. We were being tried on for size, as a person viewing a house for the second or third time might sit in a window seat and imagine reading the Sunday newspapers there.

The key to all such meetings? Consistency of message and openness of mind and manner.

And if it's not meant to be, then it's not meant to be.

Awarding the Business

This section might seem out of place in a book about how to make a pitch, but I include it in the hope that even one or two copies might find their way into the hands of clients who will one day invite pitches and make the final decision.

What I want to say is this: A huge amount of time, money, and emotion is poured into even the smallest new business pitch. Agencies work very hard to win a client's trust and confidence, and the difference between success and failure is immense. That much, everyone probably knows without my saying it. What they may not realize, though, is the difference that the act of awarding the business itself makes to the quality of the new relationship.

When Isuzu hired Goodby, Berlin & Silverstein in 1991, its selection team did so in a most unusual way. More than a week had elapsed since we made our pitch, and since the incident with Andy's mobile billboard we had heard nothing from either the client or the consultants. We then received a phone call on a Tuesday, telling us that the senior people from the client side wanted to have a conference call with us, first thing Thursday morning. Would we all be available in our offices to take part in that call?

Of course we made ourselves available, and the call was set up for 9 on Thursday morning. At the appointed time, we assembled in Rich's office and waited for the phone to ring. Each of us had prepared notes based on questions we thought they might ask, and our CFO had joined us to address any possible questions on compensation.

At five past nine, the phone rang. It was the receptionist, saying that a Mr. Kern from American Isuzu Motors was in the lobby.

In the lobby? What the heck was he doing there? Rich headed downstairs to see.

A few moments later the phone rang again. Rich spoke: "You'd better come down. All of you."

In the lobby we found Isuzu's pitch team: Fritz Kern, Dick Gillmore, Jerry O'Connor, and Mark Darling. They had brought with them a large case of champagne and enough glasses for everyone in the agency. They had also brought the title papers to the two Isuzu cars they had lent our agency for the duration of the pitch. The cars, along with the Isuzu business, were now ours.

A couple of years later our new clients from Unum Insurance arrived in person to award us their business. A phone call, they said, would not have done justice to all the work we had done, and they wanted the relationship to start the way they meant it to carry on. They flew all the way from Portland, Maine, to San Francisco to tell us that.

Such acts, however, are all too rare in our business. Accounts are most often awarded after long, drawn-out periods of alternating silence and negotiation, and sometimes by the time you have won you wonder why you ever wanted it so much in the first place. With Isuzu, though, and later Unum, we started our relationship with the clear sense that our clients were as excited about it as we were.

In the grand scheme of things, the gesture was perhaps relatively small. But it communicated their appreciation for what we had already done and their eager anticipation for what was to come. From that day forward, we would have done anything and more for those clients, and it showed in both the work we produced and the results we achieved.

CHAPTER NINE

- **The Perfect Pitch**
  - London's winning bid for the 2012 Olympic Games

The Finish Line

At 7:48 P.M. local time on July 6, 2005, the president of the International Olympic Committee (IOC), Dr. Jacques Rogge, stood at a podium in the Singapore Convention Center with a large, white envelope in his hand. Behind him, also standing according to tradition, were his fellow IOC members. On the floor of the hall, eyes fixed upon the envelope that seemed to be taking him forever to open, were the heads of the National Olympic Committees from around the world and the International Federations that represent each Olympic sport, winter and summer alike. This was the 117th Session of the IOC, and Jacques Rogge was about to announce the decision on which city had been chosen to host the 2012 Summer Olympics.

Also on the floor of the convention center were delegations from the five cities that had submitted bids to host those Games. Toward the back were those who, earlier in the day, had presented on behalf of Moscow, New York, and Madrid. Now depleted in number and understandably subdued, they had learned through three rounds of voting that their bids had been rejected. Moscow had recorded the lowest number of first round votes. In the second round, New York had come last. In the third, it was Madrid's turn. As each city was eliminated, another vote was taken among the members of the International Olympic Committee, with those who had voted for the eliminated city now switching their vote elsewhere. Now only two cities remained: London and Paris.

As Rogge looked out from his lectern, he saw the grey-suited delegation from Paris to his right, arms around each other's shoulders. To his left was the London delegation, in stone Jeff Banks-designed bespoke tailored suits, not touching each other because British people rarely do that in public. What the French and British delegations had in common was that most of their number could scarcely breathe. At stake was much more than two weeks of athletic competition. National and civic pride was on the line, with monarchs, presidents, prime ministers, and mayors having taken up the cause of the competing cities in the run-up to the vote. In raw business terms, the 2012 Olympic Games was estimated to be worth some eight billion dollars. The legacy of improved infrastructure and sporting facilities that a successful Olympic Games leaves behind would benefit future generations of inhabitants and visitors. The cost of losing, already felt so viscerally by the delegations from Moscow, New York, and Madrid, was measured in the opportunity lost, the millions of dollars spent, and the weeks, months, and years of work that their presentations had represented.

Crowded in front of the London and Paris delegations, poised to record reactions to Rogge's imminent announcement, were some 50 photographers and cameramen from the world's media. Only three of these cameramen were positioned before the British. The remaining 47 had their cameras trained upon their French counterparts, several of whom seemed confident enough of victory to have brought bottles of champagne into the hall with them.

"That doesn't look good," England soccer captain David Beckham whispered in classic British understatement to his neighbor, Sir Bobby Charlton, England soccer legend. Both had flown to Singapore to lend support to the London bid. Could the press, and even the Paris delegation themselves, have been tipped off before the results of the final vote were announced? All around them, their London bid colleagues were numb, expecting the worst.

Finally, Rogge succeeded in extricating the card from the envelope. If a 200-meter final had started at the moment he first tried to break the seal, the winner would by now have been well into his lap of honor.

"The International Olympic Committee," he read, his face impassive, "has the honor of announcing that the Games of the Thirtieth Olympiad in 2012 are awarded to the city of . . ." It seemed as if he paused; even if that pause were measured in milliseconds, it was long enough for everyone in the Singapore Convention Center, and millions of others watching live from all corners of the earth, to imagine him saying the word, *Paris*.

"London," he said.

Floating Votes

One week before the final presentations, London's *Evening Standard* newspaper ran an article about the faint hopes of its city's "underdog" team. "According to the latest betting," it read, "Paris are 1-6 on to win next week's vote. Given those sort of odds, it would be understandable if Seb Coe* and his London team had decided not to board the plane for Singapore on Monday." Throughout the bidding process, Paris had been the favorite, but as London 2012 chief executive Keith Mills had said many times as he sought to inspire his team, the final vote was "Paris's to lose." A bid is won, he argued, "in the last six weeks, the last six days, the last six hours." Everything depended on the London team's lobbying efforts in Singapore in the days leading up to the final presentation, and the quality of the 45-minute pitch to the International Olympic Committee.

The reason why that final presentation was so important, and why I have chosen to focus on it as the culmination of this book, is that the rules surrounding Olympic bidding have changed dramatically since the scandal surrounding Salt Lake City's bid for the 2002 Winter Olympics. To avoid a recurrence of such an embarrassing situation, International Olympic Committee members were banned from even visiting any of the bidding cities without the permission of Jacques Rogge. The bids were thus evaluated by IOC-appointed commissioners—a combination of IOC administrative staff and external experts—who analyzed detailed technical submissions (London's, submitted in November, 2004, ran to three volumes, with 17 chapters covering details as diverse as projected temperatures, wind speeds and wind direction at various facilities in August 2012, and how they proposed to cater to athletes whose diets were restricted by their religious beliefs).

The commissioners visited each of the five cities in the months leading up to the final presentation. With the cities receiving feedback on

---

*Lord Sebastian Coe, two-time Olympic champion and now London 2012 bid leader.

these evaluations and inspections in June, and even hearing firsthand the core elements of their competitors' bids at meetings of National Olympic Committees and International Federations that took place during the bidding process, there was a good chance, that by early July, the *content* of each of the bids would not differ greatly. The playing field was as level as it had ever been, and this meant that marketing and communications strategy was vital, and the planning and delivery of the pitch on July 6 was more important—for all of the competing cities—than ever before.

The stark reality was that every one of the 106 voting IOC members (by tradition, the president does not vote) would have decided on their first choice city before they entered the room. They would probably have decided on their second and third choice too. But the London team knew that if they received enough votes to make it to the fourth round, there would be maybe 10 to 20 floating votes up for grabs. Without attracting a large number of those floating votes, London could not win.

All the work leading up to the Singapore presentation had been designed to secure London's place in the top four, the top three, and the top two in three successive rounds of voting. The organizers were confident going into the last few days that their bid had the power to defeat those of Moscow and New York in the first two rounds. Paris was clearly the most formidable opponent, but Madrid too was a serious contender, buoyed by levels of public support considerably higher than those expressed by Londoners. If London could then defeat Madrid and get to the fourth round, success depended on being able to persuade more of those IOC members who had voted for Madrid to cast their next vote for London rather than Paris. Eight years earlier, when Athens had been awarded the 2004 Games, the final margin of victory over the competing city of Rome had been just one vote.

With a fair wind and a flawless presentation, London's bid leaders believed that they could capture enough of these floating votes to win. This would require them to take some risks, but in the position of underdog they believed that it was better to go down in flames than to try to play anything safe.

Preparation

The countdown to the final presentation began in earnest in May 2004, when London, Paris, Madrid, New York, and Moscow were officially selected as the five candidate cities. London had submitted its candidacy in June 2003, but the Paris bid had been active for at least two years before that, and New York's 2012 bid had been operational for eight. New York had fought off competition from other American cities for the nomination of its National Olympic Committee, and so was much further forward in its planning.

When London 2012 director of marketing David Magliano joined the bid team in 2003, he was convinced that the hard work and energy required for London to make up ground on its rivals might actually be an advantage. While others worked tirelessly on the technical aspects of the bid, he created a core team who would be responsible for crafting its message. He believed, as I have stated elsewhere in this book, that the number of people involved in decision-making is inversely proportional to its quality and efficiency. He thus formed a "kitchen cabinet" comprising himself, chief executive Keith Mills, communications director Mike Lee, and bid leader and former Olympian Sebastian Coe. Working closely with this team (in the kind of consultative capacity described in Chapter 7) were former IOC marketing director Michael Payne and filmmaker Stewart Binns. This team was responsible for ideas; responsibility for implementing those ideas in the form of the final presentation script fell to another, smaller group. Working with David Magliano in this group were: Chris Denny, a marketing specialist and lawyer by training, who was hired for his ability to construct an argument; Nick Varley, a sports writer and journalist who was to take on the lion's share of the scriptwriting; and Michael Dalziel, a production specialist who was responsible for coordinating the work of companies providing photographic and video materials for the final presentation.

When David Magliano and I first met, early in 2006, he described an approach to the presentation that was broad and nonspecific in its early months. "We were continually locking things away for use later," he said, and although this didn't necessarily involve the use of yellow Post-it notes, this "grazing" principle was essentially the same as the one proposed by James Webb Young. The presentation didn't come into sharper focus, with real structure and meaning, until April, May, and June immediately preceding the presentation.

The first task of the bid team was to understand the audience. The 107 members of the IOC represented 90 different nationalities. The average age of a member was 65, and more than 20 were in their eighties. This had important implications for both the tone and the content of London's presentation. Tonally, it had to speak to these members in a manner that reflected the values of their generation, and which adhered to the strict protocol of IOC meetings. As the language of Jacque Rogge's announcement suggests ("The International Olympic Committee has the honor of announcing . . ."), these are very formal affairs, where words have to be carefully chosen to show the appropriate deference to those who govern the world's greatest sporting spectacle. As for content, the presentation had to suggest a legacy that could be left for the Olympic movement by a vote for London, but perhaps more important still, a legacy that could be left by those older members who might not have many more opportunities to influence important decisions. These people wanted to be remembered for something, and David and his team understood from the start that London's bid needed to become a lightning rod for that desire.

The other key feature of this audience was its deep involvement with the Olympic Games. Seventy percent of the IOC's members were former Olympians, some of whom had competed as far back as the last time the Games had been held in London, in 1948. Jacques Rogge himself had represented Belgium as a yachtsman at the Games of 1968, 1972, and 1976, and had played rugby for his country. London's was the only bid that had an Olympian—two-times-gold-medalist Sebastian Coe—as bid leader, a man whom IOC members would regard in many ways as one of their own.

To understand the way that previous bid presentations had been constructed, David, Chris Denny, and Nick Varley watched videos of a number of past presentations by winning and losing cities. A common theme was the way every presentation began with a film designed to show how wonderful their city was; in other words, they were saying "Let's talk about us." It was a mistake that the Paris team would ultimately make again, but London stuck rigidly to David's belief that the aim of the presentation should be to engage the audience by talking about what interested *them*. Why was London's bid in the interests of the Olympic movement in general, and the IOC members in particular?

If, as David and his team hoped, the race came down to a final vote between London and Paris, it was important to know the relative strengths and weaknesses of the two bids. London's presentation should be designed to counteract any perceived weaknesses of its own bid and to undermine (subtly and very politely, of course) the perceived strengths of the Parisians.

The list of Paris's strengths was, as the French would say, *formidable*. The founder of the modern Olympic movement was a Frenchman, Baron Pierre de Coubertin, and the official language of the Olympic movement, like that of international diplomacy, is French. In the "Stade de France," Paris had one of the world's best sports stadiums, and in 1998 this stadium had been the venue for the final of soccer's World Cup, a competition hosted very successfully by France. (When the French national team beat Brazil in the final, the celebrations in the city rivaled those that had greeted liberation and the end of the Second World War.) Paris had hosted the Olympic Games two times before, in 1900 and 1924. It had thus been waiting a very long time—a quarter of a century longer than London—to host another Games. In the intervening years Paris had bid unsuccessfully twice, so the bid for the 2012 Games represented their third attempt. There was a feeling among those close to the IOC (which the French bid team did not seem inclined to contradict) that if Paris was rejected once more it might not want to bid again. Imagine a city like Paris *never* hosting another Games. It was too terrible to contemplate!

Could London match this? Well, London too had hosted two previous Summer Games, in 1908 and 1948, and the English had been active supporters from the very start. (King George V was an honorary member of the founding Congress in 1894). While London itself had not bid for the Games since 1948, it was in fact Britain's *fourth* bid in 20 years, after two bids from Manchester and one from Birmingham. Only Sweden could match that level of enthusiasm without reward. As for a stadium to match the Stade de France (the absence of which led the French spin doctors to refer to London's bid as "The Virtual Bid"), and having to talk about other facilities that were no more than a figment of an architect's imagination, this presented a more significant problem. The answer proposed by the "kitchen cabinet" was, as David Magliano described it to me, "to change the decision criteria" used by IOC members to evaluate the bids. London would use existing world-class venues like the soon-to-be-completed Wembley stadium (for football), Wimbledon (for tennis), and Lord's, the home of cricket (for archery), and create temporary venues in iconic locations such as Horseguards Parade (for beach volleyball) and Greenwich Park (for equestrian events). All the other facilities would be purposely built for athletics in a way that would make the Stade de France seem obsolete.

Such decisions were highly strategic in nature and would later be brought to the IOC members' attention very explicitly in the presentation. This would be the presentational equivalent of a nuclear explosion. As we will see, however, they were also brought to life more implicitly through clever use of language and visuals—the invisible but arguably more dramatic effect of the nuclear fallout.

As the presentation began to take shape, a three-tier intellectual framework started to emerge. The bottom tier was what David refers to as the "rational, technical part," which was designed to address the logistic issues of interest to the IOC members. Every city would be covering this ground, and London had to find ways of setting itself apart on the key dimensions. Four areas were deemed to be critical: stadiums, accommodation for visitors (including the "Olympic family" itself), transport, and accommodation for athletes. New York had long been talking about the "X" shape that defined its proposed infrastructure, and Paris had a much-touted model of a village and two clusters of venues around the city's *peripherique*. London's proposal focused on central (as opposed to peripheral) venues, and an athletes' village "within sight of the Olympic flame."

The distances that both spectators and athletes had to travel in Athens, to venues quite removed from the city center, had been widely regarded as a weakness of the 2004 Games, and London's bid team was keen to leverage those recent memories in support of its own organizing principle. London 2012 would be organized for the benefit of athletes by making sure that they could train and compete close to the Olympic village, for the benefit of spectators by giving them venues in the center of one of the world's great cities, and finally, for the benefit of the Olympic Family (IOC members, members of International Federations and National Olympic Committees, as well as sponsors and the world's media) by making legally-binding agreements that guaranteed low, fixed prices for all Olympic Family rooms. For IOC members and others from nations without the resources of the U.S.A. or U.K., this was a powerful and unique promise. Before the Athens Games, hotel prices had risen five-fold as owners sought to make the maximum possible profit from the Olympics. Such profiteering would not be repeated in London.

The second tier of the presentation would be more abstract and emotional in nature. This was "The Magic of London."

First, London would try to persuade the IOC members of the advantage of holding the Games in a truly multicultural city. More than 300 languages are spoken each day in London. More students come from overseas to study in London than to any other city in the world. Six million young people from around the world visit London each year. This was potentially a competitive advantage—even though it could never be suggested explicitly—against both Paris and Madrid, where racial tensions were neither unknown nor infrequent in their occurrence.

Second, London would welcome IOC members and the Olympic Family and "treat them like royalty." When the IOC's Evaluation Commissioners visited London in February, they were invited to dine with the Queen at Buckingham Palace. The presentation would make it clear that IOC members themselves might expect similar treatment in 2012. As David Magliano admits, this was "a fawning, obsequious show of respect and deference," but it was based upon a powerful insight. Many members of the IOC did mix regularly with royalty (Britain's own Princess Anne, the Princess Royal, is an ex-Olympian and current IOC member) and with members of the political and cultural elite, and they saw themselves very much at that level. Fawning and obsequious it might have been, but in the spirit of making a message personal, it had the potential to be very powerful.

The third element of "The magic of London" was the city's passion for sport. Every weekend hundreds of thousands of Londoners fill soccer stadiums, and once a year half a million of them line the streets to cheer on participants in the world's greatest marathon. Not only Londoners, but Britons in general, watch more sport and play more sport than any other nation on earth. Britain, the cradle of sport in the modern era, codified rules for rugby, rowing, wrestling, soccer, boxing, and many other sports. Britons attending the Athens Games in 2004 (who included Prime Minister Tony Blair and his wife, Cherie) were exceeded in numbers only by the resident Greeks. In a London Games, the IOC could be sure of stadiums filled by spectators with a strict sense of fair play, who would not leave when their own athletes were eliminated.

Finally, London 2012 promised a legacy for the community of which IOC members could be proud. Urban regeneration was offered by the creation of affordable housing in the Olympic village, a community with sport at its heart in the spirit of Pierre de Coubertin. London 2012 also offered a legacy for elite sport, with the Olympic Stadium and other facilities in the proposed Olympic Park becoming the permanent home of the London Olympic Institute, "a new world center for sporting excellence." Note: a *world* center, not a British center, which would house national governing bodies, medical experts, and educators, and provide facilities for young athletes from around the world to train.

The final tier of the presentation, in David Magliano's words, was "the difference between a good and a great presentation." It's what he called the "killer" part of the presentation, and for a very long time he didn't know what it was. He knew what he wanted: a simple, human idea that would both tie together the disparate parts of London's rational and emotional promise and give the presentation an inspiring theme. He also knew that he and his colleagues had all the raw materials they needed to develop this idea, rather like Watson and Crick had all the information they needed to identify the double helix structure of DNA, or my colleagues and I had everything we needed for a Porsche strategy before we took our trip out to the ballpark. All David lacked was the idea itself.

"We had been in a room breathing our own exhaust fumes for too long," he said later.

When the idea came, it was not from a meeting of the "kitchen cabinet" or David's presentation group. It was not suggested by e-mail or over a long distance telephone call. No, it emerged in a plain, old-fashioned face-to-face conversation between David and Sebastian Coe on the subject of television licensing. The IOC has a relatively small number of revenue streams: sponsorship, TV rights, and some licensing money from Olympic-branded goods. Television rights account for a large proportion of this revenue, and looking at viewing figures for recent Games, David could see the steady erosion of youth ratings. With the exception of businesses that provide products like retirement homes, dentures, and funeral services, an ageing audience is generally regarded as a bad thing, and the IOC was rightly concerned. Seeing a connection between London's magnetic appeal to the world's youth and this problem facing the Olympic brand, David suggested that the core message of London's bid should be about attracting younger viewers to Olympic television coverage.

"Seb," he says, "told me that I was missing the point. There was a much bigger problem to address than attracting young people to watch Olympic coverage on television: It was attracting young people to participate in Olympic sport. That's the real challenge, and his argument was that if you can address that, then the television ratings will follow."

At that moment they both knew exactly what the presentation had to do. The task of London 2012 was to inspire young people around the world to participate in Olympic sport.

The Passage of Time

At the very beginning of the competition, when the five candidate cities were announced, a so-called protocol order was established. Paris was first, New York second, Moscow third, London fourth, and Madrid last. This would be the order at the final presentation in July 2005, but it would also be replicated on other occasions when the cities were invited to address smaller Olympic Family gatherings. One such event took place in Berlin in April, where members of the International Federations that govern all Olympic sports met at "Sport Accord." Some twelve IOC members—who also happened to head International Federations—were present at that meeting. In June, a meeting of National Olympic Committees was held in Ghana, at which a few more IOC members were present in their other roles as National Olympic Committee representatives. These meetings were both a blessing and a curse. The blessing was that the meetings allowed some contact with IOC members who would later have a vote, and they also gave the candidate cities the opportunity to test-drive parts of their final presentation. The curse was that the teams from the competing cities would also be there and would see the presentations. The conundrum for London 2012 was how much to reveal in front of the competition and the world's media.

In the end, the time available for presentations was so restricted (a mere ten minutes in Ghana) that it precluded more than a general update on technical preparations. Much more useful were the opportunities that could be engineered for individual conversations with influential figures. Needless to say, these were exploited to the full.

By this stage, David Magliano's assertion that London's late entry into the race might be advantageous was looking somewhat prescient. After several years as favorites, Paris was playing safe in the interest of protecting its lead. New York was plagued by arguments over the construction of a new Olympic stadium, and Madrid's bid had been dealt a terrible blow by the terrorist attack of March 2004. London had momentum, or "The Big Mo," as Josh Lyman would say on *The West Wing*.

In Ghana one very important lesson was learned about the way that the candidate cities' final presentations would be governed. While the French presentation in Ghana was allowed to run six minutes over the allotted ten minutes, the timekeepers stopped New York's presentation at eleven minutes. Michael R. Bloomberg, New York's mayor, had flown all the way to Ghana and didn't even get the opportunity to speak. With a presentation previously timed at 22 minutes, London's team spent the duration of Moscow's presentation cutting furiously. It was clear that if presentation duration was policed this forcefully in July, then discipline was the number one priority. If London's presentation built to a climax—as any good presentation should—then it would be suicide to risk being cut off before the climax could be delivered.

Version 35

When Her Royal Highness the Princess Royal took the stage on July 6, the script she held, and which David Magliano knew word for word, was in its 35th version. Those 35 versions included seven significant rewrites, with the others representing substantial changes to certain parts. David knew version 35 word for word because he, Chris Denny, and Nick Varley had literally agonized over every one of them. Director of Communications Mike Lee and the other members of the "kitchen cabinet" had seen every significant new version. Advisor Michael Payne had been through it several times with a fine-tooth comb.

The script was developed with the idea of inspiring the world's youth to participate in Olympic sport providing its narrative arc. This idea had to support, and feed from, the rational and emotional benefits that London 2012 could offer the Olympic movement. The presentation had to state this idea and these benefits simply (in language that was not colloquial, and that was in accord with the protocol of the

IOC), approachably, and in ways that IOC members would not expect. And it had to do it in no more than 45 minutes.

A critical decision that had to be made was the composition of the presentation team itself. Sebastian Coe—as bid leader, a former Olympian, and a politician—was an obvious choice. HRH the Princess Royal had not played a presentation role in previous U.K. Olympic bids, but her position as an IOC member, former Olympic athlete, and the daughter of the primary resident of Buckingham Palace made her participation highly desirable. The third athlete to present would be Denise Lewis, the heptathlon champion from the Sydney Games who, in addition to being warm and engaging, has possibly the finest six-pack I have ever seen on a woman. She would talk about London 2012 from the athletes' point of view.

It was essential for Sir Craig Reedie, the chairman of the British National Olympic Committee and an IOC member, to speak because, like the Princess Royal, he could address his fellow members as a friend and colleague. And while the Olympic Games is about sport, and although it was considered an advantage for London's bid to be seen as representing the interests of youth rather than those of politics (Paris) or big business (New York), politicians also had an important role to play. No Games could be a success without the support of national and local government, and thus three influential politicians were lined up to help sell the bid. Foremost among these was Prime Minister Tony Blair, who from the start had been active in supporting the bid and seeking cross-party endorsement. He was to be in Singapore for a few days before the final presentation, lobbying on the bid's behalf, but while French President Chirac was to present on behalf of Paris, Blair's responsibilities as host of the G8 Summit meant that he would have to return home at the critical time. He would speak on behalf of the British government by video, supported by his Olympic Minister, Tessa Jowell. Making the case for the city of London itself would be Mayor Ken Livingstone, whose previous resistance to rehearsing, or speaking from a script, had evaporated in those few minutes of panic in Ghana.

In another demonstration of meticulous planning, former Olympic triple-jump champion Jonathan Edwards was drafted as a stand-in to represent any of the designated speakers who might be taken ill on the day and unable to perform. His own, personalized version of every part of the presentation was prepared (so, for example, he would not be in the embarrassing position of saying "I'm Denise Lewis, women's heptathlon champion from the Athens Games" or talking in language that only a Prime Minister might use), and he rehearsed every part with other members of the team.

Beyond what the speakers would say, visuals would have to be prepared to support the points they were making, and videos made for punctuation (as a relief from talking heads) and to dramatize key messages. Michael Dalziel had set up a working relationship with an event production company early in the process, and a massive data bank of photography had been built. While other cities worked with big-name filmmakers like Steven Spielberg (New York) and Luc Besson (Paris), the London team decided to work with a little-known production company, New Moon. New Moon's Daryl Goodrich and Caroline Rowland had worked on an earlier film for London 2012, and the team felt that a good working relationship should override other considerations. Five films were made in June: a film to introduce the theme of inspiring youth; Tony Blair's part of the presentation; a film about the proposed infrastructure of the Games; another about the "magic of London" to act as little more than a break; and a closing film that developed the youthful inspiration theme. Again, David Magliano gave a pretty good impression of being a control freak, bouncing back and forth between edit suites in that last month, "making sure that every shot was perfect."

Every pitch needs a control freak at the helm.

Singapore

Ten days before the final presentation, the London team traveled to a resort on Singapore's Sentosa Island. Here, individual speakers were coached and the finishing touches made to the presentation. No fewer than ten complete rehearsals were held, with understudies filling in if the feature speaker was unavailable. There first were Sebastian Coe, Denise Lewis and Craig Reedie. Coe and Reedie had to leave before the others to participate in the lobbying effort ahead of July 6, but Ken Livingstone and Tessa Jowell rehearsed several times. Even HRH the Princess Royal rehearsed three times, which is notable because royalty and rehearsal do not generally walk hand-in-hand. Presentations were literally timed to the second, with redundant words and phrases being removed to save two seconds here, five seconds there.

David Magliano invited different audiences to each of the rehearsals, and found that he increasingly spent the rehearsal watching the audience rather than the presenters. While they might later describe their reactions differently, the body language of audience members spoke volumes about their level of interest and engagement. It was clear which parts of the presentation required more attention or more energy on the part of the speaker. Even at this stage, small details were being changed. Slides screened behind the speakers would show every Olympic summer sport at some point in the presentation, and individual slides would move according to changes in copy and emphasis. At one point David's suggestion of a change was met with applause from all of his colleagues: he had no idea why they were reacting this way until they said that the slide he had just asked to be changed was in fact the only one that survived from the very first version of the presentation. They had all been waiting for its day of reckoning. In another part of the presentation they were using a shot that showed an athletics audience waving flags; this picture was changed to one in which the crowd were waving the flags of South American nations—a subliminal message to those South American members who might support Madrid in the early votes but who might later become the floating votes that London needed to win.

Detail. Detail. Detail.

In an interview in the *Financial Times* after the successful bid, David Magliano described how the members of his core team prepared for their presentation. The final hours were not spent worrying, or rewriting, or even rehearsing. All the important work had been done up front, and now everyone's primary responsibility was to be relaxed.

Speaking of Sebastian Coe, David said, "Seb didn't want to watch the other presentations. We couldn't make any on-the-hoof changes, so he stayed in his room, reading the newspapers and playing jazz music very loud. Every now and then I would pop in to see him. The last 48 hours, I just tried to keep my head clear. We just had a very strong sense that we could do it."

The Presentation

On July 6, London presented fourth, at 2.30 P.M. local time. First to walk to the podium was HRH the Princess Royal.

"Mr. President, dear colleagues," she began, according to convention. *"Thank you for this opportunity to present London's bid.*

"We stand before you today with a great sense of history. We are proud of our country's long and unbroken partnership with the Olympic Movement." (This, right up front, was a defense against the Baron de Coubertain factor.)

"A partnership which dates back to the founding Congress of 1894, of which my great-grandfather, King George V, was an Honorary Member. An interest and enthusiasm which continues today. And I'm delighted to have been asked to convey to you a special message from Her Majesty The Queen. Her message reads: 'I have been impressed by the way everyone has united behind London's bid. As a country, we share a passion for sport, and we also share a desire to welcome you to London in 2012. I was delighted to welcome the Evaluation Commission to Buckingham Palace earlier this year and I very much hope to welcome each of you to the Palace in 2012.'

"Message ends. Now, let me hand over to our colleague Craig Reedie, Chairman of the British Olympic Association."

Short, but sweet. But note how many of the key themes she introduced: Apart from the symbolic significance of a member of the Royal Family and an IOC member actively campaigning on London's behalf, she stated Britain's case as founding supporters of the Olympic movement, refuted concerns about low levels of public support for a London

Games, and introduced the emotional messages of "passion for sport" and "We'll treat you like royalty."

"Thank you, Your Royal Highness," said Craig Reedie. To everyone's surprise (including, I suspect, members of his immediate family), he said this in French. Given the notorious Anglo-centricity and limited language skills of most Britons, for a member of the London team to be speaking in another tongue—and doing so reasonably fluently—was nothing short of shocking.

"Mr. President," he continued in French, carefully observing the correct protocol, *"Dear colleagues, let me begin by paying tribute to our fellow Candidate Cities. We are honoured to be competing against four great cities. I know that each of them could host wonderful Games because, like many of you, I have attended summer or winter Games in each of their four countries in the last 25 years."*

This was the equivalent of a diplomatic knife in the back. What he was doing was reminding IOC members that even if New York, Madrid, and Paris hadn't staged Games in recent years, Los Angeles, Atlanta, Salt Lake City, Barcelona, and the French city of Albertville had. And he knew that, in particular, IOC memories of the Albertville Winter Games could not be described as "glowing."

"Our dream today is to bring the illustrious title of Host City to our country for the first time in 64 years. We are proud to say that our athletes have competed at every Games since 1896. From Athens to Athens." (He picked up where his Royal colleague left off; this is what David Magliano refers to as a "timebomb of pleasure," whereby an idea is seeded by one speaker and returned to by another. The second time it seems familiar, eliciting an "I've always thought that/known that" reaction from the audience.) *"And we are also proud,"* he said, *"to be the birthplace of Paralympic sport."* (Having checked that very important Paralympic box, he reverted to his native English.)

"No country in recent times has made a greater effort than Britain to host the summer Games. This is our fourth bid in 20 years. It was conceived by the NOC." (In other words, London 2012 was an athletes'

bid, not a political bid.) *"We have been involved throughout and developed the bid with the total support of Mayor Ken Livingstone and the Government of Prime Minister Tony Blair.*

"We have learnt from each of the three previous bids." (Unlike British bid teams in the past, we have learned from our mistakes and from your feedback.) *"We understand the recipe for magical Games. A superb technical plan. A breathtaking atmosphere in our capital city. And a vision to realise fully the power of the Olympic Games."* (Note his description of the presentation's three-tier model, creating expectations that will be met by later speakers.)

"In a moment, bid Chairman Seb Coe will outline that vision. And how it will make a unique and lasting contribution to the Olympic Movement. Olympic champion Denise Lewis will describe the special experience London offers the athletes. Mayor Ken Livingstone will describe London's meticulous preparation to guarantee the delivery of the Games. Prime Minister Tony Blair will guarantee total Government support. And Olympic Minister Tessa Jowell will explain London's sporting legacy."

As he read out the names of his fellow presenters, their pictures appeared on the big screen behind him. Sebastian Coe and Denise Lewis were shown with the Olympic rings, others with the London 2012 logo. Tony Blair was pictured at a London 2012 event, the picture chosen to emphasize his continuous involvement.

"The British Olympic Association has just celebrated its centenary. Mr. President, we appreciate that if you grant the Games to London you will place in our hands the Olympic spirit. We will guard that spirit. We will cherish it. And we will proudly hand it on. To young people like those in this film."

Like the Princess Royal before him, Craig Reedie had spoken in short, easily digestible sentences. He had laid out the ambition for the presentation and the order and content of what would follow. It was a classic case of "telling them what he was going to tell them," before his colleagues told them and finally told them again what they just told them.

The first film* opened on a close-up of an African athlete at the start of a race.

The athlete toyed with a wristband as he waited to take his marks.

"To make an Olympic Champion," said the voice of Sir Ian McKellen, *"takes eight Olympic Finalists."*

The athlete took his place on the starting blocks.

"To make an Olympic finalist takes eighty Olympians."

"To make an Olympian takes 200 national champions."

A younger athlete waited nervously in a locker room, fiddling with the same wristband. It was the athlete from the film's opening, at a younger stage of his life and athletic career.

"To make a national champion takes thousands of athletes."

The film cut to a younger boy, running barefoot, somewhere in Africa. He wore the same wristband (Figure 9.1).

"To make an athlete takes millions of children around the world inspired to choose sport."

In an African village, a small, unathletic-looking child was seen throwing stones with his friends. His wristband showed that he was the same child, even younger. He stopped as a police car passed, but then his attention was caught by a radio commentary of the final of the 100-meters in the London 2012 Games. A Nigerian athlete was fulfilling his boyhood dream and winning the gold medal.

The film faded.

"Mr. President, Members of the International Olympic Committee," said Lord Sebastian Coe, looking tanned and relaxed at the podium (Figure 9.2). *"To make an Olympic champion takes millions of young people around the world to be inspired to choose Olympic sport."* (Just in case they had missed that in the film.) *"In the past, London and the Olympic Movement have come together when there were serious challenges to be faced. In 1908, London delivered the Games and the first*

---

*This, the entire presentation, and other London 2012 films can be viewed at the London 2012 website: www.london2012.com or on the BBC's website, http://news.bbc.co.uk.

FIGURE 9.1 Visual of young African athlete.
© London Organising Committee of the Olympic Games, 2006.

FIGURE 9.2 Sebastian Coe presents.
© Bongarts/Getty Images 2006.

purpose-built Olympic Stadium to the tightest of the schedules. In 1948, our predecessors reunited a devastated world through sport. And their legacy was the first volunteer programme, an idea still at the heart of the Games."

The explicit message here, over black and white footage of those Games, was that London had a history of positive legacy. Implicitly, he was suggesting that London had stepped up before at times of crisis. Now it was payback time. He prepared to lay out the challenge that the London presentation would address:

"Today, London is ready to join you in facing a new challenge. And to provide another enduring sporting legacy. Today's challenge is tough. It's more complex. We can no longer take it for granted that young people will choose sport. Some may lack the facilities. Or the coaches and role models to teach them. Others, in an age of 24-hour entertainment and instant fame, may simply lack the desire. We are determined that a London Games will address that challenge. So London's vision is to reach young people all around the world. To connect them with the inspirational power of the Games. So they are inspired to choose sport.

"I'm delighted we have with us today representatives of the next generation. Here on stage, Amber Charles, an emerging basketball player. Amber delivered our candidate file to Lausanne last year." (Amber, a young mixed-race child from the community that would most benefit from the Games, joined Coe at the podium.) *"And in the audience, thirty of her contemporaries, aged from twelve to eighteen."* (The children waved to the IOC members. It was maybe a bit cheesy, but it stood in stark contrast to teams of men in grey suits. Coe savored the moment.)

"Why are so many here, taking the place of businessmen and politicians? It's because we're serious about inspiring young people. Each of them comes from east London, from the communities who will be touched most directly by our Games. And thanks to London's multi-cultural mix of 200 nations, they also represent the youth of the world. Their families have come from every continent. They practice

every religion and every faith. What unites them is London. Their love of sport. And their heartfelt dream of bringing the Olympic Games to our city."

On the screen behind him, Coe was pictured with Tony Blair at a London 2012 community event. With his words he had repeated the "killer" idea of the presentation and introduced the key themes of London's multiculturalism and passion for sport.

"Mr. President. Technical excellence is essential in delivering the Games. London's bid takes that as its starting point. So we are delighted that the Evaluation Commission judges our bid to be 'of very high quality.' " (This was an important acknowledgment of the Evaluation Commission's findings, and a reminder for any IOC members who had not actually read their report.)

"But we aim to go much further. Allow me to outline the three principles which have guided this bid.

"First, we want to deliver a magical atmosphere. An electrifying experience for competitors and spectators. To provide the uplifting spirit which distinguishes the Olympic Games from other sports events." (This was an attempt to connect to the older members of the audience, for whom this spirit was a guiding force.) *"And that magic begins with the venues. Which is why we have carefully selected them in line with the needs of the International Federations, and the recommendations of the Olympic Games Study Commission:*

"Existing world-class venues." (Defense against Paris's "Virtual Bid" spin.)

"Spectacular city centre locations." (An attack on Paris's Peripherique plan.)

"And, most importantly, our decision to create an Olympic Park. A Park containing nine state-of-the-art venues. And the IBC and MPC." (Broadcast and Press centers, which had never before been situated in an Olympic Park.) *"All just seven minutes from central London. Our Park will also contain the Olympic Village. We will put athletes, Olympians and Paralympians, at the heart of our Games. They will live within sight of the Olympic Flame."*

From these vital technical points, which represented unique features of the London bid, Coe adopted an air of humility. This was not what many IOC members might have expected of a British bid.

"Our second principle is to be your best partners. We have listened and learnt. We are a better bid as a result. Thank you to all of you who have helped us in our quest. We established our own Athletes Commission.* We worked just as hard to understand the needs of all those upon whom the athletes depend. IOC members. The National Olympic Committees. The International Federations and technical officials. Sponsors and the media. Every single member of the Olympic Family."

In other words, everyone in the room and their families and friends. He was checking boxes and gaining their attention before delivering tangible evidence of what this spirit of best partnership meant. As David Magliano put it so succinctly when we first met, the spirit of what Seb was saying was, "The answer's yes. What's the question?"

"For example, we know it is much harder to negotiate hotel room rates after the host city has been selected. So, we already have legally-binding agreements which guarantee low, fixed prices for all Olympic Family rooms. With no minimum stay. This alone will save you millions of dollars in accommodation costs."

Dollars in their pockets, that's what best partnership meant, and again in using dollars Coe was using Olympic currency rather than that of his own country.

"Our third principle is to deliver a lasting sporting legacy.

"We know the Games must offer more than just 17 days of world-class sport and celebration.

"So, in London every sport will have a legacy.

"We'll come back to this later.

"Now, let's see more about our plans."

---

*The Athletes' Commission had originally been called the "Athletes Advisory Group," but the name had been changed to one more favored by the IOC. "Commission" is a very Olympic word.

The issue of legacy was very important, but this was not the most logical time to talk about it. Olympic Minister Tessa Jowell would talk about it later.

A second film now played, with former tennis star turned TV presenter Sue Barker taking the audience on a tour of London's Olympic facilities. While much of what she showed was animated, it was cleverly mixed with real locations to give the sense of it being anything but "virtual."

When it finished, it was Denise Lewis's turn to speak. At one time the most nervous of the presenters, her many hours of rehearsal had paid off. Now she appeared calm and collected.

"Mr. President, Members of the International Olympic Committee. I'm Denise Lewis, Olympic Heptathlon champion from the Sydney Games. I have the pleasure of speaking on behalf of the London Athletes Commission.

"I was eight when I was inspired by the Moscow Games." (This was an implicit message that she had been inspired by, among others, Sebastian Coe. Moscow also happened to be one of the Games at which Jacques Rogge had competed.) *"I dreamt of emulating the athletes I watched. And my dreams came true when I competed in Atlanta, in Sydney, and in Athens. Like every Olympian, I have unforgettable Olympic memories. And we in London are determined every athlete will leave our city with friendships and memories which last forever.*

"Our Athletes Commission had to answer one fundamental question: how do you give athletes the best possible Olympic experience? We said: give us the best Village in the most convenient location. Everything else follows. Our Village is within walking distance of nine venues. In London, athletes will compete, not commute. The Village is inside the Park to guarantee the athletes a special experience. Take it from me: It makes all the difference to be as close to the action as possible. In fact, the whole London plan was conceived with our input. Everything athletes need was designed in from day one. Training venues. Security. And, of course, the needs of Paralympians. These are the things athletes want. When a fraction of a second, or a fraction of a

centimetre, can be the difference between winning and losing and can change your life you appreciate that the small details have been worked out years before. That's why we athletes are proud the Evaluation Commission praised our contribution."

Here she turned to face the members of the Evaluation Commission, a sign of respect. In just one paragraph of text Denise Lewis had emphasized that athletes were at the center of London's planning. And she had addressed most of the questions the former athletes in the audience might have had. All the boxes had been checked.

"In London your athletes will compete in venues packed with passionate fans, renowned for their sense of fair play." (A key point, this was where the visual of South American flags appeared.) She moved to another key point: *"Thanks to the city's diversity, there will be supporters from every Olympic nation. Every athlete will have a home crowd."* (Finally, she provided a further reminder of Britain's history with Paralympic sport.) *"And every Paralympian will enjoy a fantastic atmosphere too, from British crowds famous for their love of Paralympic sport. You, and every athlete in 2012, will never forget the magic of London."*

The magic of London was now brought to life in a short film that was really little more than an interlude masquerading as a tourist brochure.

London Mayor Ken Livingstone now took center stage.

"Mr. President, Members of the IOC. I am Ken Livingstone, the Mayor of London. That film has given you a flavour of our city. But it is only a flavour. London is a city which welcomes the world with open arms and an open mind. A city which wants nothing more than to welcome the Olympic Games."

The "open arms" reference was a subtle dig at Paris and Madrid, with their less-than-exemplary record of racial harmony. At this point in Livingstone's speech was the direction, "Pause." It was a reminder to him to pace his delivery.

"A city in which 300 languages are spoken every day and those who speak them live happily side-by-side. It is a city rich in culture, which will stage a spectacular Olympic festival. A city with sport at heart,

where every weekend hundreds of thousands of fans fill our stadia. Where every year half-a-million people line the streets to watch the world's greatest marathon."

Again, Livingstone was directed to pause, to let the three key points he had just made sink in. He had a fourth:

"And it's a city which is a magnet for young people from all over the world. London is already their number one destination. Six million young people visit every year. More of them choose London for their education than any other city. The organisers of Saturday's Live 8 concerts would tell you, if you want to mobilise the youth of the world, start in London." (A picture of the previous weekend's Live 8 concert filled the screen, with London's Hyde Park filled with hundreds of thousands of young people.)

"As London's Mayor, I know that what you want from me is to take whatever measures are necessary to deliver a safe, secure, and superb Games. That is what I am committed to do. Because I know if I fail you, I fail our city."

That was all the audience needed to hear from the Mayor. But he also wanted to address a perceived negative of London as a host city.

"For example, in transport which we know is vital for a successful Games. Our bid locates as many sports and facilities as possible in one place: the Olympic Park. That Park is exceptionally well-served by public transport. It has nine existing rail lines. The tenth line will be completed in 2007. In fact, every single competition venue is served by existing public transport. And the entire transport network is already benefiting from a 30-billion-dollar investment before 2012." (Like Coe, he was using dollars as his units of currency rather than British pounds.)

"The regeneration of the area around the Olympic Park is already under way." (This statement was accompanied by a picture of Barnes Wetlands, which is in fact on the other side of London, but no one seemed to notice.) *"The Games guarantee this regeneration will create a community where sport is an integral part of everyday life. A model for twenty-first century living. The embodiment of the philosophy of Pierre de Coubertin.*

"The Park will be an environmental showcase." (Another important box checked, thanks in part to the audience's memories of Barnes Wetlands.)

"The Games will dramatically improve the lives of Londoners. Now, please allow me to introduce our Prime Minister, Tony Blair."

The Prime Minister appeared in a video, wearing a dark blue suit and his London 2012 tie, in a room at Number 10, Downing Street. He spoke in French, both deferential and unexpected. This had been David Magliano's idea. Somewhere he had read that Tony Blair was a fluent French speaker, and when he asked if Blair was willing to do it, he had agreed readily. It was a stroke of genius. France's President Chirac had spoken only in French.

"Mr. President, International Olympic Committee members, distinguished guests. I am sorry I can't be with you in person. My responsibility as host of the G8 summit, which starts today, means I must be back in the U.K. It is the only reason I am not at your historic session. I was, however, honoured to meet many of you over the last few days, and delighted to renew old friendships.

"Last year I was privileged to attend the superb Olympic Games and Paralympic Games in Athens. And proud to be one of 20,000 Britons, the largest group of overseas spectators."

The film cut away to footage of the Prime Minister and his wife, Cherie, standing and applauding in Athens' Olympic Stadium. France's President Chirac and U.S. President Bush had not been in Athens. Their interest in the Olympic movement had strangely emerged more recently.

"Athens inspired me and taught me much about the Olympic Movement. Our goal is to witness its power in London."

Blair, like Craig Reedie before him, now reverted to English for the rest of his presentation.

"It is a unique honour to act as Host City. I also understand it is an honour which comes with a great responsibility and which requires the highest levels of cooperation with the IOC.

"My promise to you is that we will be your very best partners. All of us who have made guarantees to you are ready to deliver on them now.

On security. On finance. On every single undertaking we have given. If you award London the Games, I pledge to you personally we will continue to give the highest level of support to Seb Coe and Keith Mills as they lead the Organising Committee, backed up by our Olympics Minister Tessa Jowell. My entire Government and the main Opposition parties too are united behind this bid. It has total political support. It is the nation's bid. It has excited people throughout the country. More than three million have already volunteered their support."

The commitment of the British government to the bid was vital; Blair had also confirmed the commitment of any future government of an opposition party, and emphasized the broad base of support the bid enjoyed among the British people. Every sentence he spoke was immensely significant, but he had yet to play his trump card.

"And that support goes beyond our shores too. We were honoured to receive the endorsement of the most inspiring statesman of our age: Nelson Mandela." (The video cut away from Number 10, Downing Street to show Blair and the world's most admired statesman together, smiling and laughing.) *"He said this: 'I can't think of a better place than London to hold an event that unites the world. London will inspire young people around the world and ensure that the Olympic Games remain the dream for future generations.'"*

Mandela's words provided both a ringing endorsement and concise summary of London's message. For shock value his appearance was right up there with the British Prime Minister speaking French.

"Those words remind us that as leaders, in government or sport, we have a duty to reach beyond our own time and borders. To have a vision which serves those who come after us."

This was pure flattery. Blair was saying that the IOC members were leaders in the same way that he and Nelson Mandela were leaders. And that the IOC had as much of a responsibility as Presidents and Prime Ministers to serve future generations.

He then moved to his summing up: This was London's key message and the proof that the city and nation could deliver.

"Our vision is to see millions more young people in Britain and across the world participating in sport, and improving their lives as

a result of that participation. And London has the power to make that happen. It is a city with a voice that talks to young people. And, with more than 1,000 foreign media correspondents based here, it is a city with a voice that is heard all around the world. It is that unique combination of strengths which London offers a global plat-form for the Olympic message to young people. Not just for the 17 days of the competition, but for the years leading up to the Games, and beyond."

The video ended and the British government's most senior remaining representative in Singapore, Olympic Minister Tessa Jowell, stepped up to the microphone. Originally the idea had been for the young basketball player, Amber Charles, to speak on behalf of young people in the communities that would most benefit from London hosting the games. In the end, however, the team decided against this on the executional grounds that it might have been interpreted as a stunt, and, strategically, because they needed someone with political gravitas to talk about the Olympic legacy. It was Jowell's role to reassure the committee on the progress that had already been made in developing athletic facilities in London, and to seed some new ideas that might appeal to IOC members who were also involved in International Federations and National Olympic Committees.

"Mr. President, Members of the International Olympic Committee. I am Tessa Jowell, Olympic Minister.

"London is already investing huge sums in sporting infrastructure. You see it at the new Wembley Stadium. And the new arena at the Millennium Dome, both 2012 venues. You see it in the three Olympic Park venues already being developed. The Aquatics Centre and the Velodrome will be ready in 2008. The hockey facility soon after. There are only two permanent venues left to develop: an indoor sports arena and the Olympic Stadium. The stadium will be a purpose-built home for athletics for generations to come. Set in the biggest new urban park in Europe for 200 years."

As Jowell talked about these facilities, pictures of them appeared on the large screens. The transitions between the PowerPoint slides were designed so that animated facilities were presented in exactly the same way as existing facilities. Psychologically, test audiences had said that it made the proposed facilities look as real as the existing ones.

"But we know a successful Games has to offer more than just 17 days of spectacular sport. So, London offers much more. And our legacy will be immediate. The Olympic Stadium will become the home of the London Olympic Institute a new world centre of sporting excellence. It will house national governing bodies, medical experts and educators. And it will be an international resource for National Olympic Committees. Offering young athletes from around the world the opportunity to learn and train."

This was an offer to both the International Federations who ran the sports, and the National Olympic Committees who were responsible for their countries' Olympic teams. London's facilities would be available to individual athletes and coaches for training and medical care. These facilities could also be used, she went on to say, to host future international competitions in a variety of sports. This was an extremely important point, as many sports were restricted to just a few cities capable of hosting their world championships.

"The Stadium and the four other permanent venues in the Olympic Park will allow London to host world championships and elite competition in many sports. Each of the venues has an agreed and clear long-term future. Each has a 25-year business plan already in place. And London's legacy will reach beyond London. Our aim is to serve the ambitions of the Olympic Movement."

One of the greatest ambitions of the Olympic Movement has long been to hold an Olympic Games in Africa or South America. This has been impossible to date because of the limited facilities available in any one country on those continents, but one of London's key technical proposals was the design of temporary, relocatable venues that could be packed away after 2012 and sent anywhere the IOC wanted to use them. This was an idea that could make the dream of an African or South American Games a reality.

"The experience gained in designing and using state-of-the-art relocatable venues will help efforts to stage future Games in every

continent. So, London is committed to a legacy for sport in Britain. And to a far-reaching legacy for the Olympic Movement."

In the course of the presentations so far, the same points had been made several times, but each time from a slightly different perspective. It was now up to Sebastian Coe to draw it all together in an emotional finale. Before he spoke again, a final video was shown.

It began with the same small African boy who had featured in the opening video, throwing stones on a dusty street and having his attention drawn to the commentary on the London 2012 100-meter final.

The film now cut to a young Chinese girl, sitting on the floor of a small apartment, watching gymnastics. Somewhere in South America, a young boy watched cycling. And in Russia a small girl was transfixed by swimming. All from the London 2012 Games. Shots of running shoes, gymnastic slippers, a bicycle, and a pair of blue swimming goggles followed.

Now the young Russian girl was at the side of the swimming pool, adjusting the same blue goggles before belly-flopping unceremoniously into the water. Swimming breast stroke, she went below the surface (Figure 9.3). But with each stroke, each time she surfaced, she was

FIGURE 9.3 Inspiration.
© London Organising Committee of the Olympic Games, 2006.

older, stronger, until she was a young woman in Olympic competition. So too the Chinese gymnast ran onto the mat and with each flip left her childhood behind and brought her dreams closer to reality. The South American boy rode his bicycle through the market place in his village and into an Olympic velodrome. And finally, back in Africa, the young boy with the wristband—in a reversal of the opening film—grew up and into athletics, national championships, and finally the Olympics.

The film ended with him on the line at an Olympic 100-meter final. The starting gun sounded, and the film faded to black.

Originally the film had closed with a super that said, "Choose London. And inspire young people everywhere to choose Olympic Sport." This had been cut to shave four seconds from the presentation in order to ensure, along with numerous other cuts of similar length, that Sebastian Coe would be able to deliver his closing words in their entirety.

"Mr. President, Mr. Honorary Life President, Members of the International Olympic Committee," said Sebastian Coe. (His reference to the Honorary Life President was a tribute to Juan Antonio Samaranch, the former President of the IOC, a man much revered by South American IOC members.)

"I stand here today because of the inspiration of the Olympic Movement. When I was 12, about the same age as Amber, I was marched into a large school hall with my classmates. We sat in front of an ancient, black and white TV and watched grainy pictures from the Mexico Olympic Games. Two athletes from our home town were competing. John Sherwood won a bronze medal in the 400m hurdles. His wife Sheila just narrowly missed gold in the long jump. That day a window to a new world opened for me. By the time I was back in my classroom, I knew what I wanted to do and what I wanted to be. The following week I stood in line for hours at my local track just to catch a glimpse of the medals the Sherwoods had brought home. It didn't stop there. Two days later I joined their club. Two years later Sheila gave me my first pair of racing spikes. 35 years on, I stand before you with those memories still fresh. Still inspired by this great Movement."

Sebastian Coe was the only one of the bid leaders who could have done this, and to tell his personal story in that way was a device as powerful and memorable as Tony Blair's use of the French language or the appearance of Nelson Mandela speaking on behalf of London. It was proof that London's strategy could work—who could argue with the only man to have taken gold in the 1500-meters at consecutive Olympic Games?—but it also made the strategy personal, not only to Coe, but to most of the IOC members who would remember their own moments of Olympic inspiration. That story of Coe's journey to the Olympics was the story of London 2012.

"My journey here to Singapore started in that school hall and con-tinues today in wonder and in gratitude. Gratitude that those flickering images of the Sherwoods, and Wolde, Gammoudi, Doubell, and Hines drew me to a life in that most potent celebration of humanity: Olympic sport. And that gratitude drives me and my team to do whatever we can to inspire young people to choose sport. Whoever they are, wherever they live and whatever they believe." (In other words, he was saying, sport is at the heart of this bid: Olympic sport. We care because we have experienced what it means ourselves.)

"Today that task is so much harder. Today's children live in a world of conflicting messages and competing distractions. Their landscape is cluttered. Their path to Olympic sport is often obscured. But it's a world we must understand and must respond to. My heroes were Olympians. My children's heroes change by the month. And they are the lucky ones. Millions more face the obstacle of limited resources and the resulting lack of guiding role models."

He had emphasized the problem facing the Olympic Movement, but this time, with the reference to his children, he had made it personal once more. How many of his audience have children or grandchildren who would rather play video games than run? Who are their heroes? He was asking them to look into their own lives to understand the size of the challenge, and to see the power of London's proposed solution.

"In my travels over the last two years, speaking with many of you, I've had many conversations about how we meet this challenge. And I've been reassured and I've been uplifted to see that we share a com-mon goal for the future of sport. No group of leaders does more than you to engage the hearts and minds of young people." (In addition to

flattering them as a group, he was telling them that even if they didn't share his goals for Olympic sport, their colleagues did.)

"But every year the challenge of bringing them to Olympic sport becomes tougher. The choice of Host City is the most powerful means you have to meet this challenge." (The unspoken message? Don't waste it!) *"But it takes more than 17 days of superb Olympic competition. It takes a broader vision. And the global voice to communicate that vision over the full four years of the Olympiad. Today in Britain's fourth bid in recent years we offer London's vision of inspiration and legacy.*

"Choose London today and you send a clear message to the youth of the world: More than ever, the Olympic Games are for you." (The use of the command, "Choose London today" was by no means accidental. David Magliano was trained as a hypnotist, so he should know.)

"Mr. President, Members of the International Olympic Committee. Some might say that your decision today is between five similar bids. That would be to undervalue the opportunity before you. In the past, you have made bold decisions. Decisions which have taken the Movement forward in new and exciting directions. Your decision today is critical. It is a decision about which bid offers the vision and sporting legacy to best promote the Olympic cause. It is a decision about which city will help us show a new generation why sport matters. In a world of many distractions, why Olympic sport matters. And in the 21st century, why the Olympic ideals still matter so much.

"On behalf of the youth of today, the athletes of tomorrow, and the Olympians of the future, we humbly submit the bid of London 2012.

"Mr. President, that concludes our presentation. Thank you."

As the IOC members applauded and Coe left the podium, some of those in the audience might have pondered the end of his presentation compared to that of the last speaker from the Paris bid team.

"On behalf of the youth of today, the athletes of tomorrow, and the Olympians of the future," said Coe, *"we humbly submit the bid of London 2012."*

The Paris presentation had ended with a similar appeal, a similar structure. But it had an entirely different orientation.

Paris needs the Games.

Paris wants the Games.
Paris loves the Games.

Paris's presentation was not about the Olympic Movement. It was about Paris. And therein lies a lesson for us all.

Celebration

As Jacques Rogge fumbled with the envelope in Singapore and the bid team held its collective breath, millions of Britons watched live on television. They watched in their homes, in offices, in bars, in yacht clubs that would host Olympic sailing events, and in Trafalgar Square, where a crowd of thousands saw the coverage on big screens.

The BBC's commentator, Barry Davies, asked, "Has the best presentation, which London's certainly was, won the day?" The picture was split into three: The largest part, on the left of the screen, was devoted to Dr. Rogge in Singapore. On the right was the crowd in Trafalgar Square. Below them a similar crowd awaited the result outside the Hotel de Ville in Paris.

Finally Rogge spoke. "The International Olympic Committee has the honor of announcing that the Games of the Thirtieth Olympiad in 2012 are awarded to the city of . . . London."

The Singapore convention center erupted, and with it Trafalgar Square and every home, office, bar, and sports club in Britain where televisions were tuned to the announcement. In Trafalgar Square, Kelly Holmes, the women's 800-meter and 1500-meter champion from the Athens Games, danced for joy on stage as her fellow Olympians embraced and people in the crowd wept.

"We've done it!" commentator Davies exclaimed, momentarily forgetting the BBC's rules about impartiality. "London have won it! They've disproved the theory that you cannot win on the day, you can only lose on the day! They've won with the most inspirational presentation, surely, ever seen on such an occasion! Wonderful! Well done, Sebastian Coe and his team, Ken Livingstone, there, the Mayor of London, Keith Mills, the Chief Executive. They're all going mad here . . .

and I'm sure Dick Palmer,* who's been with the Olympic Games since he was almost born . . . almost since he was born. I'm getting the sentence the wrong way round, but my goodness me, London have got it the right way round! The Games are coming to London for the first time since 1948! Absolutely brilliant!"

In the final vote, London garnered 54 votes to Paris's 50. In the previous round London had led with 39, followed by Paris with 33 and Madrid with 31. While one third-round vote for London had been lost, enough of Madrid's floating votes had been gained to protect London's lead and give the city the Games.

"Was there any material we had that they didn't?" David Magliano said, a few months later, with the clarity that only hindsight can offer. "No. Maybe we just did a better job with the same material."

I watched the announcement with my family in a cottage on the same Welsh coast where years before I had proposed to my wife. When we had stopped jumping on the sofas, and laughing at Barry Davies's comment that Tony Blair must really be looking forward to welcoming President Chirac when he arrived late to the G8 Conference, I told my kids that some of the older children at their school—some of whom are already national champions in swimming, hockey, and other Olympic sports—may actually be competing in London's Games in 2012. They began to talk about the children who they thought had the most chance of making it, and then inevitably the conversation turned to their own chances of competing at the tender ages of 16 or 17. What sport would give them the best chance of competing so young? (Not swimming, I hoped, please? The swimmers train so early in the morning.) And then I found myself

---

*The London 2012 Technical Director and former General Secretary of the British Olympic Association. He had carried the British flag at the Moscow Olympics in 1980, and was on the platform in a nonspeaking role in Singapore. By a strange coincidence, I remember him rescuing my model airplane from a tree when I was about four years old. He happened to be married to my mother's best friend.

wondering at the power of a presentation that could become so personal, so immediately, for so many of us. London 2012's story was the IOC's story, the athletes' story, the children's story, *my* children's story.

Such a story, I thought, might provide a hell of a good way to finish my book.

ACKNOWLEDGMENTS

I would like to thank a number of people without whom I would not have contemplated writing this book, let alone been able to finish it.

About two years ago, an editor at Wiley, Richard Narramore, called and asked me if I had any interest in writing a second edition of *Truth, Lies & Advertising*. When I said that I couldn't think of anything else to say about planning, he encouraged me to write something related but new. For some reason I agreed, and he has since been a constant source of motivation and good ideas. Thank you, Richard, for your patience and support. I would also like to thank Wiley's Linda Witzling for her guidance through the production process, and all the people at Cape Cod Compositors.

Along the way, I have been helped greatly by Peter Cowie, with whom I worked in his capacity as new business director at JWT in London. He's a born new business guy, blessed with brains, enthusiasm, and good humor, and he has been generous with both his time and experience. He also introduced me to some other terrific people. Camilla Honey, who does have one of the best names in the business, runs a company named JFDI (do track her down and ask what this stands for), specializing in improving marketing communication agencies' new business performance. She read an early draft of the book, and I thank her for both her perceptive comments and her encouragement. Peter Cowie also introduced me to the remarkable David Magliano, Director of Marketing for London's 2012 Olympic bid team. Although he probably had many better (and more lucrative) things to do, David was willing to meet with me and talk about the bid process and presentation in great detail. As the London bid exemplified virtually everything I wanted to say about great presentations, it was wonderful to be able to hear the inside story. Thank you, David, both for making this book more interesting and for giving my kids something to dream about. Thanks, too, to Michael Dalziel at London 2012 for his help with visuals for Chapter 9.

Of course I could hardly write about new business and presentations if I hadn't been lucky enough to witness and participate in some pretty good ones myself. Thank you, therefore, to Chris Powell and Chris Cowpe, who let me make my first new business presentation after only two years in their agency, and allowed me to make another even after I screwed up the first one.

In my years at Goodby, Silverstein & Partners, I was fortunate to work with Jeff Goodby and Rich Silverstein, whose creative brilliance and humanity made everything about new business easier and more fun; with Colin Probert and Harold Sogard, who could always be relied upon to ask the really difficult questions; and with a host of others too numerous to mention (if you worked at GS&P between October 8, 1989, and December 31, 1999, I mean you), who consistently made the impossible seem almost routine. In the context of GS&P it would be wrong not to also mention Andy Berlin, who played a powerful role in growing the agency in its early days, and who remains a formidable new business presence. Working with Andy might not always be straightforward, but it's certainly never dull.

I would like to extend my sincere thanks to all the people mentioned above, and also to Sir Martin Sorrell, my current boss. Since I joined WPP in 2002, Martin has given me an extraordinary amount of freedom. Not only has he tolerated my desire to write books as well as work for his company, he has actively encouraged my writing and given me time to focus solely on it when deadlines were approaching. He has also given me free rein to work on the projects where I feel I can make the greatest difference. I'm very grateful for both his confidence in me and his ongoing support. It's a privilege to work for him.

My greatest thanks are for my parents, Bridgett and David Steel, and for my wife, Lynda. My mum and dad kindled and fanned my love of reading and writing, and instilled in me both a healthy work ethic and respect for the opinions of others. I couldn't have wished for better parents—not so good that I didn't want to leave home, but maybe that's good parenting too.

Throughout my career, Lynda has supported me during all the late nights and absences from home, not to mention the general grumpiness that has accompanied the busier and more tiring moments. She encouraged me to write this book even though both of us knew I didn't really have time to do it, and continued to do so when family illnesses, construction projects, and finally the death of her father threatened to derail more than just this project. Without her I would be less than half a person; I wish that everyone could be so lucky.

Finally, a big "thanks" to you for reading this far. If you have any observations—good or bad—about this book, or indeed any offers of new business, I would be very pleased to hear from you. I can be reached at jsteel@wpp.com, a mailbox that I check three times a day except on weekends and during vacation.

BIBLIOGRAPHY

If you look at this bibliography before reading the book, you might be forgiven for wondering why I have included some of the titles listed below. After all, this is a book about business, for business people. Shouldn't all the titles in the bibliography be found in the business section of your local bookstore?

Well, that would be boring, wouldn't it?

Perfect Pitch is about influencing people and selling ideas. And the people who know most about that are not necessarily to be found in my own business, or indeed in what we would commonly define as "business" at all. So while you'll find advertising industry legends like David Ogilvy, Howard Gossage, James Webb Young, Jeremy Bullmore, and George Lois listed below, you will also find books on writing, public speaking, storytelling, politics, crime, and science. You'll even find books on prostitution (*Tart Cards*); fishing (*A River Runs Through It*); flying (*West with the Night*); Japanese tradition (*Memoirs of a Geisha*); and cricket (*The Art of Captaincy*). I can assure you that the selection of these books is not as silly as it may sound. If and when you read any of them, you will discover that these strange choices are not really about prostitution, fishing, flying, Japanese tradition, or cricket at all. Instead they are about what it really means to be a human. They demonstrate the value of being able to put oneself into another's shoes. They bring to life the art of gentle manipulation and persuasion. They are also very well written and presented. And if you read them with an open mind, valuable lessons for presentation, business, and life alike, will abound.

While business books can help you find a structure for understanding marketing issues and preparing presentations, the really *big* ideas, the ideas on which the success of your presentations rests, and the interesting anecdotes that bring them to life, will almost always be found outside the business world. When aspiring agency planners ask me what they should be reading to improve their minds, I sometimes don't even mention my own book. (I'm not embarrassed by it—it's simply true that I'm not a fan of business books and if I hadn't written it myself, I very much doubt that I would have read it.) Instead, I tell them to subscribe to *The New Yorker* and a quality newspaper, and read all the good novels that time allows; to wallow in fine writing and ideas; to be simultaneously stimulated and relaxed; to bring ideas from real life to which their clients might easily relate.

Finally, on the assumption that many of you will have to travel by road, rail, sea, or air to make at least some of your presentations, I have included *The Worst-Case Scenario Survival Handbook*. Because you never know.

Archer, Caroline. *Tart Cards*. New York: Mark Batty, 2003.

Bendinger, Bruce, ed. *The Book of Gossage*. Chicago: The Copy Workshop, 1995.

Brearley, Mike. *The Art of Captaincy*. London: Guild, 1985.

Bullmore, Jeremy. *More Bull More. Behind the Scenes in Advertising (Mark III)*. Henley-on-Thames: NTC Publications, 2003.

Feldwick, Paul. "A True Story: The Birth of a Great Campaign." *Market Leader* (Winter 2005): 30–33.

Golden, Arthur. *Memoirs of a Geisha*. New York: Vintage, 1997.

Halliwell, Edward. "Overloaded Circuits. Why Smart People Underperform." *Harvard Business Review* (January, 2005).

Humes, James C. *The Sir Winston Method*. New York: William Morrow, 1991.

Khan-Panni, Phillip. *Stand and Deliver*. Oxford: How to Books Ltd, 2002.

Klein, Joe. *The Natural: The Misunderstood Presidency of Bill Clinton*. New York: Broadway Books, 2002.

Lamott, Anne. *Bird by Bird*. New York: Anchor, 1995.

Lois, George. *What's the Big Idea?* New York: Currency, 1991.

Machiavelli, Niccoló. *The Prince: And Other Political Writings*. London: Everyman/J.M. Dent, 1995.

Maclean, Norman. *A River Runs Through It*. Chicago: *University of Chicago Press, 1976*

March, Robert H. *Physics for Poets*. New York: McGraw-Hill, 1996.

Markham, Beryl. *West with the Night*. London: Virago Press Ltd., 1984.

McKee, Robert. *Story*. New York: HarperCollins, 1997.

Morgan, Adam. *Eating the Big Fish*. New York: John Wiley & Sons, 1998.

Noonan, Peggy. *On Speaking Well*. New York: Regan Books/Harper Perennial, 1998.

Ogilvy, David. *Ogilvy on Advertising*. New York: Random House, 1983.

Ohmae, Kenichi. *The Mind of the Strategist*. New York: McGraw-Hill, 1982.

Piven, Joshua, and David Borgenicht. *The Worst-Case Scenario Survival Handbook: Travel*. San Francisco: Chronicle Books, 2001.

Roman, K. and J. Raphaelson. *Writing That Works*. New York: Quill, 2000.

Steel, Jon. *Truth, Lies & Advertising*. New York: John Wiley & Sons, 1998.

Toobin, Jeffrey. "The Marcia Clark Verdict." *The New Yorker* 72(26) (September 9, 1996): 58–71.

Tufte, Edward R. *The Cognitive Style of PowerPoint*. Cheshire, CT: Graphics Press, 2003.

Tufte, Edward R. *The Visual Display of Quantitative Information*. Cheshire, CT: Graphics Press, 2001.

Tufte, Edward R. *Visual Explanations*. Cheshire, CT: Graphics Press, 1997.

Watson, James D. *The Double Helix*. New York: Mentor, 1969.

Weissman, Jerry. *Presenting to Win*. Upper Saddle River, NJ: Prentice-Hall, 2003.

Wheatley, Margaret. *Leadership and the New Science*. San Francisco: Berrett-Koehler Publishers, 1992.

Wypijewski, JoAnn. ed. *Painting by Numbers. Komar and Melamid's Scientific Guide to Art.* Berkeley: University of California Press, 1997.

Young, James Webb. *A Technique for Producing Ideas.* Chicago: NTC Business Books, 1996.

INDEX

ABOUT THE AUTHOR

The Facts—and the Fiction

In 1984, Jon Steel wrote to 20 London advertising agencies seeking a job in account management. He was rejected by 19 of them, in one case with the words that he "looked and spoke as if he'd just come up from the country." At the twentieth, Boase Massimi Pollitt, he was fourth on a shortlist of three, until the first-choice candidate withdrew his application to take a better-paid job in the City.

Twenty-one years later, he is still in the business that was so reticent to accept him, and he has played a strategic and leadership role in new business wins totaling more than a billion dollars in client billings. After five years at BMP (in which time he became the agency's youngest ever Board Director), he moved to San Francisco as fledgling agency Goodby, Berlin & Silverstein's first director of account planning. There he helped grow the agency from $35 million in billings to more than $750 million, becoming a partner and vice-chairman along the way. The agency won National Agency of the Year accolades for its unique blend of strategy and creativity, and Jon was elected to the American Advertising Federation's Hall of Achievement for executives under the age of forty (although it's quite likely that this was a case of mistaken identity).

Since leaving San Francisco, he has worked for Sir Martin Sorrell at WPP's parent company in London, providing strategic counsel to a variety of group companies and clients alike. He spent one year on assignment as vice-chairman of Berlin Cameron United in New York, which resulted in a number of new business wins (including Pfizer and the global Samsung account); recognition for the agency from both *Advertising Age* and *AdWeek* as U.S. Agency of the Year; and a rather unhealthy balance in his frequent flier account. When British Airways executives invited him to lunch at the House of Lords to recognize his contribution to their business, he decided that he was indeed flying too much, returned to his old job at WPP in London, and resolved never to fly on business again. (More than 18 months later, the resolution still holds.)

In the course of his career, Jon has won more than 90 percent of the client business he has pitched (a rare record in an industry where one win out of three is considered good), and over the years has also convinced a lot of clients to buy campaigns that quite frankly scared the crap out of them.

Jon is the author of *Truth, Lies, and Advertising* (John Wiley & Sons, 1998), which remains one of the best-selling books on advertising and has so far—for reasons that elude him—been translated into nine languages including Turkish and Hungarian. He is a board member of the AdCenter at Virginia Commonwealth University and of the Gorilla Foundation, a nonprofit primate research organization based in California. He has also lectured on marketing and advertising matters at the business schools of Stanford University and the University of California, Berkeley.

He now lives in Somerset, England, with his wife, Lynda, children Cameron and Hannah, and a menagerie that includes a diabetic cat, a pony that has to be sedated to have its hair cut, and a neurotic budgerigar.